The complete make-up artist

Working in Film, Television and Theatre

Penny Delamar

First published 1995 by
THE MACMILLAN PRESS LTD
Houndmills, Basingstoke, Hampshire RG21 2XS and London
Companies and representatives throughout the world

ISBN 0–333–58604–2   0038573

A catalogue record for this book is available from the British Library

Typeset by ⏃ Tek-Art, Croydon, Surrey

Illustrations by Penny Delamar and Tek-Art

Printed in Hong Kong

10 9 8 7 6 5 4
03 02 01 00 99 98 97

Note on products

The solvents, adhesives and other chemical formulae used in media make-up are constantly changing – new products become available; existing ones are improved; occasionally some are withdrawn from use for reasons of health and safety. You need to know the health and safety regulations, and to be guided by the specialist suppliers. This applies particularly in prosthetics. If a product is withdrawn, there is always an improved version or something else which will do the same job. This book refers to products relevant at the time of writing.

The solvent for cleaning brushes is referred to simply as 'brush cleaner' as the product used has been changed many times. Trichloroethane, used in the past in some medical adhesives and certain brush cleaners, is now known to be one contributor to the depletion of the ozone layer; it is likely that in time there will be a total world ban on the use of such products. Nevertheless, manufacturers are researching, improving existing products, and creating new, better and safer products for use in the future.

Provided you use products from a reputable manufacturer and a reputable supply outlet, it is safe to assume that all of the classification, packaging and labelling regulations have been complied with, and that health and safety data sheets will be supplied on request.

Advisory note

Every care has been taken in the writing and editing of this book to ensure that its content is accurate, and that the techniques described and the products referred to are safe when properly used in accordance with professional guidance and/or manufacturer's instructions. Training techniques for which special apparatus or chemicals are needed should be undertaken only in the presence of a suitably qualified and experienced teacher. Readers are urged to have due regard to health and safety considerations in applying what is learned. If in doubt, the appropriate professional advice should be sought. The author and publishers cannot accept legal responsibility for any problems, loss or damage arising from misuse of the methods or products described in the book.

When Penny asked me to contribute to this book, I had for the first time in my career to give serious thought to the relationship between the actor and his or her make-up artist.

The first thing I realised was that, just as it is said that we spend a third of our lives sleeping, so it could be said that an actor may spend up to a third of his or her working day in the make-up chair. For *The Elephant Man*, for example, John Hurt spent something like five hours a day having grotesque, elephantine features superimposed on his own face. Once, while filming in Rome, I spent two hours every morning sitting in the make-up chair with a *Teach Yourself Italian* book, listening to the Italian conversation around me. When, after three months, the filming ended, my Italian was almost fluent.

The make-up artist is someone with whom we actors spend a lot of time. So, to the huge meal of knowledge and experience Penny is offering you in this book, I'd like to add a pinch of psychology.

You, the make-up artist, are often the first person the actor sees at the early start of a long working day. If an actor is depressed, ill, nervous or going through a divorce, you will be the first to know. The face looking up at you from the make-up chair will tell you everything. If the actor *says* nothing, you will need to be a sensitive mind-reader; if she or he needs to *talk*, you'll need to be a discreet listener and confidante – no matter how boring you may find it!

The actor's face is his or her mask, and that – literally – is what is in your hands. Actors need you to understand their mental picture of the characters they are playing; your skill will help to make that image a reality. Then they can project their characters with complete conviction, confident that they *look* as they feel.

When all is said and done, when all the preparation is complete, finally it is the actor who stands in front of the camera to deliver the goods, seeking to please producers and audience alike. That is a weighty responsibility: it can put a lot of strain on someone. If an actor is rude, there's no excuse; but should he or she be irritable or difficult, *never* take it personally. Remember that in an industry where time equals money, people feel the pressure.

I'm not saying that your career as a make-up artist will be filled solely with actors sharing their life's woes or throwing tantrums. On the contrary, in the world of film and TV, which is unique, I assure you there'll be a lot of laughs. In fact, it's the laughs that keep the wind in everyone's sails and get you through long weeks of long days of shooting.

So, when you pack your kit and put in your sable brushes, your sponges, foundations and powder puffs, don't forget to pack your sense of humour – it's a crucial part of your equipment.

Cherie Lunghi

INTRODUCTION

A career in make-up is increasingly attractive, as it offers a rewarding and fulfilling way of earning a living. This book will help you to learn the basic principles of the techniques of make-up and will also, I hope, be valuable as reference when you are working professionally.

When using this book as a study guide, it is advisable to practise until you feel you have mastered the entire chapter before moving on to the next – in make-up, much depends on understanding principles rather than learning rules.

The sketches that I drew to complement the text throughout this book were drawn under pressure of time. As a make-up artist, you will learn that time is crucial. There is never much time available for you to show the director what you intend to do: you need to concentrate on giving the best illustration possible, whether it is on paper or the actor's face. Use your time in class, every minute of it, to practise and re-do make-ups until you are satisfied with the result. Never settle for less than your best.

In today's rapidly changing world, in which computers are replacing people in so many areas of work, we can be certain that no machine can ever replace the make-up artist. Once learned, make-up is a skill that cannot be taken away from you, a worthwhile possession in the changing fortunes of modern times.

Penny Delamar

ACKNOWLEDGEMENTS

The author and publishers would like to thank the following people and organisations for their assistance in producing this book:

Luisa Abel
Joyce Allsworth
James Anda
Emma Clark
Joanne Gilyead
Angus Girvan
Charmaine Gruhn
Sui Han Yau (Middi)
Mandy Hanson Asquith
Tamsin Hirshfield
Yuka Ichihashi
Marese Langan
Tracy Lee
Cherie Lunghi
Clare Mackinder
Ray Marston Wig Studio
Mauro
Malanie McLeary
Fatima Mousli (Timi)
Mary O'Dowd

Caroline O'Neill
Pam Orange
Jane Powell
Trefor Proud
Alison Rainey
Amanda Roberts
Concepcion Rodriguez (Concha)
Rosana Rodriguez
Samantha Serjeant
Sandra Shepherd
Tom Smith
Mieko Toyoda
TRESemmé
Simon Tytherleigh
Sylvia Wallis
Amanda Warburton
Wella Great Britain
Wig Specialists
John Woodbridge
Worthingtons

Photographers Nick Austin, John Gardey, Jim Marks, Rollo Snook, Holly Warburton and Graham Cooper. Lord Attenborough for photographs taken by Frank Conner from *Gandhi*, an Indo-British Films Production.

The author and publishers also wish to thank the following for permission to use copyright material:

The Controller of Her Majesty's Stationery Office for Crown copyright material.

Last, but by no means least, many thanks to all the make-up artists and models who were involved in the various technique photographs taken for this book; and David Shawyer for his support and secretarial services.

Every effort has been made to trace all the copyright holders but if any have been inadvertently overlooked the publishers will be pleased to make the necessary arrangements at the first opportunity.

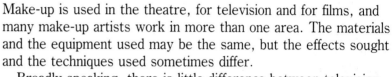

CHAPTER 1

Media make-up as a career

Media make-up as a career

INTRODUCTION

The different areas of work

Make-up is used in the theatre, for television and for films, and many make-up artists work in more than one area. The materials and the equipment used may be the same, but the effects sought and the techniques used sometimes differ.

Broadly speaking, there is little difference between television and film make-up – if you simply took a camera into the streets and filmed people without special make-up, what you would see then would be what later you would see recorded. Nevertheless, there are some important differences in practice. In television work you may be able to 'get away with' more than you can in feature films, even though a high-definition camera is very sensitive and can see more than the eye itself. The major difference is the **screen size**: a 35-foot cinema screen will inevitably show much more detail than could ever be seen on a 21-inch television screen at home. Quick-sketch comedy make-up in TV work, skilful and effective though this may be, would not be suitable for the big screen, where every pore can be seen, magnified in tight close-up. Feature films use top-quality film and effects: this is the most expensive form of media work. When a film made for the cinema is instead viewed on TV, much of the detail – and the spectacle – is lost.

In film work the make-up artist is helped by the **lighting**. Key lights are used on close-ups, and more can be achieved using 35mm (cinema film) than 16mm (TV film) stock. The make-up artist also has the advantage in film work that she is responsible only for the make-up, not for the hair, and can therefore spend more **time** on this. In television the artist is responsible for both the make-up and the hair; she is also expected to work faster than in feature films. As always, the test is simply to look in the mirror – what you see there will be what appears on the screen.

Improvements in the lighting in theatres in recent years mean that make-up has become more subtle. It is now very similar to TV make-up, and although make-up for grand opera is traditionally relatively heavy, in most modern theatre productions the performers wear only street make-up.

Specialising

As a professional make-up artist it is unwise to specialise too soon: try to remain flexible, adapting to working throughout the industry – not just in TV and films but also in theatre, fashion photography, pop promos, corporate videos, video films, documentary films, commercials and advertising.

Background study

Many other subjects provide a good basis for a career in make-up. **Drawing, painting, sculpting, hairdressing**, and **history of art** are clearly relevant; **chemistry** is useful as preparation for working in prosthetics. And for artists who wish to be able to pursue their careers across Europe and the rest of the world, **foreign languages** are always invaluable.

FACIAL ANATOMY

In order to understand how to improve or change the appearance of a face, it is vital that you understand the **bone structure** beneath the flesh.

The skull

A study of the human skull is the first lesson in the approach to make-up.

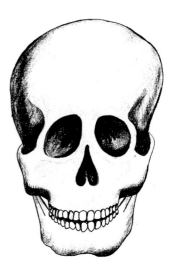

Lighting and shading

ACTIVITY: DRAWING THE SKULL
1 Using a soft lead pencil, draw the skull on white paper, noting the darkest and lightest areas.
2 Draw the skull again, this time marking in the technical names of the bones.

Now that you have a basic understanding of the *structure* of the human skull, it is time to take a look at a real face – looking at and feeling the bones beneath the flesh.

ACTIVITY: STUDYING A FACE
You will need: a fellow student to work with, two brushes – one for black, the other for white; two make-up colours, either cream or water-based.
1 Using your colleague as a model, feel the prominences and depressions on the entire face.
2 Paint in the hollows of the face with black, and the prominent areas with white.
At the end, your model's face will resemble the skull you have been studying.

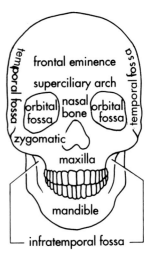

The bones of the face

TIP

When drawing shaded areas, use your finger to smudge the edges and so produce a soft effect.

Faces and head shapes

Both make-up and hair should be designed to suit the model's head and face shape. There are seven basic face shapes.

The oval face

This is generally considered to be the perfect shape – it is easy to work on, and it photographs well.

The round face

This shape needs slimming. Shading with make-up at the sides of the face will help. The hairstyle should not be full at the sides – that would emphasise the round shape. Instead, dress the hair high at the front, or straight down at the sides, to minimise the jawline.

The long face

This shape can be shaded at the chin, which shortens the apparent length. Blusher can be placed on the apples of cheeks to give the illusion of a rounder shape. Hair can be dressed full at the sides, to add width.

The square face

This should be shaded at the jawline to soften the appearance. Blusher can be placed high on the cheekbones, defining their shape, or shaded underneath for a slimming effect.

The heart-shaped face

With this shape blusher should be placed on the round apples of the cheeks. No shading should be used, except at the sides of the forehead close to the hairline. The shape can be balanced by a hairstyle that is full at the jawline.

The pear-shaped face

This is the opposite to the heart-shaped face, with the head being

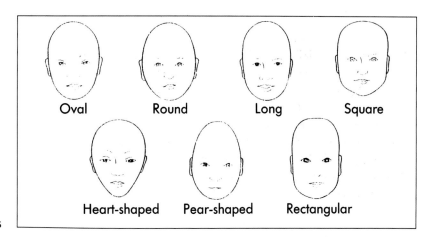

Different face shapes

narrower at the top, and the bottom half of the face being more rounded in shape. Definition can be added by shading to slim the sides of the face, working from below the cheekbones. The hairstyle should be designed to add width and height at the top of the head.

The rectangular face

In this case shading and contouring can be used at the sides of the face, especially at the jawline. The hair should not be high at the top, but used to soften the shape, with forward hair movements and fullness at the sides.

Drawing the face

The best way to understand the structure of the face is to draw it on paper. Before you start, bear the following in mind:

1 Note the *type of head* and the *shape of face* – round, long, square, oval, etc.
2 Consider the person's *character* – the expression, the set of the features, and the relation of each feature to the others. These aspects determine the model's liveliness, humour, pensiveness and so on in the sketch.
3 Look out for anything *unusual* about the face you are drawing – a distinctive nose, perhaps, or a prominent chin, jaw or lower lip. Draw what you see.

Skull make-up

> ### ACTIVITY: DRAWING THE FACE (1)
> Now take pencil and paper and begin by drawing the face of a fellow student, or looking in a mirror and drawing yourself.

The main errors made by the beginner usually are to set the eyes too high – they should be about halfway down the length of the face – and getting the eyes slightly out of line with each other.

Note that the face can be divided horizontally:

- from the hairline to the centre of the eyes;
- from the eyes to the tip of the nose;
- from the tip of the nose to the chin.

The eyes consist of two semicircles, the upper one being slightly wider in diameter and more curved than the lower. The eyes can be used to measure five areas from side to side. They are:

- the eyes themselves;
- the space between the eyes;
- the two spaces between the outer corners of the eyes and the hairline at the edge of the face.

Between the eye and the eyebrow there is roughly an eye's depth of space.

Of course, shapes and measurements vary considerably

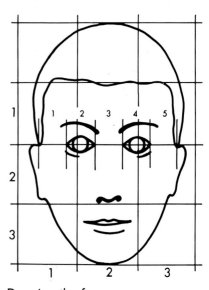

Drawing the face

between individuals. The shape of the nose, for instance, varies enormously; it can be paralled sided or wedge-shaped, thinnest at the bridge and widest at the nostrils.

When you draw the mouth, make certain that you place it such that the length of the chin and the length of the space between the end of the nose and the top lip are both correct. The bottom lip is usually fuller than the top one; the top lip is normally wider than the bottom one.

The ears are usually the same length as the nose. When viewed from the front, the top of the ear is normally in line with the bridge of the nose, and the ear lobe in line with the tip of the nose.

ACTIVITY: DRAWING THE FACE (2)

1 Take turns in drawing one another's faces from the front. Try always to achieve a good likeness.

2 Measure the relative distances and the proportions by holding your pencil between your eye and the face you are sketching. Transfer these measurements to your paper.

3 Sketch your model's face from the side, observing the profile and shape of the brow ridge, the cheekbone, the nose, the mouth and the chin.

Remember, you are not attempting a work of art, but an exercise in accurate observation and in drawing what you see.

COLOUR

A real understanding of **colour** is absolutely basic for the make-up artist.

Principles of colour

The colours we see depend on the colour of the **light source**, the colours of any **filters** used, and the colour of the **objects** that then *reflect* the light.

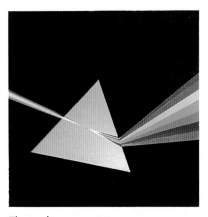

The colour spectrum

In the retina at the back of the eye, there are two kinds of receptor cells: these respond to light focused on them by the lens of the eye. One sort is responsible for colourless vision in dim light; the other for colour perception in bright light.

White light is a mixture of light of many different wavelengths. If you shine a beam of white light through a glass prism, the rays are bent according to their wavelengths and spread out to form a multicoloured **spectrum**. The spectrum can be seen if a screen is placed in its path. The order of the colours is always the same, the order that you see in a rainbow: violet, indigo, blue, green, yellow, orange and red.

When white light strikes a white surface, most of the light is *reflected*: that is why the surface looks white. When light strikes a black surface, most of it is *absorbed*. When light strikes a grey or coloured surface, some is reflected and some is absorbed – when white light strikes a red surface, for example, the surface appears red because it is *reflecting* red light, but *absorbing* light of other colours. When light strikes a transparent surface, most of it simply passes through.

From a technical point of view, make-up and paint pigments have no colour of their own: they seem coloured to us because they *absorb* light of some wavelengths and *reflect* light of others. The light reflected produces the particular colour we see.

Classifying colour

Colours are classified in three ways, according to their *hue*, their *brightness* and their *intensity*.

Hue

The **hue** of a colour represents the difference between pure colours – it is the name by which we know it: red, blue, yellow, and so forth.

Brightness

Brightness represents the range from light to dark. From any light colour to any dark colour there is a brightness scale. The scale of greys is simple because there are no hues.

The darkness or lightness of a colour – its position on the range – is called its **value**. A *light* colour has *high* value, a *dark* colour has a *low* value.

Intensity

Intensity is the range from any pure hue to a point of the grey scale. A grey-blue, for example, has a blue hue, yet it is different from the pure blue of the colour wheel. Although it is of the same *hue* (blue), it is lower in *intensity*. It is nearer to the centre of the wheel, and more grey. The colours on the outside of the wheel are brilliant; those nearer the centre of the wheel are less brilliant, and are known as *tones*. Intensity scales are of three kinds:

The scale of greys

- **tints**, ranging from any pure hue to white;

- **shades**, ranging from any pure hue to black;

- **tones**, ranging from any pure hue to a grey.

Each hue can be produced by mixing some combination of the three primary colours: red, yellow and blue. Variations can be made by adding black or white or both. Similarly, you can change make-up foundation colours by mixing them: if a colour is not warm enough, add some red; if it is too dark, add some white; if it looks too bright, add some grey (which you make by mixing black and white).

Never rely on the *description* of a make-up colour. 'Chinese yellow' is not suitable for all Chinese people, for example. 'Indian' is not automatically going to be the right base for a native of India. Train your eye to judge colours accurately – good make-up relies on your knowledge and your ability to assess colour.

The colour circle

The **colour circle** or **colour wheel** used by artists and decorators for distinguishing colours can also be applied to make-up colours, which are paints for the face.

- **Primary paint colours** Red, blue and yellow. When mixed in equal proportions, these produce *grey*.

- **Secondary paint colours** Orange, green and violet. Each of these is made by mixing two adjacent primary colours.

- **In-between colours** Made by mixing more of one colour than another, for example bluish green or greenish blue.

- **Tints** Made by adding white – this can produce colours such as opal.

- **Shades** Made by adding black – this can produce colours such as emerald.

Colour coordination

It is important that the make-up artist is careful to select and match products that **coordinate** – that is, colours that relate to one another in the completed make-up.

- **Foundation** The foundation should match the skin colour.

- **Eyebrows** The eyebrow pencil or powder should match the hair colour, or at least harmonise with it. For example, a person with ash blonde hair would need her eyebrows defined with taupe, which is a pale *grey* brown. If instead you used other shades of brown, such as browns with red in them, this would look wrong. On the other hand, a brown with ginger tones would look correct on a *red-headed* person.

- **Cheeks** In women's make-up, blusher or rouge should be harmonious with the skin tone. It should not be treated as an accessory to match the dress.
- **Lips** Lip colour should be considered in relation to the costume, as well as in relation to the skin tone and the hair.
- **Eyes** Eye colours should improve or define the eyes as well as harmonising with the total look and style.

Making the most of colour

There are thousands of colours in the world around us – however many colours you may have in your make-up box, you will almost certainly need to mix some of those in order to create the colours you need.

Mixing colours

The cleanest, clearest colours come straight from the pot, box or tube. Mixed with other colours they become muddy. As a general rule, *it is best to mix no more than two colours together*, though the result can be modified with a spot of another colour.

Primary and secondary colours

The **primary colours** in make-up are blue, red and yellow.

- Blue mixed with yellow gives a series of greens, from bluish green (more blue than yellow) to a pale, yellowish green (more yellow than blue).
- Likewise, red mixed with yellow gives a full range of oranges.
- Red mixed with blue gives a range of purples.

Green, orange and purple are **secondary colours**. The hues of the primary colours from which they are mixed will have a large effect on the result.

The colour circle

Colour coordination

Making the most of colour

Adding white

Pastel shades – such as delicate pinks, blues, greens, apricots, creams and lilacs – can be made by adding white to red, blue, green, orange, yellow or purple. If you add too much white, the colour will look chalky.

Adding black

The addition of black will create a *shade* of any given colour. It will dull any pigment you mix it with, however, and should therefore be used with caution. Mixed with yellow ochre it makes a pleasant olive green.

Adding grey

Black and white together give tones of grey. By themselves, these are cold; add a touch of yellow, brown or red to warm the colour.

Complementary and harmonising colours

Each colour has a **complementary colour**, diametrically opposite it on the colour wheel. When any two complementary colours are placed next to each other they produce a strong contrast, and each of the colours looks more vivid.

Colours that share a pigment, such as blue and green, are called **harmonising colours**: when placed next to each other they appear to blend.

If you stare long and hard at a particular colour (say, red) and then look hard at a *white* surface, you may see an after-image of the complementary colour (in the case of red, green). This is because the eye has ceased to register the original colour and is now registering the *remaining* colours in the mixture that makes up white light. This explains why it is so hard to match colours: after comparing many different samples for a long time, your brain ceases to register the correct colour.

Complementary colours can be used in make-up in these ways:

■ **Toning down** A colour can be toned down by adding a little of the complementary colour. Thus, a too-bright red can be toned down by adding a touch of green (and vice versa).

■ **Making greyer** Any colour can be made greyer by adding a small quantity of its complementary colour.

Neutral or earth colours

These are blacks, greys and browns. You will make an **earth colour** if you mix together:

● the three primary colours; *or*
● any two secondary colours; *or*
● all the primary and secondary colours.

Guidelines in using colour

Don't be tempted to use too many bright colours in one make-up as the result could be discordant. Using one or two pure colours can help to create a focal point on the face, but more than that will confuse: the eye will pass from one bright colour to the other, and because there is no contrast between brighter and more muted colours, the colours will fight for attention.

Not all cool colours are dull and not all warm colours are bright: there are dull reds and yellows, and bright blues and greens. Whether cool or warm, dull or intense, the mood can be determined by colour.

Don't worry about matching colour exactly. It is more important to get the **tonal differences** right – the degree of darkness or lightness of colours in relation to each other. Consider a black-and-white photograph. Which are the dark, medium and light areas?

THE MAKE-UP ROOM

The working area

Make-up rooms in film studios, in television studios and in theatres are custom-built to provide the necessary working surfaces, lighting and storage facilities: it is easy to move in and prepare the working environment. **On location** and on small-budget productions, however, this is often not the case: the surroundings may be uncomfortable, cramped and ill-equipped. In such situations it is the make-up artist's job to establish the working area.

- **The room** The room allocated should be well ventilated to meet health and safety regulations.

- **The facilities** There should be a mirror, a table and lights for each make-up artist. Electricity points must be adequate and checked prior to use. Close at hand there should be a wash basin with hot and cold running water.

- **The environment** The temperature and humidity must be comfortable for working and stable for the storage of make-up materials.

If such ideal conditions are not available it is essential to notify the location manager or production office promptly, and to state clearly what is required.

Health and hygiene

Once the working area has been transformed into a make-up room, it is up to the make-up artist to maintain a **safe, healthy** and **hygienic** working environment to safeguard both colleagues and models from accident and infection. Provided that you take sensible precautions, the make-up room can be kept safe and clean.

Cross-contamination via make-up

Infections, such as scabies, cold sores and styes, and other viral and bacterial diseases, can be spread via sponges, powder puffs, foundations, creams, lipstick and so on. Such diseases can also be passed on via equipment that has not been sterilised or cleaned properly. For this reason, and also because the acids in your skin could contaminate the make-up, you should not touch make-up products with your hands. Instead, use spatulas and brushes.

Control of Substances Hazardous to Health (COSHH) 1988

The **COSHH 1988 regulations** provide guidance and lay down rules about the safe storage and use of potentially dangerous substances. You should be familiar with these regulations. A copy of the COSSH regulations can be obtained from the office of your local Health and Safety Executive (HSE).

In particular you should know about the correct storage and use of cleaning agents, and ensure that the storage area is clearly identified.

Working hygienically

General preparations

- **Make-up products** should always be labelled clearly, with full instructions for use. This is to avoid accidents, such as mistaking surgical spirit or acetone for skin tonic.

- **Hazardous materials** should be kept securely, in lockable cabinets or metal trunks.

- **Wraps and towels** must always be clean and freshly laundered.

- **Individual make-up boxes** should be cleaned out regularly.

- **Electrical sockets and plugs** must be safe. If any are faulty, get them repaired immediately.

- **Tools** must be sterilised. Clean electrical equipment such as shavers, beard trimmers, tongs, electric hair curlers and the like using surgical spirit. (Always follow manufacturers' instructions.)

- **Mirrors** should be kept polished.

Before starting the make-up

- Check that you have clean powder puffs, sponges and brushes to hand.

While working

- When applying lipstick, use a **spatula** to transfer the lipstick onto a **palette**. (A ceramic tile serves as an inexpensive palette.) Then use a clean **lipbrush** to apply the lip colour from the palette.

When you have finished

- As soon as the make-up has been completed, clean any brushes in **brush-cleaning solvent**.
- **Sponges** and **powder puffs** should be washed and sterilised, or thrown away if they are particularly dirty (as they will be if they have been used for special effects work or heavy character make-up).
- Dispose of **solvent removers** safely, in covered bins.
- At the end of the working day, **work surfaces** should be scrubbed down and the floor swept.

PROFESSIONALISM

The make-up artist who always behaves professionally will be more successful than the one who does not. The best time to develop this professionalism is while you are training.

The make-up room should be a haven of calm. Models and actors need a restful atmosphere, away from the hustle and bustle of the set. The make-up artist may be the last person they speak to before going in front of the camera: it is vital that the make-up artist is unflustered in her work. Often the director's assistant will be urgently asking 'How much longer will you be?' or telling you to 'Hurry up', but you must not be distracted by such pressures.

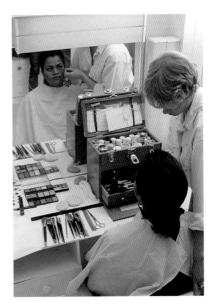

The make-up room

Efficient working

It will be easier to remain calm and purposeful if you are well organised and if your working area is clean and tidy. If everything is laid out ready when the model arrives, not only is this more pleasant but also it saves time.

Storing materials

- **Kit boxes** Keep separate kit boxes for straight make-up, casualty effects, and hairdressing. Inexpensive boxes intended for tools or fishing tackle are quite adequate.

- **Storage** Store materials in such a way that they will not be damaged, crushed, spilt or broken. Store separately any potentially messy materials, such as artificial blood, glycerine, and dirt.

- **Containers** Plastic bottles are often preferable to glass ones, but make sure that the material concerned can safely be stored in a plastic bottle. This is particularly important for substances such as surgical spirit, isopropyl alcohol and cleaning solvents.

Routine checks

- **Stock** Check your make-up stock regularly so that you do not run out of materials. Refill bottles as necessary. Report any needs to the production office.

- **Cleaning** Check that you have sufficient cleaning and sterilising fluids, appropriate to the materials you are using. (This is especially important when working on location.)
- **Labels** Ensure that the labels on all bottles and jars are clear and accurate.

Ordering materials

- **Avoiding waste** When purchasing materials for a production, take care that the products are suitable and economical. Don't use expensive brands for crowd scenes in which the actors will not be seen in close-up.
- **Special needs** Do any of the actors or models have special skin-care needs?
- **Getting quotes** When ordering facial hair and prosthetics, or hiring or buying wigs, get quotes from several suppliers. The cheapest may not be the best quality, but at least consider the options.
- **Keeping records** Keep clear and accurate records of transactions. Notify production promptly of expenses incurred.

Working abroad

- **Air freight** If you will need to have materials sent by air freight, arrange this in advance. Make sure that products are packed carefully to avoid breakages.

Clothing

- **Planning ahead** Be sure that you have sensible and appropriate clothing for the weather conditions that you may encounter where you are working.

Continuity

- **Keeping reference materials** To ensure continuity, make notes, charts and sketches to record your work, and take Polaroid photographs as necessary. These can be kept in a file or pinned to the wall so that you can refer to them as you work.

Personal appearance

Be discreet with your choice of clothing and jewellery – the artiste, not the make-up artist, is the 'star'!
   Maintain high standards of personal hygiene:

- Keep long hair tied back off the face.
- Do not use too much make-up on your own face: the artiste might think that you would also apply too much make-up to her or him!

- Wear flat-soled shoes – high heels can cause accidents in the studio.
- Do not smoke in the make-up room.
- Keep your fingernails scrupulously clean and reasonably short. Long fingernails are dangerous and make application of make-up difficult.

HOW TO SUCCEED

Checklist

In preparing for assessments on maintaining and cleaning equipment, the following list may be helpful. Check that you have covered and fully understood these items.

- The holding area for equipment and tools must be both safe and hygienic.
- Checks must be maintained on a regular basis and repairs made promptly.
- Any new electrical equipment must meet health and safety standards.
- Towels, gowns, puffs, sponges and the like must be cleaned frequently so as to ensure a supply of clean and hygienic materials to match production requirements.
- Brushes must be sterilised regularly.
- Materials must be disposed of as necessary to fulfil health and safety legislation.

Questions

Oral and written questions are used to test your knowledge and understanding. Try the following.

1 How many face shapes are there? Name them.
2 How would you improve the basic face shapes by means of make-up and hair-styling?
3 When drawing a face, where would you draw horizontal lines to help you position the features correctly?
4 What other method can help to measure the proportions accurately when sketching a face from life?
5 What are the three terms used to classify colours?
6 What colour should you add to make a colour warmer?
7 What colour should you add to tone down a colour that is too bright?
8 What are the primary paint colours in the colour wheel or circle?
9 Name the secondary paint colours in the colour wheel.
10 Which colour should you add to another to produce a tint or pastel colour?
11 Which colour should you add to another colour to produce a shade?
12 What is the complementary (opposite) colour of red?
13 When choosing colours for make-up, what factors should you consider?

CHAPTER 2

Straight make-up

INTRODUCTION

Having studied the face and learnt something about facial anatomy, you can begin some basic make-up. The most fundamental technique here is known as **straight make-up**.

Straight make-up may incorporate **corrective make-up** and **camouflage make-up**; it can overlap into beauty and fashion. Nevertheless, its real function is to enhance, to correct and to define the person's face, rather than to change it. Straight make-up is applied to news announcers, to politicians and other people being interviewed, in documentaries, in modern-day dramas, in soaps, and in comedies and light entertainment.

In general, straight make-up should be light and understated. Naturally, some women will prefer a heavier make-up, and there are always exceptions to any rule. But make-up should never be perceptible on men, and it is an art in itself to achieve a make-up look that doesn't look made-up!

It is best to think of the make-up as enhancing and grooming rather than as aiming for a high-fashion or glamorous look. Use your common sense to adapt to the situation. For example, if two people were appearing 'on camera' at the same time, and one was very dark-skinned while the other was pale in tone, it would be necessary to balance this situation for the lighting cameraman. The light-skinned person would be darkened a little to achieve a compromise.

Such a situation occurred in my own experience while Margaret Thatcher was Prime Minister. The TV crew were busy setting up in one of the drawing rooms at No. 10 Downing Street, where the interview was to take place; Mrs Thatcher was still at the Houses of Parliament, and everything had to be ready when she arrived. While the lighting was arranged, the crew were using an olive-skinned, dark-haired lady as a stand-in for Mrs Thatcher. In fact, since Mrs Thatcher has very fair hair and skin, it would have been better to have used a fair-skinned man. There wasn't time to discuss the situation, however, as Mrs Thatcher arrived and was ready for her make-up. In the small make-up room, built in Edward Heath's time, I chose a liquid foundation two shades darker than her skin tone, which surprised her. I explained the reason briefly and pointed out that she would look her usual colour using the darker base because the lights had been set using a darker skin tone. Always professional, Mrs Thatcher accepted this and went on to broadcast to India. She was surrounded by a large crowd of people and I was hovering behind them. After checking her appearance on the TV monitor nearby, she beckoned me forward, smiled approvingly and whispered, 'You were quite right.' I was touched that such a busy person, despite her many preoccupations as Prime Minister, could have such a professional eye for detail.

To practise the type of make-up needed for politicians, it is necessary to use middle-aged people as models. When practising at home, you may have parents or friends who will help in this way!

Straight make-up

PLANNING THE MAKE-UP

Make-up should always be planned prior to application. Before starting a make-up, take into account the following checklist:

- **Suitability** Make-up must match the needs of the required image.

- **Choice of colours** The analysis must be made against a neutral colour, and take into account colours to be worn, eye colour and hair colour. The hair should be well off the face and secured, and the model's face should have been cleansed, toned and moisturised.

- **Skin-care** You should check whether the model has any skin or eye allergies.

- **Timing** Assess the time needed to apply the make-up. Be realistic, and negotiate as necessary with the other personnel involved.

STRAIGHT MAKE-UP FOR WOMEN

A professional straight make-up on a woman comprises the application of some or all of the following products, applied in this order.

1 Foundation (base)

- To establish the correct skin tone.
- To obscure any differences of colour in the face.
- To provide a 'canvas' on which to work.

2 Concealer or camouflage cream

- To take away shadows under the eyes, to disguise nose-to-mouth lines, and to cover any blemishes that have not been hidden by the foundation.

3 Powder – loose translucent form

- To fix the make-up base and to take away the shine.

4 Cheekcolour or blusher

- To provide colour in the cheeks and to define the cheekbones.

5 Eyeshadow

- To provide a frame to the eyes.
- To project and define the eyes.

6 Eyebrow colour

- To define the brows.

7 Eyeliner

- To define the eyes, by painting or drawing a line close to the eyelashes.

8 Mascara

- To colour and emphasise the eyelashes.

9 False eyelashes

- Sometimes (when in fashion) to add definition to the eyes.

10 Lipcolour

- To colour the lips.
- To define or re-define the shape of the lips.

Although it is not always necessary to apply *all* of these items, it is best to consider each area in this sequence.

Equipment and materials

General

- Cleanser (milk or cream; unperfumed)
- Toner (skin tonic – for example, rosewater with glycerine for dry skin, or rosewater with distilled witch hazel for greasy skin)
- Moisturiser (unperfumed)
- Tissues
- Cottonwool
- Cotton buds
- Styptic pencil (for men's shaving cuts)
- Cream or pads for removing eye make-up
- Powder puffs
- Sponges – natural, latex, or rubber stipple (according to requirements)
- Gown
- Headband

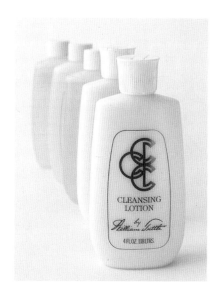

Skin-care products

Blushers and eyeshadows

Solvents

- Brush cleaner
- Nail-varnish remover

Eyelash accessories

- False eyelashes
- Eyebrow tweezers
- Eyelash curlers

Make-up

- Foundations
- Concealers
- Loose powder
- Blushers
- Eyeliners
- Mascara
- Colour ranges for eyes
- Lipsticks
- Lipgloss

Brushes

- Sable* domed brushes (¼-inch and ½-inch)
- Sable* straight-topped brushes
- Eyebrow brushes
- Eyelash separators
- Eyeliner brushes
- Blusher brushes
- Lip brushes
- Powder brushes

Brushes and sponges

*Ox, pony and goat brushes are much less expensive and are suitable for applying blusher and for brushing off powder, but they are too floppy to use when blending eyeshadow or grease or when highlighting or shading. Blending brushes *must* be sable.

Shaving equipment

- Electric shaver
- Wet razor and blades
- Aftershave, gels or creams
- Antiseptic ointment

Nail cosmetics

- Cuticle-remover cream and sticks
- Clippers
- Buffers
- Orange sticks
- Assorted nail varnishes
- Emery boards
- Nail scissors

- Nail repair glue
- False nails

Selecting the foundation

Foundations (or **bases**) are used to create a clear, healthy-looking complexion in the right colour. All blemishes and shadows should be painted out, yet the effect should be natural-looking and not heavy in texture. The eyes, cheeks and lips should be made up to emphasise the best features of the face and to minimise the less desirable ones.

Selecting a shade of foundation to match someone's skin tone is the first step and the most important one. At first this will seem difficult, but with time and practice it will become automatic.

The foundation should match the person's skin tone, and be natural-looking. At the same time it should provide an even film of colour and cover minor irregularities of skin tone such as redness. To test a foundation shade, place a tiny amount on the forehead: if the colour is correct, it will blend easily with the natural tone of the skin. This method of foundation selection is used by most make-up artists.

There is no need to have hundreds of different-coloured foundations. By using your eyes and developing your colour sense you will learn to mix a colour for any skin type. The professional brands are the best ones to use, as they are made especially for the media, they are the right consistency, and they have a wider colour choice than those made for the general public and sold in chemists' shops and department stores.

Each person's skin tone is a combination of red, brown, white and yellow, mixed in various combinations. To learn how to match a foundation colour, start by mixing a small quantity of these colours together and make an exact match for your own skin tone. Then do the same for as many other people as you can. Soon you will get used to estimating the amount of yellow in someone's skin tone at a glance. For black skins you will need more red and yellow than for white ones, otherwise the foundation will appear grey and dull.

Types of foundations

- **Liquid foundations** Used for a natural look on young or clear skin, often for beauty work. They are applied using a damp sponge. There are many types; professional products tend to be the least sticky.

- **Cream foundations** Used for older skin or for greater coverage on younger skin. They should be used lightly.

- **Panstik foundations** Used for heavy coverage, as in theatre work. These greasepaints come in palettes and as sticks; they have a greater density of pigment. Being greasy, they need powder to set them.

- **Camouflage foundations** Used for poor complexions, and to cover scars, spots and blemishes.

- **Pancake foundations** Used for body make-up and where a 'flat' look is required, as on bald heads. Pancake is normally too flat and dry for the face. It does not rub off on clothing, which makes it ideal for use on the body. It is also used for fantasy face painting. Pancakes are water-based foundations, applied using a wet sponge; they dry quickly to a matt finish. When dry they can be buffed with a cloth to give a natural-looking sheen. Pancake is available in all colours as well as in skin tones.

Liquid foundations and concealers

- **Tint foundations** Used only on very clear skin or to enhance a tan. No powder is required. Tints can look good on men's skin.

Making up the face

Hygiene

- Always work cleanly and hygienically.
- Do not re-use brushes, sponges, powder puffs and the like – keep them clean while in use; then wash them or throw them away. Throw away used cottonwool, tissues and cotton buds.
- Don't forget to put the lids back on jars and bottles when you've finished with them.

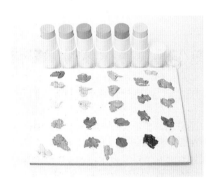

Panstiks

Preparation

1 Place a gown around the model.
2 Place tissues around the collar.
3 Put on the headband. At this point, study the face shape, the features, and the skin tone and texture. Discuss preferences, ideas and colours.
4 Cleanse, tone and moisturise the skin. If the skin is dry, allow the moisturiser to sink in. If it is oily, remove the excessive grease using tissues. (A good skin preparation is essential for the smooth application of the make-up foundation.)
5 Choose a suitable base which matches the skin tone. Test this on the forehead as the light is particularly good on this area.

Applying the foundation

Having applied the moisturiser, you are now ready to apply the foundation.

1 With a barely damp sponge (natural or synthetic – try both types), apply a small amount of the **foundation**, starting on the forehead, working down the face, lightly and evenly across the eyelids, avoiding the mouth, blending under the chin, and onto the upper part of the neck.
2 Use the clean side of the sponge to blend the edges away at

Equipment and materials
- brushes (clean) in a container
- cleanser, toner and moisturiser
- cottonwool and buds
- sponge and water in a small bowl
- foundations (assorted)
- loose powder
- concealers
- colour ranges for eyes
- blushers
- eyeliner and mascara
- eyebrow pencils
- tissues
- lip pencils
- lipsticks and lip gloss
- gown and headband
- powder puff

the hairline on the forehead, around the ears and on the neck.

3 Use a clean brush to blend the foundation evenly around the sensitive eye areas, under the nose and around the nostrils.

Setting the foundation

1 To apply **loose powder**, dip the powder puff into the powder. Shake off any excess; then tap the puff against the back of your hand, dislodging any remaining excess. There should not be too much powder on the puff at one time.

2 Roll the powder puff over the face, pressing firmly yet gently with a rocking motion, until the entire face is covered. More powder is usually needed down the centre part of the face. Don't forget the eyelids, and under the chin and onto the neck. Be very sparing on the eye areas, especially below the eyes.

3 Brush off excess powder with a large soft brush for a smooth even finish. Use the tip of the brush softly to avoid streaking the make-up.

Cheeks

To apply **blusher**, using a natural colour:

1 Feel for the top of the cheekbones. If necessary, ask the model to smile.

2 Apply blusher to the 'apple' of the cheek; brush upwards onto top of cheekbone. Use very little, simply to give the base colour some 'life'. More can be applied after working on the lips and eyes; by then you will be able to see the balance.

Eyes

To use subtle colours for a natural look on pale skin tones:

1 Lighten the brow bone with white **eyeshadow**, then with peach.

2 Apply taupe (pale grey-brown), starting at the outer edge of the eye lid and working towards the centre. Use grey to emphasise the outer edge.

Eye make-up

3 When you are happy with the blending, apply the **eyeliner**. Use grey, brown or black. Keep this subtle. Begin at the start of the eyelash growth, but not too far into the inner corners of the eyes. Pull the eyelid taut gently with your fingertip, and paint a thin line as close to the roots of the lashes as possible. If you want to blend the line, use a clean brush to do so.

4 The same method should be used along the bottom lashes. Do not draw a line further than the natural growth of lashes on the inside corner, nor further out on the outer corners than the outer edge of the eyebrow. Hold a pencil or brush to check on the distance.

The nose-to-eye measuring technique

Eyelashes

1 Apply **mascara** to the eyelashes on the lower eyelids using the tip of a brush. Stand *behind* the model. Hold the top lid up slightly, and brush mascara through the eyelashes in downward strokes and then upwards on the *underside* of the lashes. Stand further around the model and repeat the procedure for the other eye. If you aren't using a proper make-up chair with a headrest, you can rest the model's head against your body.

2 Apply one or two coats of mascara, then brush through with a clean mascara comb or brush to separate the lashes and remove any excess blobs of mascara.

Eyebrows

1 Brush through.
2 Fill in any gaps or change the shape as required, using a suitable brush and powder; a **pencil** in short strokes; or, for a heavier look, paint on strokes with 'wet powder colour'.
3 At this point, define eye and cheek colour by adding more if necessary.

> **TIP**
>
> Powder eyeshadows are also good for applying to the eyebrows.

Lips

Lips are often the hardest part of the make-up. Precision is vital. Lips should be balanced out if there are any imperfections.

Blotting, powdering and reapplying will make the lip colour last longer; loose powder can be used on top of a glossy lipstick to make it more matt. For stability, you can rest your hand on a powder puff on the face, or rest your little finger on the chin. The edges should be drawn in first, then filled in (photo on page 24).

1 Discuss the colour with the model (unless you are working to a brief).
2 **Lip pencil** can be used to define the shape first. With the **lipstick**, work from the corners up; or draw the top and bottom outline first, and then work from the corners up.
3 Lips can be evened out and enlarged; they can even be reduced if foundation is applied first. Work slowly but positively. Use the correct pressure: if you are too light you

will tickle or irritate and it will be harder to create a line; if you press too hard, however, you will move the lips. Ask the model to open and close her mouth as necessary.

4 Blot the lipstick and reapply it.

5 Check the make-up and powder again lightly, brushing off any excess with a large soft brush.

False eyelashes

From the natural look using individual lashes suitable for close-up on film to an exotic heavy-lashed look for the stage, **false eyelashes** can make an enormous difference to the eyes. For the best effect, however, they must be trimmed properly and attached as close to the real lashes of the eyes as possible.

The best – but most expensive – are made of real hair knotted onto a strip. Less expensive are the nylon ones, also in strip form. They are usually shaped, but tend to be too long for all but the largest eyes. Sometimes the eyelashes are available on long strips completely untrimmed – all the lashes are the same length.

Whatever the type of eyelashes, they should be individually fitted to the eyes and trimmed to suit the requirements of the make-up. The strip they are attached to should not be stuck too close to the inner corner of the eye, but instead further out, where the eye curves upwards and where the real eyelashes begin. The other end should finish at the place where the outer corner of the eye ends.

If the eyelashes are already shaped and you need to cut the strip, always cut the end where the lashes are *shortest*, so as not to lose the length of the outer lashes.

Preparing the eyelashes

1 To prepare the untrimmed type of eyelashes, cut them at an angle so that there is a left and a right lash, with the outer lashes about 12 mm in length and the inner ones 6 mm. Then cut every other hair about 3 mm shorter than the next, to give a feathered effect.

Applying the eyelashes

1 To apply the lashes, place the heavier, curved end on the outer part of the upper lashline, as close to the natural lashes as possible. Do not extend beyond the natural lash growth.

2 Some people use **eyelash tweezers** to place the strip in place, others prefer to use their fingers. The **eyelash adhesive** should be lightly stroked onto the underside of the strip before gently placing it on the eyelid.

3 When both sets of eyelashes have been correctly placed, and once the adhesive has dried, it will be necessary to go over the strip with eyeliner, to disguise it. Taper the end of the painted eyeline with a fine, pointed brush to make the line look natural.

4 If the natural lashes are too straight it may be necessary to

Equipment and materials

- eyelashes
- eyelash curlers
- eyelash adhesive
- eyelash tweezers
- fine brush
- cotton buds
- eyecolour (water-based)

TIP

Use a cotton bud to tap the eyelash into position.

add mascara to attach them to the false ones. Another method is to use **eyelash curlers** on the natural lashes first, before applying the false ones.

5 Do not use pencil to line the eyelids as the grease in the pencil will cause the strip to become loose. Water-applied **eyeliner** is best. Always use a fine, pointed sable-hair brush.

6 For a wide-eyed look you can attach one or two of the outer natural lashes to the corresponding false ones with eyelash adhesive. This works very well if the natural outer lashes are a bit 'droopy'.

Some false lashes are attached two or three hairs at a time. These are fixed into position by dipping each group of lashes into adhesive and placing them at the base of the natural lashes. They look effective when used at the outer corners only, or to replace a space in the natural lashline. The adhesive should be spread onto a plate or palette, and a group of hairs should be held with tweezers and dipped into the adhesive so that the base is covered. Attach each group separately, in the direction of the natural curve of the lashes. The lashes can be trimmed to the length of the real lashes and coated with mascara as normal; the result will be undetectable in close-up. Individual lashes can be placed in the same way.

There are many varieties of false eyelashes, in varying densities of thickness and length. For strong effects lashes are also available in gold, silver, red, blue, green and yellow; there are even multicoloured ones. Normally it is preferable to use brown lashes on fair-haired people and black ones on dark-haired people.

Lips

Removing the eyelashes

1 To remove the false eyelashes, take hold of the outer end of the strip with one finger; place a finger of the other hand on the centre of the closed eyelid, and peel the strip off gently.

2 Remove the bits of dried adhesive, and wash off the mascara with a cotton bud soaked in cleansing milk or **eye make-up remover**. Place the lashes back in their box.

3 If the false lashes lose their curl, wind them round the curve of a pencil: roll a tissue around this and leave overnight. They should be curled again by the next morning.

> **Equipment and materials**
> - cotton buds
> - cleansing milk *or* eye make-up remover
> - tissues

Bottom lashes may be used when the top lashes are very heavy; they were much used in the sixties. Bottom lashes can also be drawn in, using a fine brush and eyeliner; for opera, ballet and other stage work this works well. Bottom lashes are not generally used in TV and film work today as they are not fashionable, but they are still used for some fantasy and light entertainment shows, and, of course, in period or historical work where appropriate. Bottom lashes are applied in the same way as upper lashes.

Men

Men

False eyelashes are not used on men. If a man has fair eyelashes it may be necessary to use mascara in order to define the eyes. Always apply sparingly, and brush through afterwards with a clean brush to separate the eyelashes and remove excess mascara. In feature films or a long-running TV series it is better to tint a man's eyelashes, as tint will last for approximately six weeks.

An example

The following is an example of a step-by-step application of straight make-up, including false eyelashes.

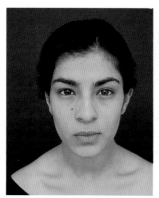
Before

Applying the foundation

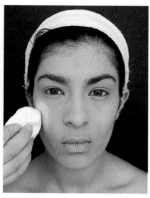
Applying the powder

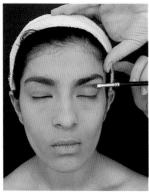
Applying eyeshadow to the socket line

Applying eyeliner

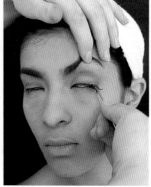
Placing false eyelashes into position

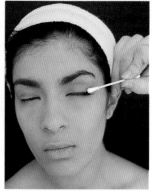
Tapping false eyelashes into position

Applying mascara to blend

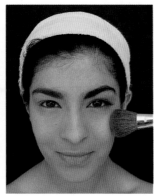
Applying blusher

Applying lipstick with a brush

Finished effect, with the hair dressed

Miscellaneous tips

Manner

- *To give confidence* Always work gently and calmly, with a friendly and relaxed manner.

General

- *To make the best use of make-up* For the maximum effect, use the minimum make-up. Apply it only when it is really needed – for example, there is often no need for an overall foundation.

Features

- *To emphasise the natural structure of the face* Use shading, both medium and light. Highlight prominent areas, such as the forehead, the cheekbones, and the shadows under the eyes. Warm the eyebrow bones by applying a light-coloured blusher. Highlight the top of the cheekbones.

- *To project a feature forward, or to diminish it* Reverse the natural shadows.

The eyes

- *To bring the eyes closer together* Put a darker colour on the eyelids, in the inner corners of the eyes.

- *To bring deep-set eyes 'out'* Lighten the socket line.

- *To 'lift' the outside of the eye* Shade the outside of the eye corner towards the eyebrow. Blend the shading away to nothing.

- *To 'lift' the eye* Apply a little eyelash adhesive to a couple of the outer-corner eyelashes and attach these to the outer eyelid.

- *To disguise stubborn shadows under the eyes* Try applying a small circle of blusher to high cheekbones, in line with the centre of the eye: this will often distract the observer's eye from the shadows.

Age

Remember: the older the person, the lighter should be both the make-up application and the colours.

- *To avoid 'ageing' the model* Don't apply too much foundation or eye make-up; don't use too much foundation or powder in creases and laughter lines; don't emphasise lines going downwards; don't light eyebag areas.

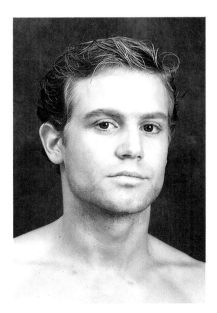

A straight make-up on a man

STRAIGHT MAKE-UP FOR MEN

The make-up for a man should be natural-looking, yet at the same time corrective and flattering. It should be subtle enough not to appear made-up to the general public, and yet should improve his image for TV cameras and newspaper photographers.

Do not apply a base all over a man's face, unless he is particularly pale or grey-looking. If it is necessary to change his skin tone, use a liquid foundation lightly, as a wash of colour, so that it is almost transparent.

The most important details to bear in mind are the shadows under the eyes and the beardline. If the latter looks too dark, it should be lightened with a pinkish, yellow or orange colour, which will neutralise and 'kill' the blueness of the beard shadow. This is necessary only on dark-haired men whose beardlines show a prominent 'six o'clock shadow'.

Grey hairs and bald or thinning patches can be darkened with make-up. Under heavy studio lights, bald heads should be made up so that they do not shine too much. Use a pancake or liquid body make-up, not grease-based products, so as to give a matt appearance.

If a make-up base has been applied to the face, don't forget to darken the backs of the hands also with pancake. (Avoid using grease or cream make-up on the hands – even after powdering, this would come off on the clothes.) The ears too should be made up as on camera they often appear too red. Be careful not to blend the face make-up too far down the man's neck as it could stain his shirt collar. Tuck a paper tissue around the neck collar whilst working under the chin and onto the neck.

Hair should be tidied with a comb or brush in the normal way. Make sure there are no stray hairs sticking out: the outline should be tidy. Hairspray may be used, also wax, gel or grease; usually, though, it is best to leave the hair looking natural, especially on an older man who is not used to using hair preparations.

If the make-up is for an interview to take place out of doors, then spraying the hair is not a good idea. I once had to make up a well-known politician for an interview which was filmed on Westminster Bridge. He had the habit, common amongst balding men, of growing his remaining hair very long and draping it over the bald part. As he was being interviewed, a gust of wind swept his hair so that it was blowing madly all over the place. The director asked me to spray it hard with lacquer to avoid this happening again. Being young at the time and so not inclined to argue with the director, I did as I was asked. When the next gust of wind came, it blew the minister's hair upwards in one stiff piece, which looked appalling. From experience you learn what works and what doesn't!

The beardline

Toning down a beardline

1 Apply a foundation, very lightly.
2 Don't remove shadows unless these are really bad; to do so tends to make the face look too feminine. A little lightening under heavy eyebags is usually enough.
3 Tone down the beard using a camouflage cream applied lightly by means of a rubber **stipple sponge**. Apply a foundation on top of this. For a *very* heavy beard shadow, an orange camouflage can be used to take away the blue; this works particularly well on Indians or men with black hair.
4 Never use blusher on a man. If colour is needed in the cheeks, apply a brown or tan colour using a **natural sponge** with a stippling movement.
5 Powder lightly and brush off any excess with a clean powder brush. To remove the powdered look, press damp cottonwool on the cheeks and the nose area. This also helps to make the make-up last longer under hot lights.
6 When standing by on the set, apply more powder only if the model's face is shining too much. If asked by the cameraman to apply more powder, don't forget to brush off the excess with a clean brush so that it doesn't look obvious.

Filling in or changing a beardline

1 Apply a bluish-black colour. Black is too hard: it is better to mix blue and dark brown from your palette. Use very little, and stipple it on using a natural sponge. A special stipple sponge may be used as well as a natural one.
2 Remember that a beardline will make the man look older.
3 If the eyes 'disappear', use eyeliner. Apply it in dots between the lashes – never paint a heavy line on a man. Use a water-based liner, and tone this down with water. Use brown or grey on fair-haired men, dark brown on dark-haired men.
4 Mascara can be used on freckly, sandy-haired pale faces, but don't use much and brush it through the lashes carefully. Use shades of brown, never black.

STRAIGHT CORRECTIVE MAKE-UP

The use of colour

A 'straight' make-up may not be sufficient in hiding defects such as scars, shadows under the eyes, and minor skin blemishes. In such cases it may be necessary also to use colour to conceal a defect. **Concealing colours** (**concealers**) are available ready-made, or you can mix your own on a palette.

■ *Too much red in the skin tone* Use yellow concealer before or after applying the foundation. In extreme cases of redness, green can be used to tone down the colour, but this should be

Toning down the beardline
(a) Before

> **Equipment and materials**
> - foundation
> - camouflage cream
> - stipple brush
> - powder and brush
> - natural sponge
> - cottonwool

> **Equipment and materials**
> - stipple sponge
> - eyeliner (water-based)
> - mascara

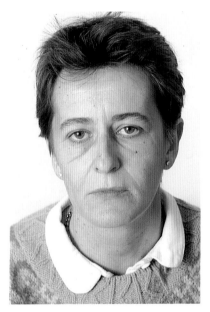

Hiding shadow under the eyes with orange (a) Before

(b) After

used with caution: green can take away so much colour that it makes the person look ill.

- *A blue-black beardline* Blue can be counteracted by applying orange, for example to tone down the beardline on a man with six o'clock shadow.
- *Blue-black shadows under the eyes* Orange works well in hiding these, on skin tones ranging from olive to black.
- *Grey shadows* Pink will take these away on pale skin tones.

Most make-up artists apply the corrective concealing colour *before* using a foundation, but it can also be applied afterwards.

Highlighting and shading

The term 'corrective make-up' also includes the use of highlighting and shading, perhaps the most important skills in the make-up artist's repertoire.

Highlighting is the blending of a shade *lighter* than the foundation in order to make a feature *more* obvious. This might be used, for example, to bring out deep-set eyes or a weak chin. **Shading** is the blending of a shade *darker* than the foundation in order to *diminish* a feature. A large nose could be shaded at the sides to make it appear thinner, for instance, or a double chin could be made less obvious by shading.

In straight and beauty make-up, highlighting and shading are often referred to as **contouring**. The process can enhance a good bone structure or, if the face is plump, give the illusion of one.

Principles of light and shade

If you draw a round circle on a piece of paper, it will appear flat. To make it appear rounded you need to add some shadow and highlighting. By placing some dark shading around the outer circle of the 'ball', and by blending this shadow to nothing, leaving a white highlight, you can make the circle look like a white ball.

If you draw a similar circle and this time add a strong colour in the centre, blending this outwards to a highlight at the outer edges, the circle will again look like a ball. This process is similar to the technique used in blending cheek colour.

(b) After

ACTIVITY: DRAWING LIGHT AND SHADE (1)

1 Throw a piece of drapery across the back of a chair, near a source of light, such as a window or a side lamp.
2 Study the light and shade in the folds of the cloth. The brightest parts will have light shining directly onto them. The darkest areas will be those where the light does not reach.
3 Using a soft pencil, draw onto plain white paper the drapery as you see it. Draw the outline first, then fill in the details of the folds, softly smudging the edges of the shading. Try to make the folds of the cloth look rounded.

The object of this exercise is to improve your drawing skills, to develop your sense of observation, and to help you become aware of the effect of light on any object.

The light from the window creates 'highlights' on the folds of the cloth.

The darkest, shadowed areas are furthest away from the source of light. The graduation of intensity makes the folds of cloth look rounded.

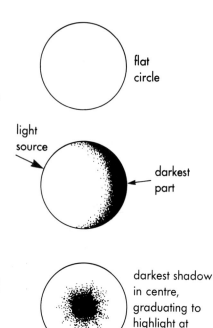

Using light and shade to make a flat circle look round

Applying these principles to make-up

Assessing what is needed

To begin the make-up, ask your model to tuck her chin down, and at the same time to look up into the mirror without raising her head. Most people will have dark circles under their eyes. On younger faces the shadows will be slight, although even children may have dark circles, either through lack of sleep or by reason of inheritance within their family.

On closer examination you will notice that there is a shadow running from the nose to the corners of the mouth. Apart from this the face may have blemishes, or patches of redness. After the foundation has been put on, you can mix a skin tone somewhat lighter than the overall colour and use this to paint in the circles under the eyes, covering any blemishes with a small brush. Blend the edges carefully. Redness can be toned down by adding more yellow to the concealing colour. (Concealing is *not* the same as highlighting, though both use a colour lighter than the base tone. The concealing colour should hide and tone in with the rest of the face tone, whereas a highlighting colour is to draw attention and to emphasise a particular feature.)

In certain contexts the performer is presumed already to be perfect for the part: the make-up is simply to make him or her as attractive as possible. This applies to the many people who appear on television but who are not actors, people such as weather forecasters, interviewers and interviewees. Slight adjustments only may be necessary, such as shortening the nose, darkening the eyebrows, or reducing a dark beardline and covering blemishes.

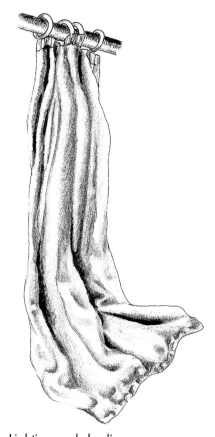

Lighting and shading

Adjusting the structure of the face

Earlier on, when you were sketching a face on paper, you learned that the ideal face can be divided horizontally: from the hairline to the eyes; from the eyes to the bottom of the nose; and from the bottom of the nose to the tip of the chin. When the balance is not ideal, make-up can be used to improve it.

- *If the forehead is too high* Darken the forehead around the hairline with a colour two shades *darker* than the base colour. The colour must be blended downwards so that it gradually disappears into the foundation.

- *If the forehead is too low* Follow the same principle, but this time you will apply a colour two shades *lighter* than the foundation. Paint it close to the hairline in a wide equal band; and, as before, blend it downwards so that there is no line of demarcation.

■ *If the forehead is too narrow or too wide* Add shadows or highlights at the outer sides, near the temples. Be careful not to shade in the temple areas too much, however. As you know from your previous 'skull' make-up, if overdone the effect will be ageing.

■ *If the chin is too long* Shade the lower part.

■ *If the chin is too short* Highlight the lower part.

■ *If the face is too flat or too round* Shading under the cheekbones is a classic aid to beauty and can make a flat or round face look more interesting.

When *drawing* you can blend edges with your fingers; when painting people's *faces*, however, it is both easier and more hygienic to use good-quality sable-haired brushes.

Remember: when selecting a colour for *shading*, use a liquid or cream two shades darker, but in the same tone as the natural skin colour; when *highlighting*, select one that is two shades lighter.

ACTIVITY: LIGHTING AND SHADING IN MAKE-UP

Try some lighting and shading on one another's faces. Try to make them look *rounder* or *longer*. Use very little make-up, the more subtle the better. It must not look painted on, but should seem like natural shadows and highlights.

ACTIVITY: MAKING UP A FACE   Time: 1 hour

Choose a type of make-up that involves the use of light and shade to create the required effect. It can be a 'beauty' make-up or one that makes your model look fatter or thinner. The idea is to choose a make-up that gives you practice in modelling with colour, either to flatter the person's face or to achieve the opposite.

1 First study the face, then decide what to do. Draw a sketch or chart, and make written notes of what you are going to do to achieve the result. Where will you put the shading? Where will you put the highlights?
2 Choose and assemble your materials. Lay them out neatly on your working space, putting clean water in a bowl and having everything ready to hand.
3 Wash your hands.
4 Place a wrap around your model to protect her clothes, and a hairband to keep the hair off her face.
5 Clean and moisturise her face. Test the skin for colours.
6 Apply the make-up.
7 Throughout the make-up, keep checking in the mirror to view

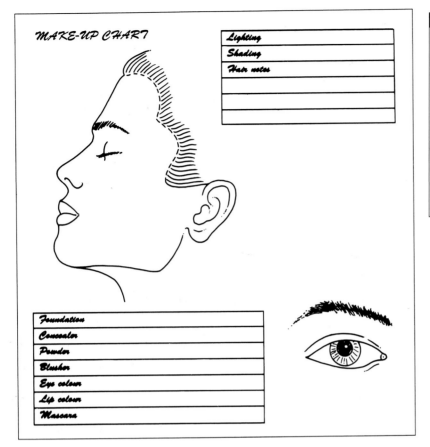

MAKE-UP CHART

Lighting	
Shading	
Hair notes	

Foundation	
Concealer	
Powder	
Blusher	
Eye colour	
Lip colour	
Mascara	

Make-up chart

TIP

Whilst applying the make-up, be considerate towards your model. Don't lean on her head with your hand. Don't jerk her head around, when looking in the mirror; if required, ask her politely to turn her head to a different angle. If applying lipstick, it may help to rest your hand on a powder puff placed on her chin.

the result and to check that the blending is balanced on either side of the face.

8 When you look in the mirror, check that the shading and lighting are not too heavy, and that the colours are harmonious and suit your model's skin.

9 Now throw away all the used cottonwool, cotton buds and tissues. Pour a little brush cleaner into a small bowl. Clean your brushes and wipe them with a tissue. Put the bottle of brush cleaner away again. Put the tops back on all of the containers.

10 If you are working in a group, seek your tutor's appraisal. It is a good idea also to look at other students' make-ups, as much can be learned from constructive criticism and praise.

11 Take photographs, for your own reference later.

12 Finally, remove your model's make-up.

Blending

Blending means *graduating the intensity* of a colour – whether it is a darker colour, for shading, or a lighter one, for highlighting. The technique of graduating a colour from its strongest tone to its lightest, until it disappears into the skin tone, is one that is used constantly in every area of make-up.

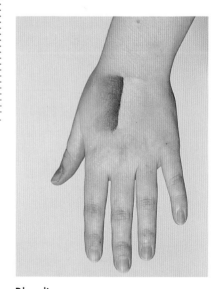

Blending

ACTIVITY: BLENDING
Practise blending by applying a line of make-up on the back of your hand.

Using a sable brush, a cosmetic sponge or your fingertips, gradually reduce the amount of colour from the darkest point to the lightest (downwards), until the final edge fades into the skin.

Corrective make-up, showing uses of lighting and shading

Before

Slimming the nose

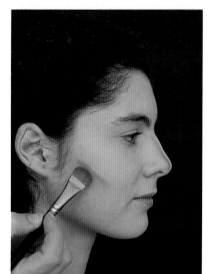

Slimming the side of the face

Finished effects

EFFECTS OF LIGHTING

Effects of lighting on make-up

Whether you are working in photography, theatre, television or film, the **lighting** is always crucial to your work as a make-up artist. Lighting is the art of painting with light and shade; it can make a set look dull or interesting. The basics of lighting consist of a main light, the **key light**; a secondary light, the **fill light**, which has less intensity and can model or sculpt the subject; and a **back light**, which separates the subject from the background.

It is not only the *amount* of light that affects the subject, but also the *direction* from which it falls. **Cross-lighting** is the illumination of the actor, on the front of his face, from two directions at equal distance but opposite angles. Cross-lighting has the effect of emphasising wrinkles on the face, and whilst excellent for an ageing make-up, it is not flattering for a 'beauty' make-up.

In *film work* the exterior work on location is natural: that is, it is the sun that acts as the key light. The secondary, or fill, light is provided by reflection or using arc lamps.

Television lighting is generally fixed on a set, with a lighting scheme similar to that used for stage lighting. Each relies on overhead fill lighting and side key lighting, with floor fill lights to lessen the facial shadows.

Lighting for *video* is generally much flatter than for cinematography: less detail will be picked up, so the make-up needs to be stronger or much of the effect will be lost.

For *still camera* work an electronic flash is used when exposing the film. This produces a very intense and rapid flash of light. The 'freezing' action of electronic flash at high speed provides sharp-looking pictures. In commercial photography this is the most widely used method.

The effects of lighting

ACTIVITY: STUDYING THE EFFECTS OF LIGHTING

Effects of lighting on make-up can be practised with normal domestic lights.

1 Seat your model under an overhead light, suspended from the ceiling without a shade. Observe the unflattering shadows in the eye, nose and mouth areas.
2 Place a lamp to one side of your model. Observe the deep shadow on the side of the face that is not illuminated.
3 Put the lamp *below* your model's face. Note the grotesque effects of unnatural-looking shadows.

Effects of lighting on colour

Light can change colours dramatically, as happens when the colours drain away from a landscape as the sun is obscured by a dark cloud. A face is never the same colour over its entire surface: it will be darker in shadow areas, and lighter where the light strikes the surface. This interplay of light and shade, and the effect this has on the colour of a facial feature, help to define the features and reveal them as three-dimensional.

ACTIVITY: DRAWING LIGHT AND SHADE (2)

With some white cartridge paper and soft pencil, and using a fellow student as a model, draw a face, putting in the light and dark areas. (Photographs can be used, but a live model is best.) Keep to the full-face pose as this avoids the problems of foreshortening of the features that arise when the face is turned away from you.

The face must not be too brightly lit; if it were, the shadows cast would be very dense and consequently harsh, making the contrast between areas of light and shade too wide. Aim at a soft diffused light, with the light source to one side of the head. This is the most flattering light: it brings out the roundness of the head and the modelling of the features.

If the shadows still look too dark, you may be able to correct this with a little reflected light placed on the opposite side to the light source. This can be achieved using a white-painted board or other white material, positioning this so that some of the light is reflected back into the shadows. Alternatively, another light could be placed on this side.

Observe the shadows and the highlights which reveal the bone structure and the contours. Note that the areas of the face most likely to be in shadow are beneath and along the jaw, and under the brows and cheeks (particularly if these are prominent). Other shaded areas are at the sides of the nose and immediately under it, especially in the depression running from the nose to the middle of the upper lip. There is usually a shadow just beneath the centre of the bottom lip, provided that the lip is fairly full. The highlighted areas are generally on top of the nose, across the forehead, and on the fullest part of the cheeks.

CAMOUFLAGE MAKE-UP

Camouflage make-up should not be confused with *concealer* make-up. Camouflage creams are used in hospitals to cover burns, scars, severe acne, birthmarks, and all conditions of the skin where normal make-up is undesirable or insufficient to cover skin discolorations.

As a make-up artist you need to understand the use of camouflage creams, because many actors and actresses have birthmarks, scars and other imperfections; the products are also useful for concealing tattoos and heavy beardlines. I once had to cover very dark freckles on a model's back for a bath-oil commercial.

It is my own view that all professional make-up artists should be willing to use their skills to help people with skin problems. This is a challenging field, offering great relief to patients and personal satisfaction to the make-up artist. Some artists specialise in such **skin camouflage therapy**, working in hospital burns units.

Products

The products used are these:

Body make-up

- **Veil** (Thomas Blake) This comes in eighteen shades: it is ointment-based, has excellent coverage, and is light in texture. It is excellent for Caucasian skin tones.

- **Covermark cover cream** (a New York company) A thick ointment base, with heavier coverage. The shades include a grey that is good for creating a beardline on men with skin grafts on the chin.

- **Keromask** (Innoxa) A fairly thick ointment base (although slightly thinner than Covermask), which is easily spread and gives excellent coverage. It is available in a range of twelve colours.

- **Dermablend** (Flori Roberts) A range of light to dark colours designed for black skins. It has a heavy consistency, and is also good for covering tattoos.

- **Dermacolour** (Kryolan) A fine ointment base allowing good coverage. It is available in a very wide range of colours; the yellows and the dark tones are particularly useful.

Before: The facial skin tone is uneven, and the body too pale; there are also very obvious scars on the stomach and arms

General hints

Experiment with camouflage creams until you understand their use. In general, use a smaller amount than you would with normal make-up. Just as two or three thin coats of nail varnish last longer than one thick layer, so with camouflage creams: each layer should be powered to set it before applying the next.

Although intended for covering extreme skin defects, camouflage creams are sometimes useful in normal corrective make-up, as for example in covering very dark shadows under the eyes or disguising a pimple. One thin layer only may be necessary.

BODY MAKE-UP

Make sure that *all* areas of the skin that may show on camera are made up to blend in with the face. Pancake or liquid body make-up should be used, in the same shade as the face make-up.

Men's ears in particular are apt to look very red if a light is placed behind them. Hands will look paler unless made up. (When making up the hands, do the backs only – not the palms.)

If there isn't time to apply body make-up, make sure that the facial skin tone matches other exposed parts of the body.

After: The face and body tone have been evened out with water-based body make-up. The scars have been made less prominent with camouflage make-up

WATERPROOFING THE MAKE-UP

When filming scenes which involve the actors working in conditions where they are bound to get wet – underwater scenes, shower scenes, rainfall scenes, swimming scenes, and so on – the make-up must be waterproof.

Camouflage make-up (as used in hospitals) is resistant to water. If camouflage make-up is unavailable, use any grease-based products in the following way:

1 Apply the make-up.
2 Apply powder.
3 Spray with water.
4 Tissue-dry, to blot the water.
5 Apply more make-up.
6 Apply powder.
7 Spray with water . . .

Repeat this process, finishing off with a final layer of powder. *Mascara* should not be used – tint the actor's eyelashes with **eyelash dye**, if necessary.

Another way of making waterproof make-up is to grind pancake to powder and mix this with sea-salt and water. Apply this make-up with a sponge. Use a large bath sponge for making up the arms, legs and torso swiftly.

MAINTAINING THE MAKE-UP

When the make-up is completed and the actor is on the set, your responsibility has not ended. It is now necessary to *maintain* the make-up you have applied, so that it remains intact throughout the shoot. Whether working inside the studio under hot lights, or outside on location in various weather conditions, it is important to stand by, ready to repair any damage to the make-up.

The make-up artist should have all the necessary tools and materials in a **small bag** or **set box**. Clear **plastic bags with zip fastenings** are useful: these not only protect your materials but make it easy to recognize them at a glance. As the set is usually dirty, perhaps with smoke machines and other effects being used, avoid leaving your kit box open or uncovered.

Check the make-up between shots, with a complete check after each meal break. Touching-up includes adding more lipstick, blotting perspiration, and re-powdering.

When the actor needs to have a complete change of costume, hair and make-up you must make arrangements with the assistant director to allow time for this.

Whether repairing the make-up or applying a new one for reasons of continuity, it is always essential to move quickly yet remain calm. The work should be done without holding up the production.

Even if you are simply blotting perspiration with a cleaning tissue or adding lipstick, it is advisable to encourage the actor to sit comfortably in a chair.

Maintaining make-up

Working on a set

To an outsider it always looks as if everyone on the set is hanging around doing nothing. This is because everyone else has to wait whilst someone finishes his or her work. Lights need adjusting, props must be moved, tracks must be laid down for the cameras to move on, and all these activities take time. So whenever you have work to do, you need to do it immediately, as others may be waiting for you.

The make-up artist should never leave the set without first informing another member of the make-up team or an assistant director. Unexpected things happen all the time: if the set is left unattended, the make-up artist is sure to be needed at that moment!

There are many potential hazards on the set, such as trailing cables and wires: to avoid accidents, always wear sensible flat shoes with rubber soles. Don't wear anything that makes a noise, such as jangling bracelets or squeaky footwear: any such sound can hold up the work.

The entire crew work closely together; by being sympathetic towards one another they create a good team. Everyone relies on the others to work well, efficiently and fast. When working under pressure in this way it is vital to establish good working relationships with everyone involved. Since intense pressure is normal on a shoot, and indeed necessary to generate the required energy, the professional make-up artist must learn to cope with stress. Consideration towards the actors, such as providing them with coffee at the right moment, can help greatly in alleviating *their* tension.

A useful item to carry when working on the set is a good-quality **chamois leather**. This can be soaked in cold water, squeezed until damp, and then sprinkled with cologne. When twirled in the air, the leather becomes ice-cold. When an actor is excessively hot you can relieve the symptoms by placing the chamois leather at the back of his neck to cool him down, which in turn helps to maintain the make-up. Small **battery fans** are also good for keeping actors cool.

REMOVING THE MAKE-UP

When the actor has finished filming the director will release him or her, and the make-up artist must remove the make-up. With character or special-effects make-up this can be time-consuming and may involve the use of special **solvents**. With straight corrective make-up the procedure is simpler, and merely involves cleansing, toning and moisturising.

An unperfumed simple **cleansing milk** or **cream** should be massaged onto the face and then wiped with **tissues** or **cottonwool**. Cottonwool soaked in warm water and squeezed until damp is good in cleansing the face efficiently. On men's faces it is better to use tissues, as cottonwool often sticks to their beardline. Some male actors prefer using **baby wipes**.

Toner should be applied after cleansing, to remove traces of grease. **Moisturiser** can then be applied to the face (especially on women). Many men prefer simply to wash their faces with soap and water: make sure you have a clean **towel** available.

HOW TO SUCCEED

Checklist

In preparing for assessments on straight corrective make-up, the following lists may be helpful. Check that you have covered and fully understood these items.

Applying make-up
- Correction of all faults is in relation to the image reflected in the mirror.
- The foundation covers the skin to a colour and texture to match the model's own skin, suited to the on-screen image.
- All colours and the foundation must be well blended to achieve a natural look, to avoid sharp lines or edges, and to suit the on-screen image.
- Where necessary, other exposed parts of the body must match the facial skin tone.
- Application of make-up must observe all health and safety regulations, and avoid both contact to the inside of the eye and any cross-contamination.
- Any adjustments made must suit the intended medium.
- All make-up and shading must achieve an appropriate look and colour and enhance the image on camera.
- All applications must be correct for the type of make-up and for the effect required.
- The order of application must be correct to maintain and maximise the effects on each application.

Maintaining the make-up
- Maintenance must be swift, efficient, and timed to cause minimum disruption to the actor and the production.
- Adjustments must be made, where necessary, in consultation with the production team, taking account of variations in lighting conditions.
- Maintenance must be of a level and frequency appropriate to the production needs.
- Maintenance must meet all continuity requirements.

Removing the make-up
- Cleansers and other materials must be suitable for the artiste's skin type and for the type of make-up to be removed.
- The artiste's own preferences concerning materials should be checked prior to cleansing.
- The artiste must be adequately protected.
- The artiste's skin must be restored to an acceptable condition.

- Removal must observe all relevant health and safety legislation and procedures.
- A good relationship must be maintained with the artiste throughout, to ensure her or his continuing co-operation.
- Removal must be as quick and efficient as is practicable.
- All removers, chemicals and other materials must be stored carefully, observing all relevant health and safety regulations.
- All materials soiled with solvents must be placed in allocated containers and disposed of safely.

Note The criteria for applying, maintaining and removing make-up apply equally to work in fashion, advertising and theatre.

Questions

Oral and written questions are used to test your knowledge and understanding. Try the following.

Straight make-up

1 What three things should you do to the face before applying a foundation?
2 What are the differences between liquid, cream and pancake bases?
3 How would you test a foundation shade to see whether the colour matched the person's skin tone?
4 What are the various types of sponges used for applying foundations?
5 When trimming false eyelashes prior to application, how would you achieve a feathered effect?
6 What colour of false eyelashes would you normally select for a blonde-haired person?
7 How would you curl false eyelashes?
8 Where would you use pancake on a man?
9 Why is it inadvisable to use hair lacquer on a man's hair when filming outside in a gale-force wind?
10 Which technique of application would you use to apply cheek colour on a man?
11 What colours would you use (or mix) to fill in or change a beardline?
12 Describe the method of application you would employ when using eyeliner on a man.
13 Which colours would you consider on a blonde-haired man, for (a) eyeliner, (b) mascara?

Lighting and shading

1 What effect does shading with make-up have on the face?
2 What effect does highlighting with make-up have on the face?
3 How would you use highlighting and/or shading techniques: (a) to make a large nose look smaller; (b) to reduce a heavy jawline; (c) to strengthen a receding chin?
4 Describe what 'blending' means.
5 When would you use blending techniques?

CHAPTER 3

Working in fashion and advertising

Fashion (the model has long hair which has been wrapped round the head to make it look short)

Fashion

INTRODUCTION

A **photographic make-up artist** works with a photographer and models. It is the photographs that are the end product, so every make-up artist keeps a **portfolio** with examples of her best and latest work.

Fashion work can be fun, as you work with good-looking models, and usually in attractive locations. Because of this it is highly competitive. An enthusiastic interest in fashion is essential; the make-up artist should be not only abreast of current fashion, but ahead of it.

To get started you need to do **tests** for photographers, as a way of getting experience and photographs to show your work. Tests are unpaid, but should eventually lead to paid work. It may take a year or two to assemble photographs of a high enough standard to convince photographers and agencies that you should be given professional work.

Most fashion make-up artists tend to work through **agencies**. If you are taken on by an agent, your portfolio or book will be shown to potential clients. When you are given work by such a client, the agency will take part of your fee, as **commission**.

Even when established, a fashion make-up artist might have to attend six interviews in one day; at each interview the potential clients will be choosing from several make-up artists' portfolios. As with all areas of make-up work, perseverance and the right attitude are important.

Kinds of fashion work

Fashion work is of several kinds, each with its own technical requirements.

■ *Catalogue shoots* In **catalogue photography** speed is important: the aim is to photograph as many outfits as possible in one day. A typical session would involve preparing the hair and make-up for three girls in one and a half hours.

■ *Portrait work – editorial* **Portrait work** involves making up well-known people to be photographed for magazines or newspapers.

■ *Fashion shows* Known as **catwalk make-up**, make-up for

fashion shows is to enhance the appearance of models who are showing off a designer's collection for the coming season. The fashion shows are live, before invited audiences.

- *Glamour photography* In **glamour photography** the pictures aim to advertise cosmetics, clothes or other products in glossy magazines. The photographs *must* make the product attractive, so that it will sell.

Differing requirements

Sometimes the make-up has to be subtle, so that it does not detract from the clothes. At other times it may be more daring and stylish: it depends on the brief. On a *cosmetic* shoot, the make-up itself is the product being sold, so plenty of time is allowed to get it right.

Photographic work may take place in the photographer's studio, or on location somewhere. For those who enjoy travelling, location shoots can be some of the most exciting parts of working as a make-up artist.

Once you have applied the make-up, you need to *maintain* it. Models need to change their clothes, and also to eat and drink, all of which may disturb the make-up. In addition, problems may arise from the hot lights in the studio, which can cause perspiration, or from the weather on location, with sun, wind, rain, and extremes of heat and cold all affecting the make-up.

TIP

When maintaining the make-up for a shoot, always apply more powder to the model *before* it looks necessary. This way the make-up does not have time to deteriorate.

Professionalism

Presentation is always important for the make-up artist, but for the artist working in fashion it is crucial. You yourself must look presentable, and your equipment must be scrupulously clean.

Planning, too, is vital. Be sure to prepare thoroughly in advance. Make written notes of what you will need, and assemble all the necessary materials before the shoot. In planning the make-up, remember to think about light and shade, even when using colour.

> ### ACTIVITY: PLANNING LIGHT AND SHADE
> Look at a colour palette. Think of it as shade and highlight. If you were to take a photograph of it, using black-and-white film, which colours should show as shadows, which as mid-tones and which as highlights? Which tones are lighter and which darker than the foundation colour you are working with?

PREPARING THE MAKE-UP

Try always to make life easy for yourself – don't complicate things unnecessarily. As far as possible, plan everything in advance: the shape of the eye colour, the type of make-up, the colours, base and liner you will use, and so on. You should know before you start exactly what the end result will be.

For all make-up, the basic questions to ask yourself are these:

1 Why am I using this product?
2 Why am I applying it to this area?
3 Why have I chosen this colour?
4 What will the result look like?

APPLYING THE MAKE-UP

The foundation

Choosing the foundation

TIP

If the model has dry skin, use a cream foundation: panstik is suitable for dry skin. If the model has greasy skin, use a water-based liquid foundation.

When testing the foundation to find the right colour, apply a little on the model's forehead or jawline.

In photographic work it is common to select a foundation one shade darker than the natural skin tone. If the shot involves exposed body areas, always be guided by the skin tone on the neck, chest, arms and legs.

'White' skins tend to have more yellow in them than is often realised. Often they are darker in the centre of the face, and lighter around the edges.

'Black' skins tend to have more orange in them than one might suppose. They are often lighter in the centre of the face, and darker around the edges.

In choosing the foundation the object is to select an in-between shade, one that will balance the skin tone to achieve an 'even' base. On the whole it is usually better to choose a slightly *darker* base for white skins, and a slightly *lighter* one for black skins.

Blending the foundation

Blend the foundation well around the edges of the face and on the neck area. Don't apply much foundation to the cheeks, and make sure that what you do apply fades down the sides of the face until the edge disappears.

Apply foundation right into the eyebrows to avoid edges appearing. The brows can be coloured in afterwards.

Checking the foundation before powdering

If any imperfections show, apply more foundation. If you have worked the foundation in well, however – a little at a time, concentrating on one area before beginning the next – it should be right first time.

Always work to the same routine: *forehead, centre, sides, neck*.

Powdering

To set the foundation and prevent shine, use a little powder, but not too much at a time: the foundation must not 'clog'. The powder blots any superfluous moisture.

Be careful not to put too much powder on the eye areas.

Eyeshadows

Brush the eyelids to remove creases before applying **eyeshadow**. *Press* the colour on exactly where you want it; *do not flick the brush*. Blend the edges with a clean brush to diffuse the lines.

The lips

To paint the lips, face the model straight on. When using a strong colour such as red, use a **lip pencil** to get a perfect shape before applying the lipstick. For a natural effect, use a soft coral pink and add some powder: mix these on a palette to give a soft matt appearance.

Always use the same **lip brush**, which should be shaped, to apply a lipstick. Using a favourite brush in this way will give you maximum control.

When applying lipstick, start at the corner of the mouth. *Roll* the brush, following the shape of the lips.

Lip pencils

Sometimes matt-looking lips are in fashion, sometimes glossy. When using gloss the lips need a firm borderline, to prevent the gloss from sliding. Strong-coloured lipstick glosses need a matching lip pencil outline applied first.

If using pale or natural-coloured gloss, use a brown pencil to outline the lips first: this adds definition.

For actresses of mature years whose lipstick would otherwise 'bleed' into fine lines around the mouth, lip pencil can be used to outline the lips.

Lip sealers

Lip sealers are products made to coat the lipstick with a transparent liquid which seals the lip colour and prevents it from smudging. They tend to sting the lips when first applied, but they are useful in scenes or shots where the actress has to eat, drink or kiss as they help to prevent the lipstick from moving.

The skin

Blusher

Blusher should be placed, depending on whether the make-up is for colour photography or black-and-white.

- *Colour photography* Apply blusher along the cheekbones, to highlight the shade of the overall skin tone.

- *Black-and-white photography* Apply blusher *beneath* the cheek bones, to shape them.

As the blusher is being used to create shading, the *shade* of the blusher is more important than its colour. Often a pinky rust colour is useful, blended well so that it is not too strong.

Fashion – a 'natural' effect

Applying blusher for colour photography

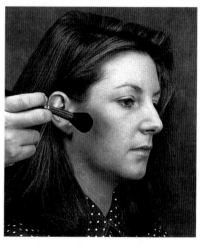

Applying blusher for black-and-white fashion photography

A black skin tone

A dark olive skin tone

A pink skin tone

The use of blushers

Blusher, or cheek colour, used to be known as **rouge** or **carmine**. It was obtained by crushing cochineal (a Mexican insect) into a red powder. Nowadays there is a vast selection of powders and creams, in every shade and tone. Sometimes it is difficult to choose which type to use.

- **Powder blushers** These are easy to apply and can be added at the end of the make-up for added warmth and colour.

- **Cream blushers** These need to be blended with a sable brush and tend to survive longer than powder types. Cream rouge is better on dry skin or on cheeks that are blemished, as it is easier to blend. Cream is also more waterproof.

- **Powder/cream blushers** This type of blusher is applied like a cream but dries to a matt finish, like powder.

Choosing the blusher

The choice of blusher depends on the colour of the skin tone:

- *Black skin tones* These need brown shades, so choose orange-browns and red-browns to enhance the skin colour. Avoid bright pinks, as these look unnatural.

- *Dark olive skin tones* These too look best with brownish blushers, shades of terracotta and russet pinks.

- *Pink skin tones* These may not need blusher at all, if the cheeks are already pink or if they tend to blush easily. Peach tones can be used to play down the colour if it is too rosy.

- *Golden skin tones* These look good with coral and peach colours on the cheeks. It is good to use pinks to offset the skin tone if this is on the sallow side.

- *Ivory and pale skins* These should not have strong cheek colours added. Shades of beige pinks and pale pinks harmonise well with this type of skin tone, which is delicate and often appears translucent.

Right: A golden skin tone
Far right: An ivory skin tone

EFFECTS OF PHOTOGRAPHIC LIGHTING ON MAKE-UP

Make-up artists work with photographers, who have preferred styles of working. It is up to the make-up artist to adapt to the way the photographer uses lights. In general, the stronger the light, the more it bleaches out the make-up.

The lights in photography draw attention to any shine, so you must always use matt colours with no glitter or shine in the pigment. The photographer will decide where he wants a shiny effect, if at all.

Always stay close to the camera in case you are needed to retouch the make-up.

MAKE-UP FOR ADVERTISING

Basic principles apply here as elsewhere. Here are a few additional points:

- *Housewives* Basic 'housewife' make-up must not overpower the product being advertised.

- *Men* When making up men, remember that the make-up must be invisible. Cover spots and blemishes, and keep make-up to a minimum.

- *Children* Children may need rosier cheeks – for a natural look, use grease rather than powder blushers.

MAKE-UP FOR THE CATWALK

From the point of view of the audience, a fashion show can be a very glamorous occasion, with attractive designs and slick presentation. Behind the scenes, however, much hard work goes unseen. The show itself is short in comparison with the time taken in preparation. And during the show, the atmosphere backstage is usually one of *frenzied* activity. Models must be ready on time and the make-up artist must work fast and confidently.

Despite this – and despite the fact that she may sometimes work on two or three shows in one day, all in different places – the make-up artist must remain cool and organised. In this she may sometimes be helped by having an assistant who can apply the foundations, sharpen pencils and the like. But what really counts is planning.

Make-up for the catwalk is usually heavier and stronger than make-up for fashion photography. There are no close-ups to consider, and the work is comparable with theatre make-up in that the audience sit at some distance from the performers. As always, the make-up must take account of the specific requirements, which in this case are those of a live show in which the models perform under artificial (and perhaps coloured) lights.

The overall look will be decided by the fashion designer, and the clothes will dictate the colours to be used in the make-up. Make-

> **ACTIVITY**
> Choose one of the following projects. Prepare and apply suitable make-up for:
> 1 a TV commercial advertising soap powder;
> 2 a Paris fashion show, where the clothes are bizarre and colourful; *or*
> 3 a close-up for a photograph advertising a lipstick.

up for such shows varies from the bizarre to the understated; like theatre make-up, it must be particularly well balanced. Lip lines must be perfect, and blusher skilfully matched.

Alternative styles in eye make-up

Fashions constantly change, so it is impossible to define or pin down a particular effect as being 'the current fashion'. Fashion always borrows from the past, and there are definite influences from other decades, adapted and changed to suit the mood of the present.

The following activities allow you to practise alternative styles in eye make-up.

ACTIVITY: BASIC LOOK FOR FASHION PHOTOGRAPHY

1 Draw a dark colour in the socket line using a matt compressed-powder eyeshadow.
2 Use the same product as an eyeliner, drawing it across the lid, above the eyelashes, and underneath the eyes at the outer corners.
3 Blend these lines up to meet the socket line, and blend them away and outwards — but no further than the point indicated by the nose-to-eye measuring technique.

ACTIVITY: A STRONG LOOK SUITABLE FOR THE CATWALK

1 Mix a dark brown or grey compressed-powder eyeshadow with water.
2 Apply it all over the eyelids, blending the edges.
3 If you find the eyeshadow difficult to blend (damp eyeshadow dries quickly), try pressing the powder with your brush, rather than stroking it on. Press the eyeshadow powder up and over the socket lines.
4 Apply eyeliner, blending well.

ACTIVITY: A SIXTIES LOOK

1 Apply white eyeshadow to the eyelids.
2 Draw in the socket lines using black pencil.
3 Blend the socket lines gently.
4 Apply grey eyeshadow to the eyelids.
5 Add white eyeshadow to the eyebrow bones.
6 Attach false eyelashes.
7 Apply eyeliner.

Far left: A cover girl
Left: A make-up for a commercial

Below left: A catwalk make-up
Below centre: A catwalk make-up
Below: Fashion photographic make-up

ACTIVITY: A NATURAL LOOK

1 Brush white eyeshadow onto the eyelids. Follow with a layer of brown.
2 Use brown eyeshadow underneath the eyes, as an eyeliner.
3 On the upper eyelids apply watercolour eyeliner, using a fine brush.
4 Comb through the eyebrows, adding clear mascara or dark eyeshadow with a thin brush.

ACTIVITY: AN ALTERNATIVE FASHION LOOK

1 Brush taupe eyeshadow over the eyelids, blending it from the lashline towards the eye sockets.
2 Try a deeper brown, drawing this slightly above the socket line. Blend it towards the inside corner of the upper eyelid, using a clean brush to fade away the edges carefully.
3 Pencil under and on top of the outside corners of the eyes, not following the natural line but extending it. Blend with a small brush.

Now try a full fashion photographic make-up. Here is one approach.

MAKE-UP FOR COMMERCIALS

The end product in **commercial advertising** may be for television or the cinema: either way, it is vital to bear in mind that each and every detail counts.

Realism is *not* what is sought. If someone hits his head, for example, no bruise will be required! No one will show any blemishes; children will look natural and perfect. The actors for such productions are cast very carefully – often they are models, chosen for their looks. Nevertheless, corrective make-up will sometimes be needed.

Working in a team

Filming commercials is extremely expensive, so everyone involved must work swiftly and confidently. Often the clients are present, watching the work; sometimes they want to get involved too, which can be difficult for the director.

As the make-up artist you will need to be relaxed and friendly with a lot of people, many of whom may be total strangers. In contrast to film, television and theatre work, the cast and crew for a commercial are thrown together simply for one day, and must 'gel' immediately. Commercial production companies like to use the same people repeatedly, to reduce this problem.

No one in this sort of work can afford to have an 'off' day: others depend on you. You need to cultivate a professional attitude and a willingness to attempt anything as asked. Usually there won't even be a rehearsal.

Children and animals often form part of the cast of commercials. To be able to entertain them between takes is a real asset in a make-up artist.

TIP

When working with young children, some crayons and paper will help to keep them from getting bored.

Planning

You should be ready to create any effect required. You may find yourself providing fashion make-up for a beautiful model in a yoghurt advertisement one day, and wigs and facial hair for a period piece the next.

Usually you will be able to find a plan for the commercial in the form of a **storyboard**, a scene-by-scene drawing showing the sequence of shots and what will appear in each.

On the set

Unless there are a great many actors, which would be unusual, one make-up artist will be expected to do the make-up and hair for the whole cast. Hands are especially important in commercials; most actors will need a **manicure**. There may be a 'hand artist' for certain shots, but this is uncommon. You should always be prepared, with a manicure set, nail-varnish remover and several shades of varnish in your kit box. If one of the cast is playing a mother, she will probably need colourless nail varnish.

Never use a foundation on young children. If the director says a child's face is too pale, resist applying a tan base immediately; instead try putting warmth into the skin by stippling the cheeks and forehead with a little blusher or warm brown. Bear in mind too that a young child will quickly get quite warm under the lights: wait to see whether this happens before rushing in with make-up. Work with the lighting cameraman, who is usually able to be very helpful in achieving the desired effect.

Don't overlook body make-up, and never forget the hands and ears. Remember – with commercials, it's all in the detail!

TIP

Sometimes an actor may nick himself when shaving. A medical 'new skin' is available from chemists, and is useful to have in your kit box.

It is useful to carry aspirins or paracetamol in your kit box in case the artiste has a headache.

YOUR OWN PROFESSIONAL IMAGE

In fashion and advertising the way *you* look is more important than any other area of the media. Your choice of hairstyle, your make-up, your clothes and the products you carry in your make-up box will all be seen as an example. The following hints may be useful:

- Keep abreast of fashion, and try to be aware of coming fashions. Everyone working in fashion is 'fashion conscious' – don't fall behind.
- Try out new products continually. Don't be afraid of rapid changes in fashion.
- Keep updating your skills on refresher courses.
- Build up good relationships with the models and photographers you work with. If you are courteous and professional, they will notice.
- How you look, how you present yourself, how you act, how you move and how you speak will all make an impression on those you work for and with. The impression you wish to convey is of being competent, friendly and trustworthy.

HOW TO SUCCEED

Checklist

In preparing for assessments on fashion and advertising make-up, the following list may be useful. Check that you have covered and fully understood these items.

- Those involved must discuss and agree the total style of make-up required.
- Techniques of highlighting, shading, and so on must be applied as necessary.
- The make-up must be maintained throughout the shoot.
- The make-up must be removed and the model's skin restored to normal at the end of the shoot.

Note See also pages 39–40 for criteria on applying, maintaining and removing make-up, which apply equally to fashion and advertising.

Questions

Oral and written questions are used to test your knowledge and understanding. Try the following.

1 When selecting cheek colour, what would be your reason for using a *cream* blusher?
2 What are the advantages of using a cream cheek colour?
3 What shades of cheek colours would you select for: (a) black skin tones; (b) olive skin tones; (c) pink skin tones; (d) golden skin tones; (e) ivory skin tones?
4 Under what circumstances would you decide not to use cheek colour at all?
5 Under what circumstances would you use lip sealer?
6 In which area of fashion work would the make-up need to be stronger and heavier?
7 Describe the sort of make-up you would apply (or not apply) to a young child when working on a commercial.

CHAPTER 4

Working in theatre

INTRODUCTION

Many make-up artists start their working lives in the theatre, usually as **wig dressers**, employed on a casual basis. In the larger theatres (in capital cities, for example) there is usually a wigmaster or wigmistress, and a small permanent team of wig dressers. Usually they help the actors with their make-up and hair as well as caring for the postiche work.

In small theatre companies and for amateur productions the actors look after their own appearance. In intimate theatre, there is often no need for them to wear any make-up at all, especially if the play is a modern one. Stylistic effects with too much make-up look old-fashioned when the audience is close to the actors, and many female performers apply normal street make-up most of the time.

In the larger auditoriums, such as the Coliseum and the Royal National Theatre in London, the tradition of employing wig dressers survives. Performances here are on such a large scale that the actors couldn't possibly be responsible for applying, dressing and maintaining the postiche work involved. In the larger houses, where the audience is at a considerable distance from the stage, the make-up has to be stronger and heavier than make-up for TV and film. There are no close-ups and fine detail is not seen, so the make-up and hair must be strong and precise.

Sometimes a make-up artist is engaged by the producer to design the make-ups for the entire cast, and – when these have been approved by the director or designer, usually at the dress rehearsal – to teach the performers to apply the make-ups themselves. This often occurs on long-running musicals, for which a make-up artist is called in every few years to revamp the make-up look when it starts to look 'tired'. Examples include the musicals *Cats*, *42nd Street* and *Starlight Express*. On *Phantom of the Opera* a make-up artist was engaged full-time to apply the special-effects make-up on the 'Phantom'.

Postiche work is very important in the theatre because a wig, beard and moustache on an actor may be most of his make-up. His character is portrayed visually by the costume and hair. Hardly any make-up will be necessary; the most important requirement will be that the facial hair and wig remain intact throughout the performance.

A make-up for the theatre: John Hurt in *Aria*

Strong female make-up for opera

Facial hair and a wig: Gertan Klauber as Nepomuk in *Pygmalion*

MAKE-UP FOR LARGE AUDITORIUMS

Basic principles

The main considerations when doing make-up for the theatre are the *distance* involved and the *colours* normally used in theatrical lights; usually these are cold colours in the blue and green range.

The principle followed in dealing with the distance is to make up the face strongly and cleanly using the basic corrective make-up techniques: 'strongly', because both the strength of light and the distance will reduce the impact of the make-up, and 'cleanly' because otherwise the facial definition will fail to 'register' at a distance.

To deal with the lighting, the face is made up in warmer tones than usual, with emphasis on the red and orange tones and on certain areas of the face.

A straight theatrical make-up: strong eyelines are used, and red is blended under the bottom eyeline to enhance the eye from a long distance

Planning the make-up

Make-up for the stage should not be heavy or overdone: the foundation can be as lightly applied as for TV and film. What matters is that the right colours and shades are applied in the correct places so as to give definition to the face.

In a large auditorium only a small proportion of people will be able to distinguish the make-up. For those seated further away from the stage, the actors' faces will be a blur. As you can't meet the needs of everyone, it is best to apply make-up that will look believable to the front section of the house. The middle to last back rows will simply view it as part of the overall picture of performance, costume, lighting and wigs.

In general, the make-up for actresses on the stage should include stronger eye make-up than would be normal for film or TV, darker or brighter lipstick, and a stronger colour on the cheeks. Bear in mind, however, that although the colours should be stronger, the placing must be exact and the blending subtle. Avoid hard lines – the eyelines, for example, must always fade to nothing at the ends. The amount of make-up used and the application should be as light as for any other area of the media.

Ballet make-up

Make-up for the ballet traditionally comprises very pale skin-tones, whitened shoulders and arms, and strong eye make-up.

EFFECTS OF THEATRE LIGHTING ON MAKE-UP

The lighting is usually set at a 45° angle to the stage and must counteract any shadows. **Overhead lighting** is also used: these lights are changed and operated during the production.

Colour gels such as 'mid-sapphire blue' are used over the lights. These 'bleach' the make-up and drain colour from the faces, so more red and warm colours have to be used in the make-up.

Make-up for the ballet

Lighting changes the make-up colours:

- *White make-up* looks blue, so cream should be used.
- *Blue make-up* looks black, so use brown.
- *Yellow make-up* looks washed-out white, so use reds, oranges and pinks.

Prior to the opening night there is a full **dress rehearsal**. This is the time when the make-up artist can check the make-up from the audience's point of view. Any shadows that need correcting can be checked, as can the strength of the colours used in the make-ups.

FANTASY MAKE-UP

Fantasy make-up is fun to do and satisfies the creative side in every make-up artist. The effect can be the simple painting of an animal face, a witch or a clown, or the design of more complex monsters using prosthetics and bald caps. Fantasy can be beautiful and charming, or dramatic and frightening.

Any materials may be used in order to achieve the desired fantasy effect, but in general it is advisable to use *grease-based* products (such as panstiks) for the stage, as watercolours tend to run when the actor gets hot. For photographic, TV and film work watercolours for the face provide excellent results, with strong, clear colours.

Ready-made prosthetic pieces such as latex noses or ears (see page 157) are ideal in creating fantasy characters such as animals. By cutting a few pieces from a broom or sweeping brush, whiskers can be stuck onto the animal face for the finishing touch.

When making up dancers for light entertainment shows, the brief given is often to create a bold, striking effect. Shiny eyeshadows, glitter, and strong colours may be used to blend with the costumes and scenery.

Of all the areas of make-up, fantasy is the one which offers the make-up artist the greatest freedom of expression. Occasionally when working in films there will be a scene such as a carnival, when everyone is in fancy-dress costumes and fantasy make-up is required. Give your creativity and imagination free rein!

Fantasy make-up for *Dr Who*

Body painting

Watercolour make-up is excellent for fantasy make-up on the body, and many visually striking ideas can be used to create stunning effects.

For a statue effect it is best to use a large bath-sized natural sponge to stipple on the appearance of stone. For a marble effect, try using Chinese brushes to paint on the colour.

Books on painting furniture and interiors are helpful for body painting. Instead of using housepaint or gold leaf, you use make-up water paints, employing the same techniques for marbling, gilding, tortoiseshell effects, and so on.

You can also paint clothes on the body, an idea used quite

frequently in photography. For this technique, it is better to use sable artists' brushes. Spraying with colour also gives good results, and is a quick method of applying one colour all over the body, such as gold or silver.

Clown make-up

As well as being fun to do, **clown** make-ups are very good for practising balance and precision. The types that are well known are the tramp and the whitefaced clown, but there is no such thing as a standard clown – each face should be individual to the performer.

The *tramp clown* doesn't have a white face. He is generally unshaven-looking, and wears old baggy clothes and a battered bowler hat. The eyebrows, eyes and mouth are painted, and he has a bright-red bulbous nose. This can be made from half a table-tennis ball, stuck on the nose with spirit gum; or by slush-moulding for a rubber nose. The mouth is painted red or white, and is drawn very large, either turning up to look happy or down to look sad.

The *whitefaced clown* is more colourful, with primary colours being used to create the design. The outlines should be drawn in black pencil, with emphasis on the eyebrows, nose, eyes and mouth.

Planning the make-up

Clowns can be funny, sad, suspicious, elegant or tragic. Bald caps with crepe hair laid on in bright colours are useful to complete the look. White stocking-tops, pulled over the head to hide the hair, make good skullcaps. Eye markings are individual, but the black cross over the eyelids is well known, as are the painted teardrop and the raised eyebrows.

Before starting the make-up, draw the proposed clown design on paper, filling it in with coloured pencils to illustrate the final effect.

Applying the make-up

Draw the design on your model with an eyebrow pencil. If using a white base, choose a pancake: this is easy to wash off with soap and water. When the foundation is dry, finish with white talcum powder.

Pierrot and Pierrette

Pierrot has a plain white face. If the eyebrows of the man to be made up are too heavy, they should be eliminated by soaping them down and applying wax or eyebrow plastic on top. Using a clown's white pancake, paint the entire face with a damp sponge, and powder when dry with white or transparent powder. The eyebrows should be well arched and black. The lips should be painted bright red in Cupid's bow fashion. Add definition to the eyes with black pencil, and two beauty spots to complete the look – one on the cheekbone near the eye, the other on the opposite side of the face, nearer the corner of the mouth. The man should wear a black skullcap, covering the hair.

For the **Pierrette** the lady is made up to look as pretty as possible. Often she wears a hat.

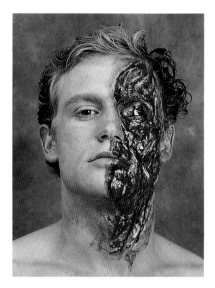

A fantasy effect using water-based make-up and directly applied gelatine

---

ACTIVITY: FANTASY MAKE-UP

1 Choose a theme, such as 'Fire' or 'Ice'.
2 Create a fantasy effect for the face, using warm colours in red, orange and yellow for 'Fire', or blue, green and silver for 'Ice'.
3 Imagine that the entire set and costumes are to be in those colours; the make-up and hair must harmonise with the overall effect.
4 Imagine that your model is a dancer. Whether for stage or TV, the make-up on a dancer will be in constant movement as she dances, so you must aim for a strong look. Use any types of material, including glitter and shine, to emphasise and highlight the face.

HOW TO SUCCEED

Checklist

See the assessment checklist in Chapter 2 (pages 39–40), which also applies to theatre make-up.

Questions

Oral and written questions are used to test your knowledge and understanding. Try the following.

1 When working in the theatre, why are the wigs and facial hair often more important than the make-up?
2 Why would you use stronger colours in theatre make-up than for photographic sessions and commercials?
3 Why are creams and panstiks more suitable for theatre make-up than water-based brands?

An animal make-up

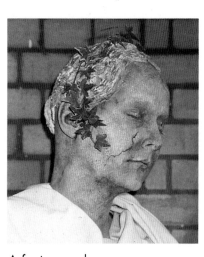

A fantasy make-up

Clown make-up

Clown make-up: Sid
Little and Eddie Large
as clowns

Body painting

CHAPTER 5

Working in television and film

INTRODUCTION

Television

In the fifties and early sixties, television was transmitted in black-and-white. With the advent of colour in 1967, the make-up changed completely. It was during the early sixties that I joined the BBC Make-up Department in White City, London. During my ten years there I worked on every type of programme, progressing through the ranks from Trainee Assistant to Assistant (after five years we were acknowledged as fully-fledged Make-up Artists), then to Senior Assistant and finally to Make-up Designer. (In those days we were called Make-up Supervisors.) Looking back, it seems to me to have been the golden era of television: dramas were numerous, and comedies full of charm. Even the chat shows were exciting, because London in the 'Swinging Sixties' seemed to be the centre of the universe: everyone who was anyone passed through our hands.

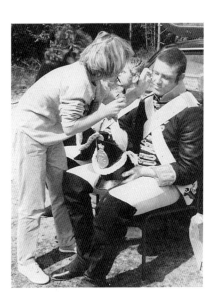

Hair work became more important; switches and other hairpieces were added to dress long swept-up styles such as the 'beehive'. Eyelashes were worn by most women – full sets of lashes above and below the eyes, or individual lashes painstakingly applied one by one.

Working in black-and-white we thought simply in terms of black, white and shades of grey. With colour, the whole concept of make-up changed. It was a gradual process: although we worked towards colour, not many people had colour televisions, so most continued to watch the programmes in black-and-white. All those on the production team had to undergo tests for colour blindness.

As colour became more common in all transmissions, skin tones suddenly became more important. It was first most noticeable when making up politicians and news announcers. For black-and-white we used to powder down a politician to eliminate too much shine or to tone down a heavy beardline. In glorious colour, however, every red nose or flushed face was noticeable. If a government minister had had a drink or two in the hospitality room before a TV appearance, this would be obvious to the viewers in their homes. More time and care was needed if make-up artists were to offset such problems. From then on we had to pay attention to the elimination of redness, and the addition of warmth through blushers and eyeshadows.

A career in television make-up

The most important aspect of working in television is to be able to work as part of a team. There is no room for histrionics behind the camera. Make-up artists must be tactful and diplomatic and remain quietly in the background.

Much emphasis is rightly laid on this aspect of a make-up artist's job, because very often you are the last person to speak to the performer before he or she appears in front of the camera. The make-up room should therefore be an oasis of peace while everywhere else in the studio is hectic.

It is important that you work fast, but it is also important that you remain calm. There should be no sense of panic. It can sometimes be hard to maintain calm confidence when an assistant is hovering nearby asking, 'How much longer will you be?' or warning 'You've got three minutes.' (It is the floor assistant's job to make sure that the performer is **on set** – that is, ready and on the studio floor – by a certain time.)

Like every other industry, television has changed and will continue to do so. The old studio system of my own youth is fast disappearing. There is neither the time nor the money for the ways of the past. Today all make-up artists must be geared to the **freelance** world and its uncertainties. It is now more important than ever for make-up artists to be trained in the different areas of make-up in order to be able to make a successful living. When I started training students for the freelance world, I realised that they would have to gain their working experience on pop promos, in theatre and doing photographic stills, as well as in television and films: the training needed to address the demands of the industry.

A freelancer has to work across the board, to be good at everything, including both make-up and hair. If you have a flair for certain areas of make-up, such as fantasy or prosthetics, that's fine, but recognise that not as many jobs require *these* skills as, say, wig dressing, straight make-up, or ageing. You are therefore wise to gain experience in *all* aspects of make-up, even if one day you hope to specialise in a particular area.

It still takes five years to become confident and worthy of the title 'make-up artist'. The work experience during those first five years will help to form the type of make-up artist you become. Freelancing is highly competitive; you need to be of the highest standard if you are to succeed. The more you learn, the more there is to discover. Explore new techniques; be willing to learn from more experienced colleagues; and never imagine that you know it all. When you become confident in the make-up field, start learning from other departments about lighting, camera and costume.

Make-up offers a truly fascinating career in television; I feel very lucky to have worked in the industry. Along with hard work there has been much pleasure and often great fun. You meet talented, interesting people; friendships form, and the feeling grows that you belong to a team – a team who, in a remote location, become your family.

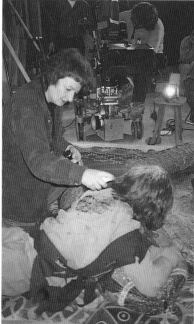

These are real aspects of make-up work, and they are good. But do not be misled into seeing this career as glamorous. If, for example, you find it hard to get up at 4 a.m., or to work all night long, don't become a make-up artist! The hours are both long and unsocial. In fact, when working on a TV film there is no time at all for a social life. Six-day weeks have become normal in the industry, and you may be required to go anywhere in the world. As well as warm, sunny locations this can include cold, damp places. Standing in the freezing cold in some isolated place at 6 a.m. is not everyone's idea of ideal working conditions. Long hours and long absences from home impose real strain on relationships with partners; very often the make-up artist is the first person to start work in the morning and the last to go home at night.

Above all, you need to be strong and healthy: you will never be able to take time off with a simple cold. The show must go on!

The assistant or trainee make-up artist

When working as an **assistant** to the make-up designer, it is important that you listen carefully, and carry out her instructions. She will already have designed the look of the make-up and hair for all the actors, including the one *you* have been assigned to look after.

Trainees and assistants should always be flexible, willing to change their approach to suit the needs of the make-up designer. Some designers will give you a free hand and allow you to use your own initiative, especially when they know your standard of work. Others will give specific instructions and even notes or charts on the individual actor's requirements.

It is always a good idea to 'chart' the make-ups you are doing when working on a long series or a film. If you became very ill, someone would have to take your place, maybe at an hour's notice. No one is indispensable, of course, but it is very difficult to take over a make-up from another artist and achieve exactly the same look without the aid of written notes, sketches or Polaroid photos.

When making up for crowd scenes – the background people known as **extras** or **crowd artists** – it is not necessary to make notes about the individual faces you make up. Here it will be a general look that you work towards, depending on the period – for the forties, for example, appropriate hairstyles, matt red lips, and emphasised eyebrows with pale skin tones for the women, and for the men short haircuts, moustaches and no beards. The make-up designer will issue instructions, the assistants must interpret them and carry them out.

Continuity is important in television: it is up to every make-up artist to maintain continuity in her hair and make-up work.

As an assistant, then, there is plenty to do. You may be left on the set to **stand by**, ready to retouch the make-up if necessary. Be sure not to leave without permission from the designer. If the director calls for make-up there should always be someone from the make-up department within view, and within earshot. In summary, your job is to support and assist the make-up designer – to be responsible, reliable, and an active member of the make-up team.

The senior assistant make-up artist

The **senior assistant** make-up artist also should provide back-up for the designer. Having had years more experience than a trainee make-up assistant, she will be given the more important or difficult make-ups to do. These are usually those for the principal actors who will have the most close-ups. She will also have such responsibilities as the designer chooses to give her – paperwork, sometimes; shopping, attending wig fittings, or contacting suppliers by telephone. This is because in the absence of the designer she would have to be able to take decisions. Whilst working as a chief assistant, she is really training to become a designer herself.

The make-up designer

The **make-up designer** is responsible for the make-up **budget** allowed. Within this budget she must plan and organise everything – how many wigs, which stock to purchase, how many assistants to hire, and the entire look of the hair and make-up.

After some weeks or days in preparation, including planning meetings with the rest of the key crew members – the director, the costume designer, the set designer and so on – she will aim to be ready for anything that is needed on the shoot. She will have **broken down** the script, contacted the actors, arranged wig fittings, and sent scripts to her chosen assistants. By the time the crew has assembled to start filming, the make-up designer should have organised everything. Make-up materials will have been purchased, tests carried out if necessary, wig and facial hair fitted and dressed, and transport and accommodation arranged with the production office.

This **pre-production work** can be a difficult period, especially if time is short. Actors may not have been cast until the last minute and there may be a frantic rush to get everything done. If the director should change her or his mind about something, rearrangement may be necessary at the last minute. The designer is responsible to the director for whatever look is required. Interpreting the director's wishes is not always easy; many directors do not know what they want until they see it. Yet whatever the director may ask for, if it relates to the make-up or the hair, it is the make-up designer's job to produce it somehow.

For special effects, such as artificial features (**prosthetics**), the make-up designer will contact a specialist, hiring out the work if the budget can meet the expense. If not, she will make the piece herself, with the help of assistants. It is for the designer to judge which is the most sensible option, basing her decision on the assignment, the circumstances and the budget.

The designer should also look after her assistants, making sure that their working conditions are up to standard, with adequate lights, mirrors, space to work, sleeping accommodation, regular meal breaks and so on. She should encourage and instruct any trainees, building up their confidence. At the same time, she must keep a supervising eye on all that is going on, remain in touch with the production office, take any new instructions from the director, and make up the leading actors.

In television each person should know exactly what his or her role is in the overall scheme. A highly professional TV crew working well together on the studio floor is a truly beautiful sight. Not every team will gel together, but at its best, with the combination of technical expertise and professional grace, it can seem like a well-choreographed ballet. To be a part of something like that, when it happens, is a remarkable and wonderful experience.

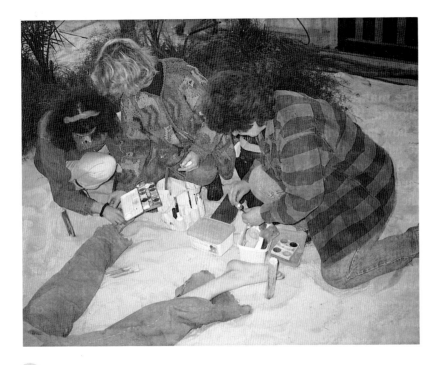

Working as a team

Working in film: Dudley Moore in
Santa Claus – The Movie

Film

When working on a feature film, the end product is destined for showing in a cinema on a big screen. The close-ups will be seen larger than life, and the make-up will be very obvious. Just as the actor's performance must be more subtle – the twitch of an eyebrow or the winking of an eye – so must the make-up.

In general, a feature film takes much longer to shoot than a television production. The cameras are heavier and the lighting set-ups take longer: filming is very expensive in both equipment and time. The average large-budget feature film will involve more people (especially if there are special effects involved), than the average large-budget television film.

One of the advantages of feature film work is that usually more time is allowed for the make-up artist than in any other medium. This is mainly because each scene takes longer to set up and light, which allows time to retouch the make-up. A second reason is that the leading actor or actress is often a well-known film star, and stars tend to get their own way! Very often they have their own entourage – make-up artist, hairdresser, chauffeur and secretary. Sometimes the star is the producer as well, so if he or she wants an extra half-hour in the make-up chair, time will be found.

Another reason why film work is more luxurious for the make-up artist is that the hair work is done by a separate person. Although on smaller film productions the make-up and hair styling may be done by one person, as in television, this is simply for reasons of economy: on larger-scale productions it would be considered detrimental to the overall standard of excellence not to have make-up and hair as separate departments.

Special effects involving prosthetics would be a further separate department of experts specialising in that field, again to ensure excellence. What the make-up artist gains in time, however, she loses in variety and interest: in television she would do the make-up, the hair, *and* any special effects.

Make-up artists who work on films will often complain about the

Nineteenth-century make-up for
Lady Windermere's Fan

long hours, the early starts (typically at five in the morning), and the amount of travelling involved. At the same time, however, they also insist that feature film work is the most exciting and the most rewarding area of their work!

PERIOD MAKE-UP

Researching the period for a production is one of the most interesting parts of a make-up artist's job. The history of the times that people lived in, what they wore, how they dressed their hair, what make-up they used and so on are continually fascinating. How authentic the final made-up look will be depends on the requirements of the production you are working on. Sometimes the style will be softened to suit current fashion, at others it will be accurate to the last detail.

In planning the make-up, pay attention to the character and age of the person whose role the actor is playing, as well as to the make-up used in the period. *The notes given below are simply guidelines*: you will need to adapt them to suit the look you wish to achieve.

Period make-up: Ione Skye as Eleanor in *Covington Cross*, an American tv series

Research

Period or historical make-up is closely tied to character work, but is also linked to fashion as the overall look at a given time was based on the current fashion. Today's fashion will be tomorrow's period or historical make-up!

The best way of researching is to study **old magazines** and **photographs**, to watch **old films**, and to visit **museums** and **art galleries**.

Prehistoric people

The Natural History Museum in London provides evidence of prehistoric people, both in reconstructions and in pictures and books on anthropology. Another source of information is the cave drawings. These, which provide visual information, are the earliest known works of art by human beings.

The earliest records of Neanderthal Man show a narrow receding forehead, with a broad flat nose and a heavy powerful jaw. The neck was heavy and the eye structure projected forward. People at this time were also very hairy. To achieve this look it would be necessary to use prosthetic appliances such as forehead pieces, and dentures to project the jaw.

The Egyptians

The Egyptian civilisation, founded around 31 000 BC, left a great deal of useful material in records of their culture. It is known that Egyptians shaved their heads and wore wigs made of hair from animals and humans, and vegetable fibres. They wore plenty of make-up and were probably the first people to use black kohl,

which is still worn today. Vegetable dyes, red clay and white lead were all used to adorn the faces of both sexes. The hair colour was usually black, but the wigs were sometimes dyed in bright shades of green, blue and red, and the eyeshadow often matched the wig.

The eye make-up has become well known through **archaeological evidence** following the uncovering of buried tombs. The famous black lines drawn around the eyes from the inner corner and extended outward in a straight line 3 cm beyond the outer corner is the classic 'Cleopatra' style. The eyelashes and eyebrows were blackened and the brows extended. The cheeks and lips were reddened with carmine, and the natural light-brown skin tone was often whitened with lead and oil foundations.

The Egyptians

The Greeks

The Greek civilisation around 350 BC offered the ideal of the perfect face, an ideal still accepted today. A painted marble head, dating from 350 BC and found in a Greek temple, depicts a fashionable lady of those days. The eyebrows are painted black, the upper eyelids reddish-brown, and dark green is used to emphasise the eye sockets. The same green is used as a strong eyeline on the lids close to the upper lashes, and extended at the outer corners. The lips and cheeks are rouged a brownish-red colour.

The women had long hair and dressed it in elaborate styles, incorporating ringlets. Combs and jewels were used to decorate the hairstyle. The men did not wear wigs either. The soldiers were clean-shaven and had their hair cut short and curled; many statues still exist which show the curled hair brushed forward. Some men dyed their hair blond or red, and many of the elders had beards and moustaches.

The Greeks

The Romans

A statue of a Roman beauty dating from the last first century shows clearly her heavily darkened eyebrows.

Most of the information about the use of make-up in those days comes from the writings of churchmen who objected to it during the early Christian period. In the fourth century St Ambrose called women 'harlots' for painting their faces. Because of the complaints of the Christian Fathers we know that for three or four centuries after the birth of Christ there were many women whitening their faces, necks and breasts, blackening their eyebrows, and dying their hair. We know also that the lips and cheeks were reddened with magenta rouge. The fashionable colours for hair were blonde and red.

Pictorial evidence shows that the average Roman man had short hair and was clean shaven. The older men, intellectuals and philosophers, had long hair and flowing beards.

The Romans

The Middle Ages

Mediaeval women used white lead to achieve a pale complexion, as the fashion for pale skins and red lips continued throughout Europe. A fourteenth-century sculpted Madonna from Spain shows plucked painted eyebrows, rouged lips and cheeks, and black-lined eyes.

Many Dutch and French paintings dating from 1447–75 show

The Middle Ages

plucked eyebrows and high, shaved foreheads.

During the fourteenth and fifteenth centuries the women wore headdresses and removed any hair growing below the hairline. When not wearing a headdress the hair was long, and dressed close to the head. The fashionable colours for hair were blonde and black, but not red.

The men had long hair in the early part of the century, with long flowing beards. By 1509, when Henry VII of England died, the men's hair was worn shorter, with the facial hair trimmed; hair had become less elaborate than earlier in the century.

The sixteenth century

The Renaissance is the name given to that period which denoted the revival of arts and science in Europe, bringing in a new style of architecture and decoration to succeed the Gothic.

In England, Queen Elizabeth favoured red hair, which became fashionable. She also favoured heavy cosmetics. According to Ben Johnson and other writers of the day, the older she became, the heavier the application of her cosmetics.

As usual, a white skin was desirable and white lead was still being used. People did not use natural plant extracts to obtain their colours for reddening the cheeks and lips, as in the earlier centuries. Since this was the new scientific age, many artists' pigments were used in their face-painting techniques, and some of these were poisonous.

During the reign of Elizabeth I (1558–1603) the influence of the Renaissance first made itself felt in England. The dress, speech, and manners of Italy became very fashionable amongst the Queen's subjects.

The sixteenth century

The seventeenth century

The French and English make-up and hairstyles became very similar when Charles I of England (reigned 1625–49) married Henrietta, the sister of Louis XIII of France (reigned 1610–43). It is important to remember that face-painting has always been confined mainly to the sophisticated society in larger cities. Country people used little or no powder and paint, and led healthier lives.

As the fashionable ladies in the English and French courts used more make-up, they started putting patches on their faces. The patches were in stars, half-moons and round shapes, cut out of black taffeta, Spanish leather, or gummed paper. Such patches became useful in covering scars or skin afflictions, and according to reports of the day gradually became excessive as women used more and more patches at a time. Famous portraits dating between 1670 and 1685 show that the fashionable look at that time was a wide fleshy face with a double chin, prominent eyes, full red lips, dark eyebrows and dark hair.

The Cavalier men wore their hair shoulder-length and curled. Their moustaches were curled, trimmed, and pomaded or waxed. Beards became shorter and neater.

Puritan men cut their hair short and round, and wore no facial hair. For this reason they were called Roundheads.

Louis XII started the fashion of wigs for men in France, and Charles II in England popularised black wigs. The men were using make-up, too. Judge Jeffreys, Lord Chancellor of England in 1678, was notorious for his extravagant use of make-up.

In Asia and Africa the make-up was entirely different from that in Europe. From writers of the early seventeenth century (1603–25), we hear that many Moorish women were observed using tattoos on their faces, and their bodies were coloured with henna.

The seventeenth century

The eighteenth century

The ladies at court continued to use heavy make-up, whitening their faces with lead paint and applying rouge heavily. They also powdered their shoulders and accentuated veins on the bosom with blue.

By now there was publicity about the danger of using white lead paint, and it was known that this eventually killed people. The fashion of using it still continued in England, however, and even more excessively in France, from where most of the cosmetics came.

The gentlemen also wore face paint, and rouged their cheeks heavily. The fashion of powdering the hair or wig was very popular; white powder or flour was used by the nobility and soldiers. Moustaches and beards were out of fashion. The hair was still worn in the pigtail (or queue), using either the natural hair or a wig. Military men did not have facial hair at this time. By 1768 the men at court were blackening their eyebrows and reddening their lips.

Women's eyebrows were plucked thin, pencilled high, and curved. Rouge was placed in a round or triangular shape. The lips were painted in a rounded shape with a 'bee-sting' effect.

The voluptuous look of the mid-seventeenth century had changed to the ideal of painted porcelain. By the middle of the century (1737–70) rouge was being placed in a round shape lower on the cheeks, in a bright pink colour. The lips were small and rosebud-shaped, with paler eyebrows than previously.

Patches were still worn, and during Queen Anne's reign (1702–14) became a political symbol, with Tories wearing their patches on the left side of the face, and Whig supporters on the right. The wigs became larger and more fantastic until a tax on hair powdering was introduced in 1795. The excesses of this period came to an end with the French Revolution.

The eighteenth century

Eighteenth-century make-up
Above left: Theatrical version
Above: TV/Film version
Left: An English Officer from the
film *Revolution*

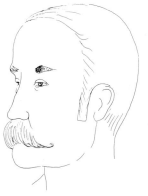

The nineteenth century —
Victorian

The nineteenth century

After the French Revolution anything associated with the
aristocracy went out of fashion. Wigs and long hair were out, and
most of the men had short hair. They began to grow sideburns
and moustaches instead, and by the middle of the century beards
also had come into fashion. Wigs were retained only for the courts
for official legal occasions.

Women wore cosmetics very discreetly, and when Queen
Victoria (reigned 1837–1901) came to the British throne there was
a complete reaction in England against the use of any paint on the
face. Women continued to use cosmetics, but since this was now
considered vulgar they had to use even more discretion. Many
cosmetics were home-made. Officially, only powder creams and
lotions were used; only stage actors and courtesans openly applied
paints.

Meanwhile the men cultivated large handlebar moustaches with
carefully curled ends. The women had long hair worn up in rolls
and curls.

The twentieth century

Make-up was being used to enhance rather than to over-paint the face. By 1913 light skin, dark eyebrows and full rosebud-shaped lips were the fashion. The hairstyles for women were still long and elaborately dressed on top of the head during the first decade. A style called the 'pompadour' was very fashionable.

The twenties

In the 1920s a short haircut called the 'bob' became the vogue and the make-up that went with it created a new look.

By 1925 the fashion was for a wistful look with soft, smudged eye make-up. The lips were painted red in a 'Cupid's bow' shape, and the eyebrows were plucked, then redrawn in a thin arch sloping downwards at the ends; this gave a sad, wistful expression to the face. The skin was still pale, and powdered to avoid shine.

From the late 1920s make-up was prepared using safe

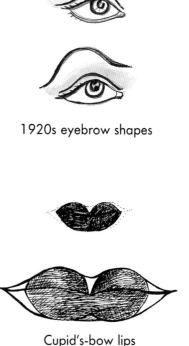

1920s eyebrow shapes

The 1920s

Cupid's-bow lips

ingredients for the first time. The men were shaving off their facial hair at the beginning of the decade, and any moustaches worn were always neatly clipped. The hairstyles were short, neat and plastered down to the head, usually in a side parting.

The thirties

In the 1930s the women started painting their lips in a more natural shape, and making the mouth look wider rather than smaller. The foundations were natural-coloured and still powdered heavily. Rouge or blusher was applied lower, under the cheekbones. Eyeshadow was blended from the eyelids up to the eyebrows, in subtle, smoky blues and browns. Lipstick was still red. The eyebrows were not too heavily plucked.

The styles were set by Hollywood films. Hair was bleached

1930s eyebrow shape

The early 1930s

blonde and waved tightly with irons, and nail varnish was used in both bright and dark colours.

The men had short neat hairstyles and moustaches of different shapes, but no beards.

The forties

In the 1940s, during the Second World War, less make-up was used in England, simply because it was unavailable. The one available item was lipstick, which was a symbol of the era. As well as red lipstick, the forties look relied on natural-looking eyebrows, brushed into shape and darkened.

The early 1940s

Women's hair was usually worn long, with more natural-looking waves than in the previous two decades. In 1941 the film star Veronica Lake set a fashion with her long hair undulating in waves and falling across one side of her face.

Postiche hairpieces were used for styles requiring curls or chignons when dressing the hair. Wigs had been used for some time, but they were unobtrusively named 'transformations'.

Men had short hair still, but cultivated waves in it using a comb and water. They too were influenced by the film stars. In England men wore moustaches, but in America these were unusual, apart from the 'Clark Gable' shape which was sometimes seen.

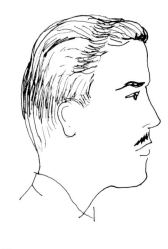

The mid 1940s

The fifties

By the 1950s make-up had become more natural-looking. The products were of a better quality, and there was more choice in colours than ever before.

The Hollywood musicals in glorious Technicolor seemed to bring a fashion in brighter skin tones, and suntans became fashionable as people were able to travel freely after the war. A fake tan for men, called 'Man Tan', was popular. Women had more choice in lipstick shades, and corals, oranges, and vivid pinks were much in demand. The eyes were not heavily made up – the look was an all-over one without particular emphasis on one feature.

The 1950s

In the mid-1950s the 'Mandarin' look arrived from Paris. The outer ends of the eyebrows were entirely plucked and redrawn in an upward sweep. The eyelines were drawn upwards at the outer corners. The rest of the face had no colour, except the lips – overall an interesting effect.

The hairstyles became shorter, fuller and curlier. Blonde was still a popular colour in American films, and the fashions were taken from the current filmstars – Marilyn Monroe, Elizabeth Taylor and Doris Day. Audrey Hepburn set a fashion for a doe-eyed look, with heavy black eyelines.

Chignons and false hair were popular, and then in 1953 the Italian filmstars started a fashion called the 'Italian cut' – a short, shaggy-looking hairstyle. This was popular for a while and then gave way to the bouffant style: a thick pageboy style, puffed out at the sides and lacquered heavily to hold it in place.

The men had shaven faces and short hair at the back and sides, with long hair at the front worn in a tuft or wave, like Elvis Presley. Crew cuts were also popular. Less conservative men wore beards and moustaches.

The sixties

The 1960s saw a decade of rebellion, in which the younger generation switched to a completely different appearance. There were many different fashions, each more bizarre than the last.

For women eye make-up dominated the decade. In 1962 the Egyptian look was fashionable, with heavy black eyelines and strong eyebrows.

In 1963 the lips seemed to disappear; no colour was added to them, and attention was focused on the heavy eye make-up.

In 1965 the eyebrows were played down as well as the lips, so the eyes were the focal point, with heavy colouring and false eyelashes. This was a very theatrical look, with heavy shading in the eye sockets and pale colour or none on the eyelids. The lips were pale. Sometimes they were painted with frosted pink or any

The 1960s

chalky-looking colour. Rouge or blusher was not used, but shading was added under the cheekbones to add emphasis to the face shape.

Men grew their hair long, and sideburns, moustaches and beards were fashionable.

Women wore their hair in elaborate styles, hairpieces being used more generally to make their hair look larger and fuller. A style called the 'beehive' became popular, and it became so large in size that it looked like a soldier's busby.

'Flower power' became fashionable, with young people 'dropping out' and rebelling against the work ethic. They were called 'hippies', and wore their hair very long and deliberately unkempt-looking.

The seventies

The 'flower power' movement lasted in England until 1975. Eye make-up was slightly softer than in the 1960s, with frosted eyeshadows and painted bottom lashes. A shiny doll-like look became fashionable, with glossy pastel colours painted on the lips, eyelids and cheekbones. The men still had long hair, though it was not popular in the workplace.

By 1975 an aggressively unglamorous look called 'punk' had swept away all traces of the sixties. Heads were fully or partially shaved, and safety pins worn through the nose. The look was deliberately hard and ugly. Tattoos started to become fashionable, and girls had pale faces with no make-up, or heavily painted eye make-up.

The 1970s

The eighties

In the 1980s the punk look gave way to the 'Gothic' look, with faces being painted white once more, heavy, dark eye make-up, and hair being gelled to make it stick up.

The rest of the population conformed to a different fashion. Hairstyles became 'big' for women, to match their expensive designer clothes with large shoulder pads.

Waves of fashions sought to create past styles such as the 1940s.

The 1980s

A unique style was the fashion for heavy ungroomed eyebrows for women, a look started by an actress called Brooke Shields who had naturally heavy eyebrows. The make-up became quite strong for women, with blusher being swept across the tops of the cheekbones. For a while, pink was used on the eyelids.

Men's hair became short again, with 1950s hairstyles in fashion. The eighties were 'boom' years and the young business people, called 'yuppies', tended to be materialistic, spending their money lavishly on their clothes and grooming. However, the 'boom' finished with the decade, and the whole world plunged into recession.

The nineties

Nostalgia became popular, with fashion adopting looks from past decades, revamping and adopting them as its own. The models on the catwalks went swiftly through a 1960s revival at the beginning of the 1990s, bringing false eyelashes back into fashion. Eyebrows were shaved off for a while and a line pencilled in, but this did not catch on with the general public. The 'grunge' look with unmade-up faces and untidy hair became popular with young people.

There have been thirties and fifties revivals, too, and hairstyles have ranged from elegant upswept chignons to braided plaits and layered bobs reminiscent of past eras. One fashion unique to the first half of the nineties (1990–4) was the fashion for large lips. Not only did the famous models overpaint their mouths to look as large as possible, but some had silicon injections to give a particularly swollen look to the upper lip.

When choosing cosmetics, many people have gone back to ancient times when the pigments used were derived from plant extracts. The popularity of homeopathic medicine has helped to promote a preference for natural-based products. On the whole, the fashion in make-up and hair is based on a natural look. This is achieved through a more skilful application of face paints than in the past.

The 1990s

Adapting fashion make-up to period styles

Some faces adapt easily to period styles. You will often hear a make-up artist remark that a certain actress has a 'period face'.

It is not always possible in period productions for TV and films to reproduce faithfully the 'correct' historical look. The effect may be distracting, or considered too ugly relative to the current fashion. Often it is necessary instead to indicate the period by conveying the *feeling* of the look. For example, in the Restoration period white head paint was used as a base: you could use a cream panstik for a heavy authentic look, but it might be necessary to use a thin, pale, liquid base so that the effect was not too theatrical. Pure white is often a problem for the lighting, making it necessary to use a beige or cream base instead. Similarly, if the period look includes plucked eyebrows but the *current* fashion is for natural, heavy brows, then the audience would not want the leading actress to look 'bizarre', even if her make-up were historically correct.

It is best to convey the look of the times using a softer version of a period rather than the harsh reality. An example of this can be seen in the film *Gone With the Wind*, where the make-up and hair are late 1930s (when the film was made) adapted to the 1770s (the supposed period of the film). As you watch classic period films, study the hair and make-up and try to work out when the films were made.

The Victorian period is easy; for this the actor should look as if she or he is not made-up at all, as make-up was not supposed to be worn. The facial hair on the men, and the women's hairstyles, are more important in conveying the historical look.

Actors must be *comfortable* in their roles. Remember, for example, that in the 1940s not *every* man had a moustache. On the other hand, if the actor is meant to be an RAF pilot, he will be more believable with a moustache since this was certainly fashionable at the time, especially amongst aircrew. Wherever possible, do try to 'get the period right'.

ACTIVITY: CREATING A DRAMATIC LOOK
From the 1920s to the present day, the dramatic effect of a pale face with defined eyebrows, blood-red lips and intense eyes has been ever-popular.

Use compressed eyeshadows, in matt dark shades of charcoal grey, dark aubergine, dark brown or black, along the eye sockets and beneath the bottom eyelashes, to give a sultry look.

ACTIVITY: CREATING CUPID'S-BOW LIPS
1 With the mouth slightly open, apply red lipstick: from the centre of the upper lip, in upward and outward curves to the apex; and then down, with a round movement, towards the corners. Do not carry the lipstick to the extreme corners, as this would make the mouth look large and wide.

Take care that the two curves are of equal size, or the lip will look one-sided. Keep the curves slightly separated, or the mouth will appear to pout.

2 For the lower lip, place the colour in the centre and then blend it to right and left. Leave as much unpainted space at the corners as in the upper lip.

ACTIVITY: CREATING A 1970s 'FLOWER POWER' LOOK

1 Use soft translucent colours (pink, orange and peach) to create a soft-focus look.
2 Use pale blue frosted eyeshadow on the eyes.
3 Leave the eyebrows bare, or pencil in thin lines.
4 Paint Cupid's-bow lips in pale colours, and accentuate with lip gloss.
5 Highlight eyebrow bones with pale colours (cream, beige or pale pink).

ACTIVITY: TWO EIGHTEENTH-CENTURY LOOKS

1 Apply an eighteenth century make-up to your model. Try to reproduce an authentic historical style, as you think it would have looked in those days. (see *Notes* below.)
2 Adapt today's fashion to an eighteenth century look. This time, show how you would do it for a film today.

Notes For the hair, use a white powdered wig with a combination of rolls and two curls. Add a piece on the top of the head to give greater height. If you do not have a wig, make one out of cottonwool to get the right effect, or spray a dark wig with white spray.

Take photographs of each make-up. Compare the results and discuss the differences.

TIME SPENT ON THE MAKE-UP

How much time should be spent on each make-up?

Time is valuable, if the **shooting schedule** is not to be held up. Ensure that you work effectively to meet **deadlines**.

How long each make-up will take must be considered carefully; a **test make-up** will determine how long you need. Liaison is essential between the costume, make-up and hair departments. The assistant director (known as the AD), who will arrange the actors' transport and arrival in the mornings, will ask how long to allow for costume, make-up and hair.

The amount of time needed to complete a make-up is often difficult to determine. Each make-up is an original design: the problems involved are variable, depending on the complexity of the design.

A rough guide

- *Straight corrective make-up, with tidy hair: man* 15 minutes.

- *Straight corrective make-up, with tidy hair: woman* 15 minutes.

- *Glamour make-up and hair: man* 30 minutes.

- *Glamour make-up and hair: woman* 1 hour 30 minutes.

- *Period make-up and hair using facial hair: man* 1 hour.

- *Period make-up and hair using wig: woman* 1 hour 30 minutes.

- *Fantasy make-up using wig: man* 1 hour.

- *Fantasy make-up using wig: woman* 1 hour 30 minutes.

- *Black eye, bruise, simple cut* 15 minutes.

- *Ageing make-up using bald cap, wig, and old-age stipple* 1 hour 30 minutes.

- *Ageing make-up using bald cap and prosthetics* 2–3 hours.

HOW TO SUCCEED

Checklist

In preparing for assessments on working in television and film, the following list may be useful. Check that you have covered and fully understood these items.

- Application must observe all health and safety regulations, and avoid contact to the inside of the eye and cross-contamination.
- Any likely contraventions of health and safety regulations must be reported promptly to production and steps taken to ensure that a qualified practitioner is present to take responsibility.
- The effect must be achieved within the allocated time appropriate to the type of production, on and off the set.
- The final effect must look realistic and natural on camera.
- The materials must be chosen to achieve the desired effect.
- Techniques must be suitable for the materials chosen and achieve the desired effect on camera.
- The artiste must be seated comfortably; the make-up process must be carried out so as to minimise discomfort to the artiste; and a good relationship must be maintained at all times to ensure her or his continuing co-operation.
- Techniques and materials chosen must meet the continuity requirements of the production.

Questions

Oral and written questions are used to test your knowledge and understanding. Try the following.

1 When researching the period for a production, where would you obtain your information?

2 When did it become fashionable for women to have a suntan?

3 When did Hollywood film stars start to influence make-up and hair fashions?

4 Before photography and films, where did the strongest influence in fashions come from?

5 When did the fashion of white-painted faces and wearing wigs come to an end?

6 When did women cut their hair short, wear shorter skirts and openly apply make-up?

7 In which period of history was it considered vulgar for women to wear any make-up, yet the men had carefully dressed facial hair?

8 Why is it sometimes important in TV and films to adapt a period look to a modern style, rather than copying it exactly?

9 Which facial features (eyes, lips or eyebrows) were emphasised in the following periods: (a) 1920s; (b) 1930s; (c) 1940s; (d) 1950s; (e) 1960s?

CHAPTER 6

Hairdressing and wigmaking

INTRODUCTION

In feature film production it is customary to employ hairdressers to design and dress the actors' hair, but in television it is often the make-up artist who is required to do the **hairdressing**. For commercials and fashion photographic work also make-up artists are usually expected to have both skills. (In theatre, on the other hand, there are usually wig departments to meet these needs, and actors will apply their own make-up.) To be able to secure work in any area of the industry – film, TV, videos, commercials, fashion photography and pop promotions – the student make-up artist is therefore wise to learn as much as possible about hairdressing.

Often you will be working with the artiste's own hair; at other times you will be preparing added hair (**postiche**) as a wig or facial hairpiece. Colleges throughout the country offer courses in hairdressing, most leading to some kind of qualification. As well as acquiring the basic hairdressing skills of cutting, setting and dressing hair, the make-up student needs to learn special skills, such as how to adapt a modern hairstyle to resemble a historical style for a period film or TV production, and how to **break down** hair so that it looks naturally untidy or dirty. You must learn:

1 how to clean, block and dress a wig;
2 how to prepare the artiste's own hair for application of a wig or hairpiece;
3 how to fit and secure the wig or hairpiece;

Wigs dressed and ready to be attached to the head

4 how to dress out the wig or hairpiece on the artiste's head;

5 how to apply and remove temporary colouring for particular hair effects.

The hairstyle

Just as lighting and shading with make-up can dramatically change the shape of the face, so the **hairstyle** can alter the shape of the head, accentuating a strong feature or disguising a weak one. A good hairstyle, in conjunction with the make-up, suggests the period, the character and the age. Equally, however, the effect of a skilful make-up can be ruined if the hairstyle is unsuitable for the character.

suitable

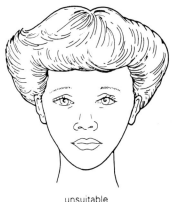

unsuitable

A suitable and an unsuitable style for a heart-shaped face

> ### ACTIVITY: STUDYING THE EFFECTS OF HAIRSTYLES
> On a piece of paper, draw a series of copies of the same head shape. Now sketch in the hair in various styles, and look at the changes the different styles make to the way the head looks.

As in other aspects of make-up, **continuity** is important. It sometimes seems in film and television work that if a lock of hair is placed differently in one shot from the next, *everyone* notices! Because of the natural movement of hair, its position must be monitored closely during filming.

Postiche

The term 'postiche' is French in origin, and includes all added hairpieces – wigs, transformations, pincurls, switches, fringes, falls, backpieces, toupees, fronts and every other kind of article made with hair.

Years ago, each hairdressing salon had its own workroom in which postiche was made to order. In this workroom student hairdressers first handled hair and learnt to appreciate its texture. They studied the way hair falls into waves and curls, and learnt to manipulate it with ease. Gradually they acquired a feel for the craft, developing knowledge and skill in the handling of growing hair and in the making of postiche. When short hair became widespread, this form of craftsmanship dwindled: few salons these days have practical understanding of postiche work, and hairpieces have now to be ordered from specialists. The demand continues in film, television and theatre work, of course; and no doubt the circle of fashion will eventually turn and postiche again be required by the public.

The make-up artist's responsibilities

For a large-scale production there may be as many as twenty wigs, plus numerous falls, headpieces and added facial hairpieces. If a character in the production ages extensively, the same actor may need several different wigs from youth through to old age. If stunt doubles are being used, duplicate wigs may be needed.

The make-up artist (or hair designer) must first specify what is required, providing drawings, diagrams, reference photographs, written notes and perhaps verbal descriptions. Each wig must include a mixture of shades of the chosen colour, otherwise it will look dull and unconvincing. With the right mixture of colours in the wig or facial hair, a character can be made to look stronger or more vibrant. Remember too that a man's hair, eyebrows, beard and moustache may not all be of the same colour.

Although some postiche can be hired, much will have to be bought. Occasionally it will be possible to **refront** an existing wig to ensure correct fit for re-use. Before hiring, several companies must be contacted and the one selected that offers the best price and workmanship. Facial hair cannot be hired, and has only a short lifespan; moustaches, beards, sideburns and eyebrows are made to order in any size, shape or colour. For a long TV series, too, purchase will prove cheaper than repeating hiring.

The make-up artist must oversee the wigmaking process and ensure that all the postiche items required are delivered on time, before shooting begins. The principal actors will need several fittings, whether the wig is being made specially or altered to fit them. During production, the wigs must be cleaned and dressed at the end of each day, ready for use on the next.

A wig with too much hair knotted into it will look false; if the hairlace at the edges is too thick or too white, this will show on camera. To understand such characteristics, to be able to judge what constitutes a good wig, you yourself need to have learnt about the wigmaking process.

EQUIPMENT FOR MAKING POSTICHE

Types of hair used in postiche work

Human hair

Human hair tends to be used solely for wigs and hairpieces. The most expensive is eyebrow hair, particularly if it is blonde, red or grey. The main countries supplying human hair for wigs are Italy and – more recently – Spain. Asian hair is more common and therefore less expensive; as it is usually dark, Asian hair needs to be lightened.

Cleaning and dyeing processes weaken the hair and make it porous. Because the hair no longer has its natural supply of oil, it does not behave as it would on the head, either in its movement or in the way it holds any curl.

When handling a swatch of human hair, it is important to keep the *root* ends of the hair (the clubbed ends) lying in the same direction.

Yak hair

Yak hair is used for facial hairpieces – beards, eyebrows, sideburns and moustaches – and for chest wigs and the like. The softer hair is from the belly of the yak, the coarser hair from the tail. Yak hair is dyed by the hair merchant to match the required colour.

If the hair needs to be curled, it can be permed on rods after the piece has been knotted. Alternatively, it can be pre-curled on rods in a pressure cooker, and dried in an oven before knotting. These processes usually result in a colour change, so the final facial hairpieces may not exactly match the hair sample. Using pre-curled hair usually gives a better finish to the moustache, but curled hair is also more difficult to knot.

Wool crepe hair

Wool crepe hair is the cheapest type of hair, and comes braided over two strands of cord which are removed before using the hair. Wool crepe hair does not have long hairs; it consists of many shorter hairs, held together by overlapping.

Colours

Wool crepe hair comes in many colours, with shades of blonde, brown, black, grey, red and white. These look natural when mixed. Unusual colours also are available, such as bright green or yellow. White braids can be dyed any colour using normal wool dyes, or sprayed with hair-colouring materials.

Uses

In the larger theatres and auditoriums, and occasionally in TV and film for extras in the background, wool crepe hair is mainly used for facial hair. It is also used in hairstyles as padding, to give extra bulk to the existing hair, whether natural or in a wig.

Preparation

> **Equipment and materials**
> - wool crepe hair
> - towel
> - hair dryer (hand-held)
> - metal comb (wide-toothed)
> - scissors (sharp)
> - tissue paper *or* facial tissues

1 Cut a piece of braided wool crepe hair, about 300 mm long.
2 Remove the two cords.
3 Straighten the hair by dipping it in hot water.
4 Wrap it carefully in a towel, to absorb excess water.
5 Dry the hair by winding it round the back of a chair and leaving it overnight; or, to dry the hair more quickly, use a hand-held dryer.
6 When completely dry, cut the hair into shorter lengths (about 150 mm).
7 Each length should be teased apart carefully, and divided into smaller widths (about 25 mm across).
8 Hold a small bunch of hair in the middle, and use a wide-toothed metal comb on the ends of the hair.
9 Using sharp scissors, cut off the straggly ends to make the strands even in length.
10 Repeat the combing and cutting with each bunch, and lay the bunches carefully on tissue paper or facial tissues. Fold over the tissues to store the hair for future use.

Mixing shades

First prepare the different shades or colours of wool crepe hair as above. Then combine them as follows:

1 Place one small mat of prepared hair on top of another.
2 Pull the ends to tug the hair apart into two sections.
3 Continue mixing the colours by laying one colour on top of another and pulling the hair apart, until the desired effect is achieved.

Real crepe hair

Real crepe hair is braided together in the same way as wool crepe hair, but consists of human or animal hair. When the cords have been removed the skeins are usually 150 mm or 200 mm in length.

The hair can be straightened by using a steam iron, and is then prepared with a hackle in the same way as other real hair. A **hackle** is a giant comb used to disentangle hair, and for mixing hair for colour matching.

Angora goat hair

Angora goat hair is very soft and fine, and is therefore suitable for specialised wigs such as period powder wigs, or for soft-looking beards such as Father Christmas beards. It is usually blended with yak hair for beards, and added as necessary to other hair to provide softness.

Horsehair

Horsehair is stiff and straight. It is used for barristers' and judges' wigs. It is also useful for adding whiskers to an animal make-up.

Artificial hair

Wigs and hairpieces can be obtained in artificially created **plastic hairs**. These are available in department stores and specialist shops. Although much less expensive than real hair (either animal or human), artificial hair is more difficult to dress. However, it is very tough and long-lasting, so many rented wigs for period work are made of artificial hair. They are suitable for theatre productions but are not used much in TV or film work as they are less natural-looking than real-hair work.

On low-budget productions, artificial-hair wigs are very useful, and do not require much maintenance. They can be cleaned by gently immersing them in lukewarm water mixed with a mild wig cleanser or fabric softener. They should be rinsed in cold water several times and then left to drip-dry naturally.

Lace

The types of **hair lace** or **gauze** range from thick theatre lace, used mainly in large theatres, to very fine laces, used by film and

TV productions and where a theatre production is to be staged in a small space such as a studio. Although the thicker, coarser types of laces last longer, they tend to allow less movement of the face, and can therefore be less comfortable for the actor.

Film and TV lace comes in two thicknesses, 30 denier and 20 denier (which is finer). It requires greater skill and care to knot facial pieces on 20 denier lace, as this is prone to tearing. Never use a piece of lace with a snag or fault in it as this will inevitably become a large hole during the knotting process. Thick lace will loosen a little once it has been cleaned several times.

The shades of lace vary slightly, from off-white to darker tones. Before knotting, lace can be stained somewhat darker using a weak solution of tea. If the facial piece is required for black skin, **potassium permanganate solution** can be used to dye the lace dark brown.

Knotting hooks

Knotting hooks come in a range of sizes. For knotting the bulk of a wig you would use a hook capable of picking up six or seven hairs at a time. For the front hairline of a wig you would use a finer hook, as here you want to pick up only one hair at a time. Facial hair likewise needs a fine hook.

The *angle* of the hook can be altered to suit the individual. **Hook holders** are made either of plastic or of brass; the latter is heavier. These too come in differing lengths.

A fairly large hook is used in whipping together with nylon thread the pleats on wig foundations and beards. Such hooks are sometimes called **whipping hooks**.

MAKING A WIG

A wig can change a person's appearance almost beyond recognition – the height of the forehead can be increased and the width extended, for example, and an actor with a bald head can be transformed with a convincing head of hair, provided that it is a good wig and properly suited to the character.

Wigs are made according to two main principles: those which can be blended to tone into the general make-up – these use a gauze or net front, the **hair lace**; and those which provide a full head of hair without the need to blend the make-up – these have no hair lace fronts and are known as **'hard front' wigs**. The wigs fronted with hair lace are used in TV and film make-up as they are more natural-looking in camera close-ups. Hair-lace wigs are very expensive; they also demand greater skill and care in fitting than the hard-fronted wigs.

The less expensive, hard-fronted wigs are used in the theatre and are easier to put on, requiring no extra attention with the make-up as the edge of the wig provides the dividing line at the hairline.

The fitting of a wig must be as perfect as possible, so meticulous care should be taken in measuring the actor or in

A period wig

Taking measurements for a wig

WIG SPECIALITIES LTD.

173 SEYMOUR PLACE · LONDON · W.I

DATE:

MEASUREMENTS TAKEN BY:

WIG MEASUREMENTS

1. CIRCUMFERENCE AROUND HEAD — ins.
2. FRONT TO BACK — ins.
3. TEMPLE TO TEMPLE AROUND BACK OF HEAD — ins.
4. EAR TO EAR OVER CROWN — ins.
5. NAPE OF NECK — ins.
6. TOP OF EAR TO NAPE OF NECK — ins.
7. EAR TO EAR OVER FOREHEAD — ins.
8. TEMPLE TO TEMPLE ACROSS FACE — ins.

PARTING ☐ RIGHT ☐ LEFT ☐ CENTRE ☐ NONE

TOUPEE MEASUREMENTS

1. LENGTH — ins.
2. TEMPLE — ins.
3. CROWN — in.
4. BACK — ins.

PARTING ☐ RIGHT ☐ LEFT ☐ CENTRE ☐ NONE

NAME:

CHARACTER:

ARTICLE

PERIOD OR TYPE OF WIG

WEIGHT OF HAIRPIECE ☐ THICK ☐ THIN ☐ SPARSE

HAIR LENGTH ☐ ins.

COLOUR

DRESSING ☐ CURLY ☐ WAVY ☐ STRAIGHT

DIRECTION OF COMBING

REMARKS

NOTE - WHEREVER POSSIBLE SUPPLY SKETCH OR LATE STILLS
OF THE ARTIST WITH THIS FORM.

selecting from stock. Once the make-up artist has begun making up the actor on a shoot, there is no time to rectify any errors in the fit of the wig.

Preparation

Although as a make-up artist you will not have to make wigs yourself, it is useful to understand the wigmaking process: this will help you when commissioning or hiring wigs.

The process of making a good-quality wig uses a special knotting hook to knot small bunches of real hair onto a **foundation** base of gauze or hair lace. This process is similar to the way in which carpets or rugs are made, and many actors refer to their toupee or wig as their 'rug'.

The foundation on which the hair is knotted is fixed to a wooden **block** with small nails called **block points**. The block is held in position by means of a clamp attached to the edge of a table or workbench. The loose hair used for knotting is held in place using a **drawing mat** or **card**.

Making a pattern

The head measurements must be taken in order to make a **pattern** of the head on which the foundation can be based. Opposite is an example of a chart used by a wig company to specify the details required in order to make a wig or toupee. Usually the actor is taken by the make-up artist to the wig company for a consultation and fitting. If this is impossible, the chart is made and sent to the wig company.

Traditionally the pattern was made by transferring the measurements of the head to a piece of paper, which was then cut and shaped. Nowadays wigmakers use clingfilm, a method which is easier and more accurate.

When the measurements and pattern are ready, they are sent to the wigmaker.

Equipment and materials
- clingfilm
- clear adhesive tape
- pencil (soft)

ACTIVITY: MAKING A PATTERN FOR A WIG

1 Prepare the head by brushing the hair back from the face, and as close to the head as possible.
2 Wrap clingfilm tightly around the head, towards the back. A single piece should be big enough to wrap the front of the head and fasten at the back. If there is a gap on top of the head, fill this in with another piece of clingfilm.
3 Now secure this with clear adhesive tape. First apply the tape over the top of the head from ear to ear, making sure it is not too tight. Next take adhesive tape from the front to the back. Then apply tape along the entire circumference. Cover the whole head in this way until the pattern feels rigid, like a stiff cap.
4 Now draw in the existing hairline with a soft pencil, from the front, around the ear, and down to the nape of the neck. If

the hair is fine at the hairline, draw fine lines. Cover the pencil line with adhesive tape to protect it.

5 Remove the pattern from the head by easing it off gently.

Making the foundation

The wigmaker cuts the pattern at the back and places it on the right-sized wooden block; the edges are then taped back together, and the pattern is fixed with points. The wooden block used to make postiche should be approximately 15 mm larger than the circumference of the artiste's head. If the block is too small it should be padded. A cut is made and tissue paper pushed through; the cut is resealed with clear adhesive tape. Further cuts are made elsewhere as necessary. Only one cut is made at a time, and never too near the hairline.

The foundation, mount or base is now made using net, gauze or silk; springs, ribbons and fasteners provide extra support and fit. **Galloon**, a type of silk ribbon, is sewn around the outline of the pattern. The foundation net is sewn onto the galloon, and this forms the shape of the wig base. For a more natural-looking frontal hairline, a galoonless edge is more suitable – this applies to wigs or hairpieces used in TV and film work.

Once the wig foundation has been made to measure, it is ready for knotting.

Knotting

As a make-up artist you are not required to make wigs, but you do need to understand how they are made in order to recognise good workmanship. **Knotting**, however, does have practical applications. One such is knotting in extra hairs to soften, and generally to improve the appearance of, a damaged or poorly knotted hairline.

Knotting is a delicate operation, requiring patience and good eyesight. It takes practice and time to become an expert knotter. To start with you should practise on odd pieces of foundation net, attached to a block with block points. It is best to use straight hair about 150 mm in length. Select a knotting needle to suit the size of the mesh of the net, and firmly secure this into the wooden handle.

Types of knotting

There are many different types of knots. The ones generally used in making a wig are described below.

Single knotting

In **single knotting**, individual knots of hair are added to the foundation net. This is the most common method of knotting when fine net is used. Different sizes of hooks can be used, depending on the amount of hair needed for each knot.

Single knotting

A small quantity of hair is placed in drawing mats with the ends protruding. A few hairs at a time are drawn out and turned over to form a loop held in the left hand; this is dampened. The knotting hook is inserted under one mesh of the lace, and one or several hairs are picked up from the loop in the left hand

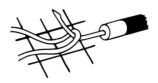

This loop is drawn under and through the hole in the lace

The hook is turned to catch the remaining ends of hair

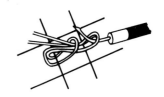

These ends are pulled carefully through the loop on the hook towards the right-hand side

The completed knot is pulled tight so that it is as invisible as possible. (Dampening the hair at the outset helps this.) Care should be taken to ensure that *both* ends of the hair are always pulled through

Double knotting

Double knots are tied to make the hair absolutely secure. The result is more unsightly as the knots are less easily concealed. Double knotting is used on the crown and large parts of the foundation, but single knotting is usually employed for the more visible parts of the wig.

Point knotting

Point knotting is single knotting the point ends of the hair. The root ends are cut away, allowing the hair to lift from the piece. This technique is useful for men's short-haired postiche, on the nape of a short-haired woman, and on light fringes.

Underknotting

After the piece has been knotted it is turned inside out on a malleable block. Single knotting is applied around the edge of the foundation, following the direction of the hair on the other side. Two or three rows of **underknotting** can be added. The wig is usually pressed when finished, using tissue paper or cloth to protect the hair.

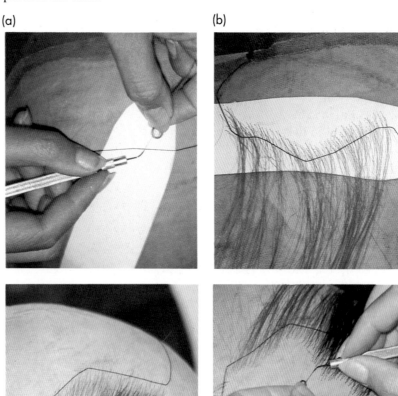

(a) (b)

(c) (d)

Knotting a hairline on a film wig

(a) Hand knotting into the hairline: a white card has been inserted to make the very fine lace visible for working on

(b) Knotting (continued)

(c) The front edge hairline completed and ready for filling in with main hair

(d) The completed front edge being checked for softness of hairline before continuing with knotting

OTHER POSTICHE WORK

Extra pieces of postiche can be added to a wig, or to the natural hair when a wig is not required.

- **Chignons** Knotted or wefted postiche, worn between the crown and the neck. They are good for adding fullness, height and shape.

- **Marteaux** Pieces of weft folded together; they are attached to the hair by means of combs or sewn loops. They are useful for adding a wave, when required.

- **Switches** Lengths of weft wound spirally around tailcord. They can be coiled, plaited and twisted, and can be used in a variety of ways.

- **Pincurls** Small pieces of weft, sewn into various curl shapes. They are useful in adding to the hairstyle when dressed.

- **Ringlets** Larger curls, also used for dressing into a finished style.

- **Swathes** Made from two marteaux, sewn end to end. They are used for encircling the head.

- **Torsades** Coiled pieces of postiche. They look attractive when added to the hair.

- **Bandeaux wigs** or **cape wiglets** Can be knotted or wefted postiche. This kind of hairpiece is used in turning a short hairstyle into a long one; it is held in position by a band, leaving the real front hair showing. It can be any length at the back.

- **Toupees** Knotted hairpieces, made to cover bald areas of the head. They are used extensively in TV and film on male actors, and chosen to match the natural hair.

- **Transformations** Hairpieces, either wefted or knotted, worn to add length or bulk to the existing hair. They are often used on men for period work.

- **Semi-transformations** Smaller pieces, also used to add length to the existing hair.

- **Wigs** The largest postiche items, covering the entire head of hair.

- **Fringes** or **frontal pieces** Wefted or knotted postiche, used on the front of the head.

- **Double-loop clusters** Wefted postiche made by winding and sewing onto a cord, and finished with loops at each end. They are attached to the head with sewn-on combs, and used to provide a cluster of curls.

- **Hidden comb** A bunch of curls attached to a hidden comb; the technique is also known as **top knots**. These may be

A chignon: view from underneath, to show the foundation with loops and a comb to attach the piece to the head

A marteau with hoops

A switch

A coiled switch

A pincurl

A ringlet

A torsade with curled ends

A bandeau wig

A frontal piece attached to a
headband

knotted pieces, but are usually wefted. The weft is made on two silks and a wire which, when folded and sewn, forms a very pliable foundation piece.

Weft work

Weft work is the weaving of hair in the manufacture of postiche. The hair is interwoven onto silks, cotton thread or wire; interweaving at the root ends forms lengths of weft. The weft is folded, spirally wound, or sewn onto a **mount** or base.

Wigs made in this way are known as **weft wigs** and many other pieces of postiche use woven or weft work.

Weft wigs and pieces are less expensive than hand-knotted pieces, although the quality of the finish is not suitable for TV and film. Weft work is useful for adding to natural hair to provide extra bulk and length in period hair work.

ACTIVITY: VISITING A WIG COMPANY

Each wig company has a staff who specialise in the various aspects of wigmaking and wig dressing. Make-up artists spend much time there, attending fittings and chatting to other make-up artists and actors they know.

It is a good idea as a student make-up artist to visit a wig company; here you can gain an insight into the making of postiche work from start to finish.

WIGS AND HAIRDRESSING IN THE STUDIO

Equipment

- Brushes
- Combs
- Heated rollers
- Tongs
- A hair dryer
- A malleable wig block
- A chin block (540 mm or 560 mm)
- A bench clamp or stand
- Galloon
- T-pins
- Long pins
- 'Short white' pins (small)
- Sectioning clips, pins and grips
- Acetone (be careful: this can be 'rough' on the lace)
- Cleaning solvent
- Surgical spirit (good for removing spirit gum)
- An artist's stipple brush or toothbrush
- An old sable make-up brush (for applying spirit gum, and for applying surgical spirit to the lace to loosen it from the skin when removing wigs or facial hair)
- Spirit gum

- A damp cloth or powder puff
- A piece of silk *or* a piece of chamois leather
- An assortment of hairnets and stocking tops
- Crepe hair
- Heated tongs and a heater
- Moustache tongs (small)
- Hair spray
- Plastic spray

CUTTING AND STYLING THE POSTICHE

When the wig or other hairpiece has been made, it is pinned onto a malleable wig block and the hair is cut and styled in the required shape. The type of setting will depend on the period or fashion; this will have been discussed during the fittings, and the wig dresser should have sketches, photographs and notes supplied by the make-up artist or hairdresser.

Postiche work is usually wet-set on rollers, and placed in a special oven to dry slowly for several hours, often overnight, until it is dry. It is then brushed out and dressed in the desired style. For wig styles that are flat, such as the finger waving which was in fashion in the 1930s, the wig is set with the fingers and placed in the oven to dry in the same way.

Protecting the postiche

When the postiche arrives from the wig company it will already have been dressed and will be ready to put on the artiste's head. It will come packed in tissue paper in a large wig box; on the lid will be the date of delivery, the name of the artiste, the name of the make-up artist, and the name of the production company which has bought or hired the postiche.

Maintaining a wig

At the end of the first day's shoot, after it has been removed, the wig will need re-dressing and the hair lace will need cleaning. Once the lace has been cleaned, the wig should be placed on a wig block to keep its shape.

Thus, the make-up artist or hairdresser must clean the wig when it gets dirty; she must then attach it to a block and re-style it, either returning it to the way it was or dressing it into a different style, according to the production requirements. Maintenance can therefore be divided into three areas: *cleaning*, *blocking*, and *dressing*. Wigs can be *built up*, using added hairpieces.

Cleaning postiche

Whether the postiche is made from human or from synthetic hair, it must be cleaned regularly and carefully. How often will depend on how long the wig or piece has been worn: if the wig is being used every day for weeks at a time, it is generally necessary to clean it at the end of each week.

Cleaning must be carried out with great care, so as not to damage the foundation and loosen the knotted hair or weft. Real-hair postiche should be cleaned in a recommended hair-cleaning solvent. Never use sharp combs, which can damage the foundation; and never use shampoo and water, as these cause tangling, and loosening of the hair knots.

Cleaning real-hair postiche

1 Make sure the room is well ventilated – open a window, as the fumes from hair-cleaning solvents are as obnoxious as those from house paint.
2 Pour the hair-cleaning solvent into a large porcelain, glass or metal bowl. *Do not use a plastic bowl*: the chemicals in the cleaning solvent would melt the plastic.
3 Place the postiche in the cleaner until the base and hair are immersed. Leave for several minutes.
4 Move the wig or hairpiece around the bowl; then lift it up, allowing the liquid to drain back into the bowl.
5 When the liquid has finished draining off, shake the piece gently and hang it somewhere until the cleaning liquid has evaporated. If the weather permits, hang it outside in the open air.
6 When dry, place the postiche on the block, ready for setting, blow-drying, tonging or applying heated rollers.

Cleaning synthetic-hair postiche

Shampoo can be used on synthetic hairpieces, as can **fabric conditioners** (such as Comfort).

1 Add shampoo to a bowl of lukewarm water. Make sure that the water is not too hot: extreme heat can damage the pre-formed curl in the hair.
2 Move the hairpiece gently in the water.
3 Rinse it in cold water.
4 Rub a conditioner, such as a fabric conditioner, into the hairpiece.
5 Hold the piece to let the water drain off into the bowl, then pat it with a towel and place it on a malleable wig block covered with plastic (to protect the block).
6 Set the hair with rollers or allow it to dry naturally, as required. The block, with a hairnet placed over it, can be placed in a warm airing cupboard or under a hooded hair dryer.
7 Most modern fibres can be set and blow-dried, or styled using hot tongs and heated rollers, but care should be taken: some artificial hair will be damaged by too much heat.

Cleaning the hair lace on a lace-fronted real-hair wig

At the end of the day, when the wig has been removed, the hairlace will need cleaning as it will have spirit gum and make-up on it.

Surgical spirit is good for removing the spirit gum, as are acetone or methylated spirits. A toothbrush, a sable make-up brush or a stipple brush may be used to apply the spirit; the brush chosen must have hairs that are stiff enough to do the job properly.

1 Pour the spirit into a small glass or enamel bowl.
2 Place the hair lace of the wig onto a clean towel, soft tissue or paper towel.
3 Dip the brush into the spirit and tap it gently onto the wig lace, forcing the dried-up spirit gum and make-up to go *through* the lace and onto the material below. Use a gentle but firm tapping motion. Be careful not to be too harsh, or the delicate lace will tear.
4 When the lace is clean, place the wig on the block, ready for blocking and setting.

> **Equipment and materials**
> ● small bowl (glass *or* enamel)
> ● towel, tissue *or* paper towel
> ● brush (toothbrush, sable make-up brush, *or* stipple brush)

Blocking the wig

1 Set up the malleable block and stand, and carefully centre the wig in position on the block.
2 Make sure that the hairline at the front is in position. Check that the hairline in front of the ears is the same length on each side of the wig.
3 Use T-pins to secure the wig at the earpieces and at the corners of the nape area at the back of the wig.
4 Cover the lace front with galloon to reinforce the hair and protect the lace from being torn. Use small pins known as 'short whites', which minimise stress on the lace. Place the pins in a triangular pattern along the tape. Run the tape around the front hairline from ear to ear. Do not place any tension on the lace itself, only on the tape. Fold the tape to suit the shape of the hairline.
5 If the wig still feels loose, add long pins at the back of the wig until it feels secure on the block.

> **Equipment and materials**
> ● malleable block and stand
> ● T-pins
> ● galloon
> ● 'short white' pins

The wig is now ready for dressing.

Blocking a hair-laced wig

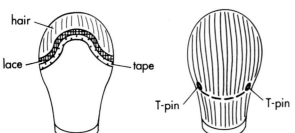

Put wig on from front to back: make sure that it is central

Attach the tape from ear to ear and secure it with T-pins at the two corners at the nape area

Tape down the lace, securing the tape with small pins in this pattern

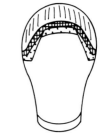

The wig blocked and ready to be dressed

Dressing postiche

Equipment

When dressing postiche you will need the following equipment.

- Hairdryers – hand and hood types
- Tongs
- Crimpers
- Flat irons
- Heated rollers
- Setting rollers
- Various hairnets
- Clips, of various sizes
- Pins, of various sizes
- Grips, in various colours (matt if possible)
- Hairbands
- Haircombs
- Scissors
- Combs, including tail, setting, clubbing, and other types
- Brushes, including bristle, vent, half-round, round and other types
- Gels
- Mousses
- Sprays
- Water spray
- Toupee tape
- Spirit gum

Finger waves

Finger waves were extremely fashionable in the 1930s. The technique of finger waving consists in moulding the wet hair into S-shaped movements using the fingers and a comb.

Finger waving a *wig* is carried out as follows:

1 Block up the wig and spray down the hair. Be careful not to get the lace or the malleable block too wet.
2 Keeping with the root direction of the hair, make the first 'wave' of the hair by combing the hair from the roots.
3 Pinch the 'crest' of the wave between two fingers, and comb the rest of the hair in the opposite direction.
4 Move your fingers down to pinch the next 'crest', then comb the rest of the hair, again in the opposite direction. Try to keep the waves an even width. (Use your fingers as a guide – two fingers are about 30 mm.)
5 Work in circles around the parting, taking the waves around the head until you reach the occipital bone. At this point continue with reverse pincurls, barrel curls, or pincurls set into the centre.
6 Secure the finger waves by applying wig tape across the 'dip' of the wave. Use a little tension and insert pins along the tape.
7 Place the block in a warm place to dry thoroughly.

Finger waving

Equipment and materials
- malleable block
- comb
- wig tape
- tail comb
- pins (large)
- hairnet

It will help if you remember the following points:

- The hair should be combed thoroughly to rid it of any tangles.
- Use warm water to wet the hair, and comb the hair on the slant backwards.
- Keep the hair wet (but not dripping) during the waving.
- Take care with the parting: it must be perfectly straight. Pin a tape along the parting to keep it neat, but do not place pins through the parting.
- For short hair, make shallow rather than deep waves.
- For a soft and natural look it is best to avoid deep waves, as these can look too hard.
- Short hair at the front of the wig can be curled separately. This gives a soft effect to the waves around the face and forehead.

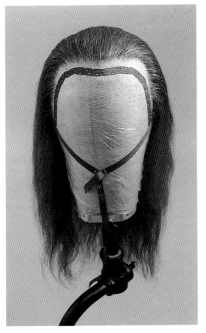

A wig blocked and ready for dressing

Complete the dressing out as follows:

8 After removing the block from the oven or warm place, allow it to cool for a few minutes.
9 Using a tailcomb, lift up a thin layer of the hair along the parting. Backcomb the hair strongly near the roots, gradually lessening the backcombing as you work towards the points.
10 Continue making divisions and backcombing until the entire wig has been worked on.
11 Comb softly over the top to smooth the hair down, and push or press the waves into position. Try not to comb out too much of the backcombing.
12 Use one or two large pins to hold the waves down at the edges.
13 Leave the hair at the parting raised: hair on the head does not naturally grow flat from the parting.
14 Adjust the final shape, place a hairnet over the wig, and return the wig to the oven or warm place for about 30 minutes.
15 Do not comb out the wig afterwards: this would remove the backcombing and leave the wig looking too flat. The top layer of hair only can be combed smooth.

Finger waving *natural hair* is a somewhat different process:

1 Make the finger waves as before, but secure them with clamps or long sectioning clips. Form any pincurls using small hairclips.
2 Place a net over the set and seat the artiste under a hooded hair dryer.
3 Do not backcomb during the final dressing out, as you would with a wig. Natural hair can be combed and pushed into position very easily, especially if the hair is finger waved with setting lotion, gel, mousse or emulsion whilst still wet.

TIP

In an emergency a wig can be dressed and waved very quickly using methylated spirits or cologne in place of water. This saves on the drying time, but it is just a standby method.

Equipment and materials
- clamps
- sectioning clips (long)
- hairclips (small)
- hair dryer
- comb
- setting lotion, gel, mousse *or* emulsion (if required)

Beehives

Beehives and **bouffants** were fashionable in the 1960s. They can be created with or without false hairpieces, depending on the artiste's own hair. They can also be filled out with crepe hair.

Equipment and materials
- heated rollers
- false hair (if required)
- brush and comb
- hairgrips
- hairpins
- tailcomb
- gel
- eyelash glue

1 First plan your beehive shape.
2 If you are using partings, set the hair in heated rollers.
3 Prepare any false hair if required.
4 Brush out the hair, and backcomb it where you want the most height. Leave free any sections to be pulled over the bulk, kiss-curled or tonged. Keep most of the hair around the hairline smooth so that the final effect is sleek.
5 Make an anchor of grips down the centre of the back of the head. Smooth the hair from the right to the left.
6 Fold over the hair from the left and coil it round, securing it with hairpins. Keep the 'fold' very tight in the nape area. Add more pins as you work up the fold, securing the hair and covering the line of grips.
7 Coil round the backcombed hair on the crown to make the desired shape; fix this with pins.
8 Check the shape in the mirror and 'tease' it with a tailcomb to change the shape slightly if necessary.
9 Gel flat any pieces to be left out in the front.
10 Any small, wispy sections of hair can be pincurled and attached to the cheeks with eyelash glue. Tong any other pieces of hair that you want to leave loose.

For added height or a different shape, use crepe hair or a hairpiece.

Wigs also can be set into beehives: a similar method is used on wigs to create an eighteenth-century look.

Building up a wig

Block your wig and begin to create a pre-planned shape. Then make a 'beehive', keeping it as flat as possible at the nape.

To attach another hairpiece, make a pincurl base with hairgrips crossing over one another to form a cross. Attach the piece to the pincurl base, then work it in with the rest of the hair. Crepe hair also can be added – use it sparingly and secure it with hairpins. Extra pieces can be used for rolls, curls or tendrils.

Chicken wire can be used for a frame. Hair can be sewn into this with needle and thread, or attached with grips. Likewise, for extra bulk crepe hair can be wrapped in netting before being secured to the wig.

As much hair as you like can be added, but it must be secured well. Take care that the extra weight is not too uncomfortable for the artiste to wear. Refer to your design and don't attach more hair than is necessary.

Hairpieces

Hairpieces add length and fullness. They may be attached as follows:

1 First assess the size and weight of the piece.
2 Make a pincurl base, either in the natural hair on the person's head or on the wig, as appropriate.
3 Attach the hairpiece to the pincurl base with hairpins. Hook a pin through the loop of the piece, pinching the pin together as you do this so that when you let it go it springs out and grips the surrounding hair.
4 Secure the hairpiece with more pins, making sure that they 'grip' into the pincurl base.

Parting pieces

A **parting piece** is attached at the centre of the hair. Always look at the piece first, however, and place it on the head in different positions in order to find out where it looks best.

1 Make pincurls on the head with the natural hair to the side of the lace of the parting piece. If there is no hair, as on a balding man, toupee tape can be used.
2 Attach the piece with hairpins, weaving them in and blending them with the natural hair for a result that looks natural.

This method can be used for toupees, and for any area of the head. The hair can be styled as required.

ATTACHING THE WIG

Before attaching a lace-fronted wig to the head, carefully remove the tape and pins in order to detach the wig from the block.

Preparing the head

1 Use grips to pincurl the natural hair – two on the crown, and one on either side of the head, forming anchors.
2 Wrap the remaining hair around the head.
3 Put stocking or hairnet on the head. Fix it with hairpins.
4 Gel or soap short hairs around the hairline.

If the wig has a parting, match the hair to it by parting it in the same way.

Attaching a wig to very short hair

When the artiste's hair is very short it is hard to make pincurls. Instead, therefore, use tiny rubber bands to secure the hair in very small tufts all over the head at the crown, nape and front hairline.

Attaching a wig to long hair

If the artiste has very long, thick hair, it is not possible to pincurl it flat. Instead, the hair should be wrapped around the head as flat as possible and covered with a hairnet or stocking top. Pins and grips can be used to secure it firmly.

A full wig: Michael Pennington in *Cymbeline*

Placing the wig

1 Hold the back of the wig with both hands and slide the wig front over the forehead.
2 Place one finger at the front of the lace to hold it in place, then pull down the back of the wig until it fits smartly on the head.
3 Holding the wig firmly on each side of the head (using the open palms of the hands), slide the wig-front back until you reach the desired hairline.
4 Comb back any stray hairs, under the lace or away from the front of the wig.

Attach the lace to the head just in front of the natural hairline so that the hair growth does not appear to be too far down on the forehead.

Fixing the lace

1 Roll back the edge of the lace a little and apply spirit gum adhesive to the forehead in three spots.
2 With your fingertip, make the gum tacky.
3 Roll the lace back over the adhesive, pressing the edge onto the head with a damp cloth (muslin or silk).

REMOVING THE WIG

Always take great care when removing a wig or hairpiece with hairlace. You must not damage either the actor's skin or the lace itself.

Method: wigs with lace

1 Loosen the lace by applying a little surgical spirit on the brush to its edges.
2 Hold the tissue pad in the other hand, below the lace so that any drops from the brush trickle onto the pad, and not into the actor's eyes.
3 Continue gentle dabbing at the lace where it has been stuck down.
4 When the adhesive has softened, the lace may be lifted from the skin at the edges and rolled back to remove any remaining adhesive.
5 Remove the hairpins attaching the wig to the head.
6 Lift the wig off from behind, holding it carefully at the sides: pull it gently forward and off the head.
7 If it is a man's wig, detach the hairgrips from the anchor points on the crown and sides. If it is a woman's wig, remove the stocking or net and then remove the hairgrips on the head.
8 If the natural hair is so short that you used tiny rubber bands as anchor points, the simplest course is to cut them off carefully with scissors.

9 Remove any remaining spirit gum on the face using mild mastix remover.
10 Cleanse, tone and moisturise the skin to remove the make-up.
11 Brush through the hair to restore the artiste's normal hairstyle.

Method: wigs without lace

Remove these in the same way as wigs *with* lace (above), but without the surgical spirit and mastix remover.

TEMPORARY COLOURINGS

Temporary colourings are often used in film and television to alter the colour of the natural hair or postiche. They can be used, for example, to disguise and cover white and grey hair, and so make the person look younger, or to paint in white and silver hair, and so make the person look older. They are also used to create exciting fashion effects.

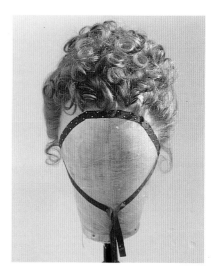

A dressed wig ready to be attached to the head

Types of temporary colourings

There are many different types of temporary colourings. Here are the best known.

- **Coloured hair lacquers** These are sprayed onto the dried, dressed hair. They can be obtained from specialist theatrical make-up shops in a wide range of colours. They wash out easily.

- **Hair colour sprays** Available in liquid or powdered forms, these also are for use on the dried, dressed hair. They too wash out easily.

- **Hair colour setting lotions** These are applied to towel-dried hair and used to set the hair. They wash out easily.

- **Cosmetic hair-colouring liquids** These are available from theatrical make-up shops, packaged in bottles or wands (similar to mascara wands). The best way to use them from the bottle is to pour some into a dish, and paint it onto the hair with a small make-up brush. The wand can be used directly onto the hair with its own applicator.

- **Hair colour crayons** These can be used directly on the dressed hair. They are useful for colouring in hair around the temples, or for filling in a bald patch on the head.

- **Gels and mousses** These are available in a limited range of colours and are easy to use straight onto the hair. They colour and condition the hair, and give extra 'hold'.

- **Hair glitter** This is available in loose form to sprinkle in the hair for a sparkling, glittering or twinkling effect. Though much of it is usually gold or silver, other colours are available.

Coloured hair

Glitter is tricky to control and goes everywhere, but it is good for adding glamorous effects to hair.

- **Hair gel glitter** This comes in a tube. It can be used on the hair or the skin. Colours are iridescent, giving strong effects under lights.

- **Hair colour creams** These are available from good specialist make-up shops. Packaged in small pots, they look like any other make-up creams. They are usually available in pink or light yellow, and are painted onto individual hairs to neutralise dark hair before applying the chosen colour. They are generally used before putting ageing streaks of white, cream and silver at the front hairline. (Without the cream neutralising colour, very dark hair always looks blue when streaked with cream, white or silver.)

'BREAKING DOWN' EFFECTS

Very often a scene may require an actor to have his or her hair dirtied or made wet. The make-up must take account of the type of dirt – whether dusty or muddy, for instance – and the effect must look realistic.

Materials for dirtying the hair

- **Powders** – dark brown, grey or black – are used for dry-looking dirt, such as coal dust. **Fullers' earth** is also useful for dirt.

- **Greasepaint** provides a greasy, matted effect.

- **Coloured hair-lacquer sprays** are useful for spraying on dark colours to 'break down' blonde hair.

Making the hair look wet

This is usually achieved using a **spray bottle** filled with water. The hair is sprayed before each 'take', and care must be taken to ensure that the continuity is maintained.

Because sets and locations are so expensive, the order in which the production is filmed makes the most economical use of these, and this seldom follows the order of the storyline. When filming rain scenes, therefore, it is always advisable to take a Polaroid photo of the actor's hair. The interior scene moments later, when the character comes in out of the rain, may actually be *filmed* several days later!

'Breaking down' effects add considerably to the realism of a scene. Co-operation is needed between the make-up and costume departments to achieve the degree of dirtiness required.

For casualty effects, 'blood' used on the hair should be of the *washable* kind: it will otherwise stain and be very difficult to wash out.

A three-quarter wig and dirt: Jonathan Pryce in *Cymbeline*

PERIOD HAIRSTYLES

As with period make-up, researching period hairstyles will involve visiting museums, art galleries and libraries, and looking at magazines, old photographs, and so forth.

Here are some simple examples, from the Egyptian period through to the twentieth century, which should serve as a useful guide. (See also pages 64–75 for some background information on period hairstyles.)

(a) The Egyptians

(b) The Greeks

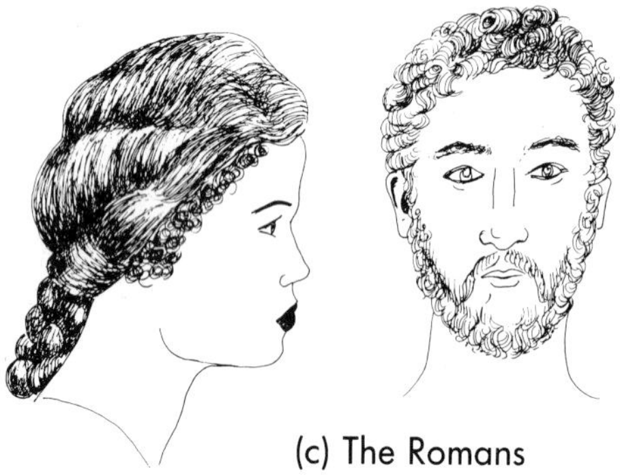

(c) The Romans

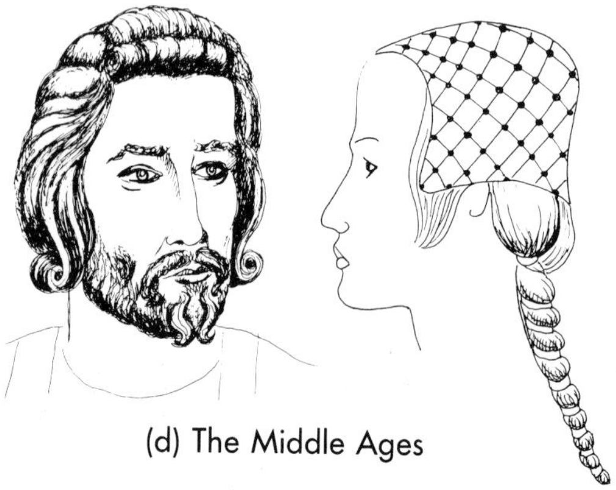

(d) The Middle Ages

(e) The sixteenth century

(f) The seventeenth century

(g) The eighteenth century

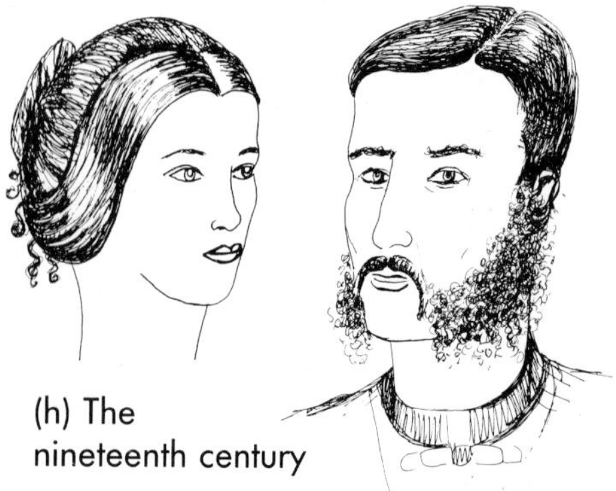

(h) The nineteenth century

(i) The 1920s

(j) The 1930s

(k) The 1940s

(l) The 1950s

(m) The 1960s

(n) The 1970s

(o) The 1980s

(p) The 1990s

Checklist

In preparing for assessments on hairdressing and wigmaking, the following lists may be useful. Check that you have covered and fully understood these items.

Postiche

- How to give details of an actor's head measurements and other information to the wigmaker.
- The difference between a weft wig and a hand-knotted wig.
- The types of hair used in making postiche, and which is suitable for theatre, television and film.

Cleaning, blocking and re-dressing postiche

- Lace must be cleaned using a solvent appropriate to the adhesive used.
- Appropriate protective equipment must be used (or worn), and ventilation must be within safety limits.
- Lace must be cleaned using a brush that will not damage the lace and that will not be dissolved by the solvent.
- Lace must be cleaned on a suitable smooth, absorbent material.
- All removers and other chemicals and all materials must be stored carefully, observing all relevant health and safety regulations.
- All materials soiled with solvents must be placed in allocated containers, and disposed of safely.
- Wigs must be placed on blocks of a suitable size to avoid puckering.
- Wig stands must be firmly secured.
- Wigs must be blocked using suitable pins and tape to avoid damaging the wig lace.
- The extent of re-dressing must be as dictated by continuity and the demands of the production.
- Where necessary, re-dressing must recreate the particular characteristics of a previous style.
- Wigs must be stored securely and safely to maintain their condition in all environmental conditions.

Removing postiche

- Lace must be loosened using an appropriate adhesive remover that is approved for use on the skin.
- Removal must observe all relevant health and safety legislation and procedures.
- All anchor points must be removed with care, once the remover has softened the adhesive and without damage to the artiste's hair or to the wig or hairpiece.
- Hair lace must be removed without tearing, stretching or fraying.
- If necessary, the artiste's hair and skin must be restored to an acceptable condition.
- Removal must be carried out as quickly and as efficiently as is practical.

- A good relationship must be maintained with the artiste throughout to ensure her or his continuing co-operation.
- All removers and other chemicals and all materials must be stored carefully, observing all relevant health and safety regulations.
- All materials soiled with solvents must be placed in allocated containers, and disposed of safely.

Questions

Oral and written questions are used to test your knowledge and understanding. Try the following.

1 When cleaning real-hair postiche, why is it necessary to have a well-ventilated room?
2 When pouring the cleaning solvent into a container to clean postiche, why is it wrong to use a plastic bowl?
3 When blocking a wig, which type of pins would you use to secure it at the earpieces and at the back of the head?
4 Which type of pins should you use to secure the wig tape along the hair lace when blocking a wig?
5 Describe how you would attach a hairpiece to a wig or natural head of hair.
6 Describe how you would attach a wig on a man or woman with: (a) very short hair; (b) very long hair; (c) medium-length hair.
7 When removing a hair-lace wig, which solvent would you use to loosen and detach the lace?
8 Describe how you would protect the actor's eyes when applying solvent to the hair lace in order to remove a wig.
9 What does 'breaking down' the hair mean?
10 What is the difference between wool crepe hair and real crepe hair?
11 What type of wig would you expect to be made of horsehair?
12 What are the advantages of synthetic-hair wigs to the make-up artist and the production?
13 What are the advantages of real-hair wigs to the make-up artist and the production?
14 When is it less expensive for a make-up artist to buy rather than to hire a wig?
15 What are the differences between hair lace used for the theatre and that used for television or film?

CHAPTER 7

Facial hair

INTRODUCTION

Facial hair plays a significant part in changing men's appearances in productions for the theatre, television and films. It can assist in creating a character, and in portraying ageing. It is also important in period make-up work (see below).

Postiche work for the face comprises **beards**, **moustaches**, **sideburns** and **eyebrows**. Beards, especially for opera singers, are sometimes made in three pieces, to ease the movement of the jaw. Exact measurements should be given whenever possible: a beard or moustache that does not fit properly can cause the actor great discomfort, and can even hinder his speech and so spoil the performance.

Facial postiche cannot be hired, for reasons of hygiene and because it has only a short life. It needs to match – or tone in with – the colour of the wig or the actor's own hair. In the latter case, the postiche maker will need samples of the actor's hair, one from the top of the head and the other from the nape of the neck.

Facial hair is knotted onto lace – thicker for the theatre, very fine for film and TV work. As a make-up artist you will not generally be expected to make facial hairpieces, but you do need to understand the procedure in order to assess the quality of work when commissioning it from others. If as a student you want to learn the art of knotting, start with a moustache – don't tackle a full facial hairpiece at the first attempt.

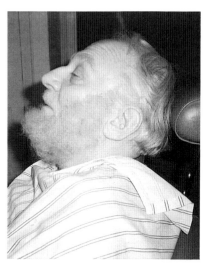

Facial hair: John Carter with his own moustache and an added full beard

Historical background

Throughout history, facial hair has been very significant in men's appearances. The practices of trimming, shaving or partially shaving the face have often had an importance beyond vanity or mere habit. All over the world, shaving has at times taken on superstitious, religious or political significance.

Shaving has not always been voluntary! Occasionally, as in England at one time, shaving has been enforced by law. Likewise, when one area was invaded by people from another, the invaders would often impose their own practices.

Marius Goring with his own hair curled and added facial hair – a moustache and a full beard

FACIAL HAIRPIECES

Making facial hairpieces

A moustache

Making a pattern

1 Place a piece of clingfilm on a flat surface. Cover it with adhesive tape to make it more solid. Cut out a V at the top, to allow a space for the nose.
2 Put this pattern on the person's face. With a make-up pencil, draw out the required shape.
3 Go over the pattern with more tape, to protect the pencil line. Use more tape to attach the pattern to the chin block.

Attaching the lace to the block

4 Place a piece of lace across the pattern and secure it around the edge of the shape using small pins.
5 Pin the lace as tautly as possible over the pattern. This makes it easier to apply pressure on the hair whilst knotting, and thus to achieve tight knots. Stretch the lace evenly so as not to distort the direction of the line of holes.
6 The moustache pattern should be clearly visible through the lace. Make sure it is not off-centre on the block: the moustache pattern should be dead straight.
7 Place the block in the wooden box so that you can work on it comfortably.

Knotting the hair

Use a knotting holder and hook to knot the hair. Be careful with these hooks; as with fish hooks, it is easy to hook them back into your skin.

8 Use yak hair for the moustache. Place the hair between two mats to keep neat. The mats have teeth on them: these should be turning towards you. Lay the hair over the teeth and push the mats together. As you pull the hair out, a bit at a time, the teeth will separate it.
9 Fold the hair in half, and dip the doubled end in water. Continue to do this as you work.
10 Decide which way you want the hair to lie. If you want the hair to lie downwards, then knot upwards.
11 When you have completed the knotting of the moustache, trim the lace and hair to size and curl it with tongs into barrel curls.
12 Dress out the moustache to the finished style.

A beard

Measuring for a beard, and taking a pattern for the beard, follows the same procedure as for a moustache. When taking the pattern and when applying the beard, the mouth should be open. Find someone whose chin you can practise on! For a production, of

---

Equipment and materials

For making facial hair
- beard block
- knotting hook and needle
- hair lace
- small bowl of water (to dip the hair into)
- drawing mats (to hold loose hair)
- loose hair (yak)
- block pins
- cradle (a wooden box in which the block rests whilst you are working)
- tongs and tong heater (for dressing the hair)

For taking measurements
- tape measure
- clingfilm
- clear adhesive tape
- eyebrow pencil (brown *or* black)

Maurice Denham with his own hair and added mutton chops and a moustache

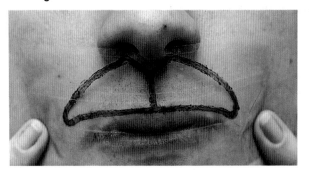

(a) The moustache pattern is traced from the model's face using a soft eyebrow pencil and clingfilm reinforced with clear adhesive tape

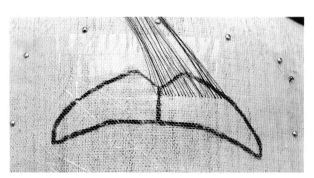

(b) The resulting pattern is taped to a malleable block and a piece of lace is pinned tautly over the pattern, with the lines of holes running horizontally. One line of knotting has been completed on the first side. The hair is knotted in an upward direction, and combed back down when completed

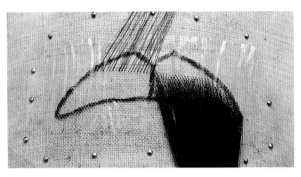

(c) Most of the first side is now complete. One row of the opposite side has been knotted, showing that the hair is knotted in a different direction

(d) One completed side of a moustache, which has been curled into barrel curls using the small hot curling tongs

(e) The finished dressing. Both sides have been curled and the hair has been combed through, trimmed to the desired length and shaped into place with the tongs. A light coating of plastic spray will help to keep the dressing in place

Facial hair equipment

course, it would be the actor's: for TV and feature films the measurements and fitting must be exact.

Making a pattern

1 Put clingfilm across and under the mouth, and up to the temples. (Leave the nose uncovered, so that the artiste can breathe!)
2 Cover it with adhesive tape, under the mouth.
3 Add tape underneath the chin.
4 Add tape from the sideburns to the jawline.
5 Add tape from the sideburns to the mouth.
6 Trim any excess clingfilm.
7 Use an eyeline pencil to draw the shape of the beard required; if possible, follow the pattern of the model's own beardline.
8 Cover the line with adhesive tape to protect it.
9 Place the pattern on the beard block.
10 If necessary, pad the block to the shape of the pattern.
11 To ensure a good fit, shape the lace for the beard into at least four pleats underneath the chin. 'Whip' or tack it into place with nylon thread or whipping nylon, using a hook.

Taking measurements

To make sure of the measurements, use a soft tape measure. Send details of these, as well as the pattern, to the postiche maker.

- The width of the sideburn (usually 25 mm).
- From the bottom of the mouth to the neck (usually 75 mm).
- From the sideburn to the point of the jaw (usually 75 mm).
- From the centre of the chin to the point of jaw (usually 100 mm).

A beard for an opera singer must be made longer than usual to compensate for the wide mouth movement during singing.

Applying and removing facial hairpieces

Applying a moustache

1 Make sure that the skin is clean and free of grease. If you are unsure, use an astringent.
2 Using a brush, apply spirit gum to the skin.
3 Tap the spirit gum with your finger until it is tacky.
4 Place the moustache in position.
5 Use a damp powder puff or cloth to press the moustache down firmly.
6 When the spirit gum is dry, comb the moustache into shape.

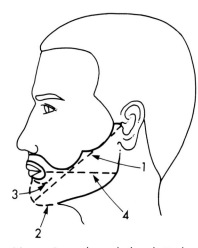

Measuring a beard: the dotted lines represent the measurements taken; the numbers show the sequence

---

Equipment and materials
- clingfilm
- clear adhesive tape
- eyeline pencil
- beard block
- nylon thread *or* whipping nylon
- hook

Equipment and materials
- astringent (if required)
- spirit gum (mastix)
- brush
- powder puff *or* cloth (damp)
- comb

Removing the moustache

1 Use mild spirit gum (mastix) remover or surgical spirit. Dip a clean brush into the remover and stipple the edge of the lace to loosen it.
2 Slowly work around the edge until the moustache can gently be eased off.
3 Use remover to clean the rest of the spirit gum from the face.
4 Clean the moustache with acetone.
5 If ageing whitener has been used, soak the hair in surgical spirit for a minute and tissue-dry it.
6 Pin the moustache to a beard block and re-dress it.

> **Equipment and materials**
> * spirit gum remover *or* surgical spirit
> * acetone
> * tissues
> * beard block
> * pins

Applying a beard

1 Position the beard on the actor's face before applying spirit gum.
2 Apply spirit gum thinly to the skin on the chin area; tap the gum with your fingertip until it is tacky.
3 Adjust the position of the beard for the actor's comfort before pressing it down firmly with a damp cloth or powder puff.
4 If a full beard, turn back the beard at the sides of the face and apply spirit gum to the skin in the usual way.
5 When securing the beard in front of the ears, lift up the actor's own hair and stick the lace underneath.
6 Comb down the actor's own hair to hide the 'join'. If the colour is different, use a toning colour to blend the beard into the hair or wig.

> **Equipment and materials**
> * spirit gum
> * powder puff *or* cloth (damp)
> * comb

Applying sideburns

Use the same method as you would when applying a beard – that is, sticking the lace under a small section of hair. On long productions and for big close-ups, it is best to cut or shave a small section of the actor's own hair after first lifting a section which can be allowed to blend over the adhered lace.

There should be no visible gap between the sideburns or beard and the natural hair.

Tonging and dressing facial hairpieces

1 Pin the facial hairpiece on the beard block.
2 Heat a tong (small size). Test it on tissue to check that it is at the correct temperature.
3 Start at the top of the hairpiece, taking a section at a time, and tong the hair. Make sure that the hair is lifted at the roots.
4 Pin the dressed section out of the way.
5 When all the hair has been tonged, comb it into place. If necessary, spray it with hair lacquer.
6 Plastic spray, used sparingly, is useful in keeping an elaborately shaped moustache in place. Moustache wax can be used to pinch the ends of a moustache into a fine point.

> **Equipment and materials**
> * beard block
> * small moustache tongs (No. 1 irons)
> * electric tong heater
> * tissues
> * pins
> * lacquer (if required)
> * plastic spray
> * moustache wax (if required)

Cleaning facial hairpieces

Facial hairpieces *must* have all the spirit gum removed from the lace before they can be dressed ready for using again. Acetone is the best solvent for cleaning hair lace.

1 Place the piece, lace down, on a lintless towel or muslin pad.
2 Use a wig-cleaning brush soaked in acetone to press the adhesive out of the lace and onto the towel. Use brush cleaner to remove any make-up, or stroke the lace gently with a muslin pad soaked in acetone. Do not brush the lace hard or you will tear it.
3 Using the stiff bristles of the brush, stipple onto the lace to force the surgical spirit through the holes of the net.
4 Move the piece to a clean area on the towel, and repeat the process until the lace looks clean.
5 Allow the hairpiece to dry out thoroughly before re-dressing it.

A toothbrush can be used to clean the lace.

Another way of cleaning lace, which is quicker and used in theatres, is to make a pad from cheap muslin folded around a flat wad of cottonwool which has been soaked in acetone. A similar pad, soaked in mild spirit gum remover, is used for cleaning the spirit gum from the actor's face.

There are also special creams for removing adhesives from the face; these are used by some make-up artists.

A beard and moustache

APPLYING FACIAL HAIR DIRECTLY TO THE SKIN

Instead of using hair knotted onto lace, another way of adding facial hair is by applying it directly to the face. An art in itself, this process has two great advantages: when facial hair is laid directly onto the actor's face it is impossible to tell that it is false, as there is no lace edge to conceal; also, with the right tools and sufficient expertise, a make-up artist can create any style at a moment's notice when there wouldn't be enough time to commission or make the piece. The addition of laid-on hair is a skill with other applications, including the overlaying of hair on the edges of hair laces to change the shape of a hairpiece or to soften a hard-looking line.

Preparing the hair

The hair as received from the supplier is straight. In this condition it is very difficult to spread evenly, so to be able to spread and control it it is necessary to treat the hair first.

1 Crimp the hair with the No. 1 tongs.

Hackling the hair

1 Draw the hair through the teeth of the hackle to separate the different lengths.

2 Place these in the teeth of the hackle in order of the colours, very much like paint on a palette.

Mixing the hair

To achieve a natural effect with facial hair you need to mix several colours together. A head of hair, even of black hair, is made up of hair of several colours. Never lay a one-tone beard or moustache: this would look phoney.

1 By mixing hair carefully you will be able to achieve any of the colours and tones that occur in natural facial hair. Take care not to *overmix* the hair, however, or you will make only a nondescript colour – in this respect the process is very much like overmixing paint.

Equipment for directly applied facial hair

Laying the hair

A sidewhisker

Your equipment should be clean and laid out neatly.

1 First place a fine cutting comb under the man's own sideburns and lift them upwards to expose the skin underneath. Secure the comb in position by placing it over the top of the man's ear.
2 Using the brush, paint a thin layer of spirit gum onto the desired shape of the sidewhisker.
3 Wipe the scissors on the acetone pad, to remove any spirit gum, then wipe them on the Vaseline pad to coat the blades lightly. This helps to prevent the build-up of gum on the blades, and should be repeated frequently during the process of the laying.
4 Now draw the hair from the hackle, holding it between the thumb and forefinger of the *left* hand if you are right-handed, and the *right* hand if you are left-handed.
5 Taking the scissors in your other hand, spread the hair onto the gummed area by rolling the hair between the forefinger and thumb, and lightly tap the ends of the hairs so that they adhere to the gum.
6 Cut these hairs to the required length.

Note that you lay hair *starting from the bottom and working upwards.*

Hackling the hair

Hair held between the thumb and forefinger

> **TIP**
>
> The correct way to hold the scissors is with the thumb and third finger. The bottom blade is held steady by the third finger; the upper blade, operated by the thumb, performs the cutting.

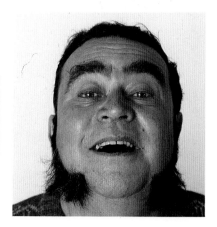

Side whiskers

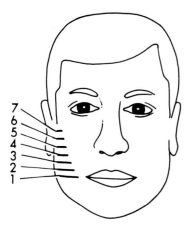

Laying hair for side whiskers

Equipment and materials
- spirit gum
- hackle
- scissors
- towel
- comb (large-toothed)
- eyebrow tweezers

TIP

When laying hair for beards, start with mid-deep brown, then work through mid-brown to light brown, and use blond for the last few strands.

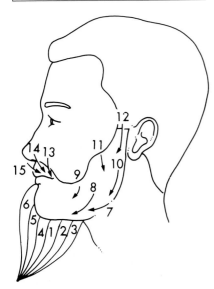

Directly applied laid-on hair: the arrows show the direction of growth; the numbers show the position and sequence of application

A beard and a moustache

For a beard the process is similar. Note that soft edges are produced by thinning out, and by using lighter-coloured hair. Never make an actor look bland and dull by using one colour. With black beards, add a little white or red to give colour, interest and life to the character.

1 Apply spirit gum under the chin in the desired shape.
2 Draw the prepared hair from the hackle, applying it to the face as described above for sidewhiskers. Use the darkest colours underneath, fanning out the hair with the forefinger and thumb.
3 When it has adhered, cut the hair to the required length.
4 Mix in a lighter colour, and keep applying a small section at a time. (Always mix some light hair into dark hair.)
5 Work up towards the mouth, adding the lightest colours.
6 When a fairly large area has been covered, use a towel to press onto the hair firmly. (For extra pressure, gently use your thumbs.) This secures the hair and gets rid of the extra gum and the odd loose hairs.
7 Start to apply the moustache, section by section.
8 As you work up the side of the jaw, start thinning the top hairs out, and use a lighter colour of hair.
9 When finished, use a large-toothed comb to gently comb through the beard and moustache.
10 Cut the hair into the shape required. Use eyebrow tweezers to remove unwanted hairs.

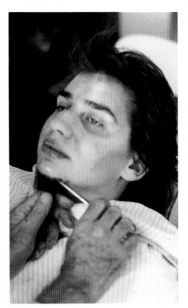

Laying on a beard and moustache

(a) Applying loose hair under the chin

(b) The hair has been applied and is trimmed into place, ready to be dressed with tongs

Dressing out the beard and moustache

The laid-on beard and moustache need to be styled (dressed out).

1 Heat the tongs. Test the temperature on a tissue: if the tongs singe the tissue, wait until the correct temperature has been reached.
2 Use the hot tongs to dress the hair. Rest them on a comb held in the other hand, to avoid touching the face with the tongs. Start at the roots and, using the tongs, shape the beard.
3 Turn the underneath layers upwards.
4 Trim and style the beard to the shape you want. Bring hair down to cover any gaps.

> **Equipment and materials**
> * heated tongs
> * tissues
> * comb
> * scissors

APPLYING LOOSE HAIR TO A BLOCK

Yet another approach is to apply loose hair directly to a fibreglass or wood block. This is a good method to practise before attempting to apply hair directly to the skin.

When using yak hair (as is normally used for film work), the hair is hackled and applied in exactly the same way as it would be if applied directly to the face. Once the hairpiece is complete, and when the spirit gum is dry on the block, the beard and moustache can be eased off in sections, using a brush dipped in acetone or spirit gum remover to loosen the gum. It helps if you first spray the facial hair to maintain its shape. The piece can then be applied to the artiste's face with spirit gum, and pressed down with a lintless towel or clean, damp powder puff.

Yak hair is expensive, so it is best for beginners to start by using wool crepe hair. This type of hair comes in braid form: it can be straightened with tongs or by wetting the cut length and drying it straight. When straightened the hair is mixed and shaped by hand, and cut at an angle before sticking it to the block with spirit gum. As before, the hair is then trimmed into the desired shape and sprayed to keep the shape intact. After this it can be removed from the block and applied in one piece to the face.

HAIR STUBBLE

Although it is possible for an actor to grow a short stubble by simply not shaving for a few days, it is often necessary to create one. Because filming is seldom in the same order as the storyline, continuity often demands that the actor be both clean shaven and unshaven in the same day's work! It might seem common sense to film his 'unshaven look' scenes first, but this is not always possible.

Although at a distance the look can be simulated with make-up, in tight close-up for feature films it is necessary actually to be able to see the hairs sticking out of the face.

Applying the stubble

Equipment and materials
- short cut-up real hair (3 mm long)
- piece of hair lace
- powder brush (soft)
- wax (stubble paste)

1 Spread wax thinly on the face, following the natural beardline.
2 Have some finely chopped hair (human hair is best) in a bowl. Place a small piece of hair lace (70–100 mm square) on the wax and press it on.
3 Start at one side of the face, where the beardline begins, on a level with the ear. Dip the soft powder brush onto the prepared hair stubble so that it picks up the hair evenly on the tip of the brush. Stipple the brush onto the hair lace held against the skin. Use light movements to convey the hair *through* the lace, onto the wax below.
4 When you have finished, pull off the lace *very* carefully, leaving the hairs attached to the wax.
5 Move on to the next section, covering the entire beardline using the same method. The moustache and chin areas are the hardest to do.
6 If any small areas are missed, it may be necessary to apply more wax and go over these sections again. Tiny areas can be strengthened with dark greasepaint and a small pointed brush.

Applying beard stubble

(a) Cutting the hair finely – about 3 mm in length

(b) Darkening the natural beardline with greyish-blue greasepaint. The greasepaint is then powdered, and a fine stipple wax is spread onto a small area of beardline

(c) The hair lace is stretched across the skin and the loose hair stippled through the hair lace with a soft brush. The hair lace is then pulled away, leaving the hairs sticking out. This is repeated, a small section at a time, across the beardline

(d) The final effect, showing the beardline completed on one side

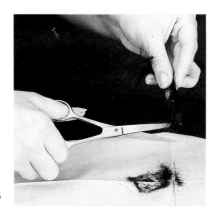

(a)

(b)

(c)

(d)

Remember to take the growth down onto the neck under the chin, as far as the Adam's apple.

Another way of applying stubble is to darken the beardline with greyish-brown compressed powder; then apply the wax on top; and finish off by applying finely chopped wool crepe hair using a brush. This method is excellent for the stage and television, but in close-up shots for feature films it is ineffective: the hairs do not stick out from the face as they do when using hair lace.

Facial hair, using six pieces, dirtied down: Michael Pennington in *Cymbeline*

Removing the stubble

1 To remove hair stubble, apply cleansing cream to the beardline and scrape off the hair and wax with a spatula or palette knife.
2 Finish off with normal cleansing, toning and moisturising, to restore the artiste's face to normal.

> **Equipment and materials**
> - cleansing cream
> - spatula *or* palette knife
> - moisturiser

HOW TO SUCCEED

Checklist
In preparing for assessments on facial hair, the following lists may be useful. Check that you have covered and fully understood these items.

Applying loose hair to skin or a block
- The skin must be thoroughly clean before application.
- The artiste must be sufficiently protected.
- The artiste must be encouraged to be quiet and still throughout the application.
- The adhesive must be appropriate to the type of skin or the block, to the hair to be applied, and to the removal techniques.
- The lie of the hair must follow the direction of the intended dressing and must imitate a natural effect.

Applying facial hair on lace

- The skin must be thoroughly clean before application.
- The model must be sufficiently protected.
- The model should be encouraged to be quiet and still throughout the application.
- The adhesive must be appropriate to the type of skin.
- The adhesion of the facial hairpiece and its edges must be precise.
- The edge of the hair lace must completely blend into the skin.
- The shape and style must achieve the desired effect and match or blend with the hair or wig.

Questions

Oral and written questions are used to test your knowledge and understanding. Try the following.

Loose hair

1 When applying loose hair directly to the face to make a beard, which type of hair would you use?
2 How would you treat the hair before applying it to the face?
3 Why would you mix different colours of hair?
4 Describe the process of mixing the hair.
5 How would you produce soft edges when laying a loose-haired beard?
6 Draw a man's profile, showing the direction of hair growth.
7 Where on the face do you start laying the hair for a man's beard?

Hair on lace

1 Describe how you would measure and make a pattern for a moustache knotted onto lace.
2 When dressing facial hair, why is it necessary to test the temperature of the tongs on paper tissue?
3 When cleaning facial hair, why is it better to use a stippling movement than a brushing action on the hair lace?
4 When making a moustache, in which direction should the holes on the lace lie when pinning it over the pattern?
5 Which solution would you use (a) to remove a moustache from the face, and (b) to clean the lace?
6 What are the different ways of cleaning the hair lace?
7 Why is it important to dampen the folded yak hair as you work?
8 What should a good beard have to ensure a snug fit?
9 What is used to dress the yak hair into barrel curls?

CHAPTER 8

Special make-up effects

INTRODUCTION

By applying material directly to the skin, and then shaping and colouring it, many special make-up effects can be achieved. The best known, and perhaps the most impressive visually, are **casualty injuries**.

There are two stages:

1 applying and building the material to create the effect;
2 finishing the effect with colour and texture.

MODELLING WITH WAX

Sometimes modelling a feature with light and shade is not dramatic enough, and a three-dimensional effect is needed. In such circumstances **putty** or **wax** can be used to change the shape; **mortician's wax** is generally used for this purpose. The wax is covered with a special liquid **sealer** and allowed to dry, and can then be made up to blend with the rest of the face.

Nose shapes

Although wax may be used anywhere on the face, it is generally most successful in changing a nose shape. A very small amount can product a striking change in appearance and does not hinder an actor's ability to speak. If used too far up, between the eyes, however, the wax will lift and look unnatural when the actor smiles or frowns. It should therefore start below the bridge of the nose and blend naturally at the edges to a thin consistency.

Wax is tricky to use, but modelling becomes easier with practice. Keep your hands cool and dry or the wax will become too sticky to work with, rather like making pastry.

Method

Stage 1

1 Make sure that the skin is grease- and oil-free.
2 Apply a thin coat of wax to the nose, as a base for further application.
3 Soften a small ball of wax with the fingers.
4 Mould a rough shape and apply it to the nose. Work cleanly – keep your hands cool to prevent the fingers from becoming

A car accident victim: the wound on the cheek was built up with wax and painted white to look like bone in the middle of the wound

---

Equipment and materials

- wax
- artists' modelling tools (wooden and metal)
- water
- powder
- moisturiser
- sealer
- camouflage make-up *or* a grease-based palette
- foundation
- various make-up materials for the finished result
- isopropyl alcohol (to clean the brush when using sealer)

Nose shapes

too sticky. (Dip your fingers into a bowl of cold water from time to time.)

5 Use a modelling tool to blend the edges so that the join is invisible.

6 Work up and out from the natural bone and nose shape. Don't work up the bridge of the nose (between the eyes): wax here would wrinkle with any natural movement.

7 Build width, keeping a contoured shape without ridges.

8 With a modelling tool or your fingers, blend the wax into the natural shadows and folds of the real nose. Work quickly and positively. For the best result, use the minimum wax.

9 When you are satisfied with the shape, use your fingertips to smooth a little moisturiser or cleansing milk onto the surface to keep the wax smooth and remove any tackiness. Use the tip of your finger to smooth away any imperfections.

10 Apply texture, if needed, using a rough towel, orange peel, or a stipple sponge. This will give an open-pored look.

11 Apply a thin coat of sealer with a brush. Allow this to dry.

12 Apply a second thin coat of sealer with a brush. Again, allow this to dry.

13 Apply a third thin coat of sealer: this time, tap a little translucent powder onto the surface while it is still tacky. This will prevent any shine from the sealer and wax showing through the make-up. Use a soft mop brush loaded with powder, tapping the stem of the brush so that the powder drops onto the sealer, making it matt.

Stage 2

When the top coat of sealer is dry, make-up and colour pigmentation should be put on top to make the wax look like living flesh. Be sure to match the surrounding skin tones.

14 Study the colours and tones of the surrounding skin on the face.

15 Make a mental note of any other pigmentation marks, such as freckles, broken veins or redness.

16 Camouflage make-up provides good coverage, or you can use your normal grease palette. Use a soft sponge or brush to apply rose, pink or red to the wax; be careful not to dent the wax. Use more pink and red than you would imagine necessary: this is to give the effect of blood flowing beneath the surface. Wax always appears too pale on camera, paler than it does to the naked eye.

17 Powder gently, using a soft brush; then apply some yellow and brown colour with a soft sponge. Powder again.

18 Apply foundation colour all over the face in the usual way, and be careful when applying it on top of the wax nose. Check that the nose blends in naturally with the rest of the skin tone.

19 Powder the face and apply the rest of the make-up according to the required style.

TIPS

When applying foundation to wax noses, it is helpful to add a little moisturiser: this makes it more pliable, and easier to spread.

When stippling on pink and red colours, remember that the wax is opaque: it will take plenty of colour to match the skin tone.

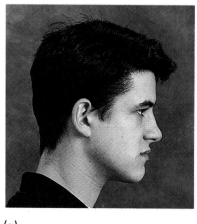

(a)

(b)

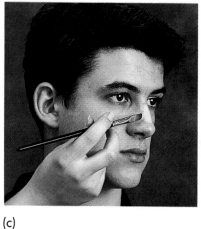

(c)

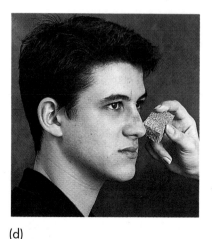

(d)

(e)

Changing the shape of a nose using wax

(a) Before

(b) A small amount of wax has been applied

(c) Blending the edges with a modelling tool

(d) Applying colour to match the surrounding skin tone

(e) Foundation and powder have been applied for the finished effect

When the entire make-up is complete, check the nose. Make sure that the shape is rounded and natural-looking from all angles. A little more wax can be added to hide any imperfections. Remember to add colour tones, base and powder to any extra application of wax.

In warm weather, the wax will become very soft and sticky. Keep dipping your fingers in cold water to prevent stickiness. Throughout the make-up, wipe tools regularly with isopropyl alcohol. Clean the brush used in applying the sealer by keeping it in isopropyl alcohol.

Guidelines

Before you start, study the nose you are going to change and choose a shape that will look natural. If the face is small, do not plan a huge nose, as this would *look* false.

Don't use too much wax – if you do it will be harder to shape and blend. Take care in modelling the wax, or it will look like a stuck-on blob.

Avoid blending the wax onto the cheeks: it is much harder to hide the edges there. Confine the work to the bridge of the nose.

Theatre work

For stage work it is usual to apply a layer of spirit gum to the natural nose before applying the wax: this prevents the wax nosepiece from falling off during the performance! When the gum is tacky, a small amount of cottonwool can be used as a bond. The wax is placed on top and modelled in the usual way.

Other uses for wax

Wax can be used to build up any area of the face provided that there is not too much movement of the underlying muscles. The most effective places are bony areas such as the cheekbones, the chin and the forehead.

Blocking out eyebrows

Wax is very useful for blocking out eyebrows, as for an eighteenth-century period make-up. Before applying the wax, use a bar of soap to flatten down the natural eyebrows. This will prevent the hairs from poking through the wax.

1 Wet the end of the soap bar and use it to flatten the eyebrows firmly to the skin.
2 When the soap has dried, use a modelling tool or spatula to apply a thin layer of wax on top of the soap.
3 Seal the wax using one or two applications, allowing each layer to dry.
4 Colour the wax with make-up and apply foundation colour to the entire face. Make sure that the eyebrow areas match the foundation colour.
5 Paint in the new eyebrows with brush and greasepaint. (Pencils are not successful on wax as they are too sharp.)

Equipment and materials
- soap bar
- wax
- modelling tool *or* spatula
- sealer
- foundation
- greasepaint and brush

TIP

When drawing eyebrows on wax, use a *ruler* to make sure that the brows are evenly matched. It is surprisingly difficult to get both eyebrows the same if you are not following the natural brow bones.

Blocking out eyebrows

(a) Eyebrows have been pressed down with soap to flatten them; wax is smoothed on top with a modelling tool. A sealer is painted on top of the wax

(b) When the sealer is dry, camouflage make-up is used on top and the whole face is ready to be made up

(a)

(b)

CASUALTY EFFECTS

Basic casualty effects are called for on many types of productions, ranging from medical documentaries, through drama, to horror videos. All of the materials used can be obtained from professional make-up suppliers, but many can be made by the make-up artist using kitchen ingredients. Thus, **latex**, **mortician's wax** and **scar plastic** are specialist products used to build up three-dimensional effects on the skin, but most of the other materials can be found in food stores: they include gelatin powder, vegetable colourings, glycerine and petroleum jelly (from chemists), coffee granules, cereals, and black treacle.

Plan the effect

It is easy to get carried away when doing casualty make-up. Over-enthusiasm may result not only in 'over the top' effects but in effects that are difficult to reproduce. *It is essential to be in control* and to suit the effect to the production's needs. In a horror film it may be fine to go all the way, but restraint should be exercised in more realistic dramas. So before splashing on a lot of blood, remember that your design comes first, and consult the director. However impressive or convincing the effect, the director won't thank you for creating a horrific slit throat for a 'prime time' series when children may be watching.

TIP
Don't paint yourself into a corner. Stay in control. Always take notes.

These are the questions to ask before applying the make-up:

Wounds

1 How obtrusive is each wound to be?
2 What caused it?
3 How will it heal?
4 How can you repeat it?

Bullet wounds

1 What calibre was the gun?
2 From how close was the shot fired?
3 Is the casualty dead or alive?

Bruises

1 Where are the bruises to be positioned?
2 How old are they?
3 What caused them?

Equipment and materials

- Barrier cream
- 'Blood' – different brands and colours; running blood; congealed blood (black treacle or blue food colouring will help in darkening the blood)
- Spray containers
- Medicine bottle droppers

- Palette containing red, blue, yellow, green and black
- Greasepaints
- Scar plastic
- Latex
- Mortician's wax
- Sealer
- Spirit gum, spirit gum remover
- Vaseline, KY Jelly, gelatine, glycerine
- Coffee granules
- Collodion
- Tear stick
- Black cotton
- Scissors

Water sprays

A **spray bottle** with a fine nozzle filled with water is useful for refreshing blood on wounds during fight scenes. It is also used on the hair to refresh hair gel and to reactivate it during the course of a day's shoot.

For heavy fight scenes the spray can be filled with half water and half glycerine to provide perspiration. If you put a fine layer of Vaseline on the actors' foreheads first, the mixed glycerine and water will adhere to the area and not dry too quickly.

Gelatine

Gelatine is very useful in casualty effects and can be directly applied to the skin. It can be coloured red to provide an excellent 'blood' which doesn't run. It is harmless to the skin and provides fast, effective results.

Basic recipe for direct application of gelatine

> **Equipment and materials**
> - gelatine powder
> - glycerine
> - water
> - colouring (pancake scrapings, powder pigments, etc.)

1 Use equal amounts of gelatine powder and glycerine, plus water and colouring. Mix the gelatine and glycerine together, and heat them gently in a saucepan on a stove, adding a small quantity of water at a time. (It is easier to add water gradually than to add gelatine.) Heat gently until the mixture has clarified.
2 When clear, add the colouring. Add a little more water until you are happy with the texture.
3 Test by putting some first onto a plate, and then applying it to the back of your hand. *Be careful not to burn yourself.* The mixture should be warm enough to be liquid when it is applied, cool enough to be harmless to the skin, and thick enough to set quickly.

Colouring effects

The gelatine can be coloured in advance, to give a flesh effect, or for use as blood which stays in place, or, using additional colour, as a burns effect. This can be achieved by adding food colouring – red, for a blood effect – into the gelatine mixture. It is also easy

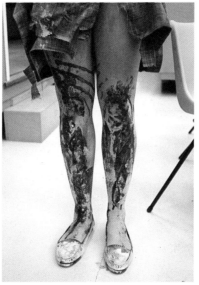

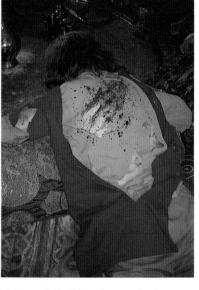

(a)

(b)

to colour the gelatine once it has been applied to the skin and has become firm to the touch. Powdering, and painting with watercolour paints on top, produces a good effect. Other substances can be mixed in for added textural effects – dirt and gravel, even glass fragments, splinters, and so on. It will all wash off with soap and hot water.

Gelatine is easy to apply, using sponges, brushes or modelling tools to transfer the gelatine straight onto the skin. For a really firm hold you can use spirit gum on the skin before applying the gelatine on top. The beauty of using gelatine is that it is completely harmless to the skin, and provides an excellent translucent look which is very effective.

Recipes for 'blood'

1 Flour, water, red food colouring – vary the proportions to make the 'blood' thicker or thinner.
2 Red and yellow food colouring, Karo clear syrup, methyl paraben (preservative) and photoflo (from darkroom suppliers).

Recipe for wound filler

Use black syrup, red food dye, and something to bind it – fine breadcrumbs, for example, crushed cereals or talcum powder.

Health and safety

All the materials you use for special effects should be treated with respect. Some of the materials can be harsh, and damaging to the skin: always test them first on a less delicate area of the artiste's skin, such as the back of the hands. Before using spirit gum, latex or scar plastic on the face, apply a good barrier cream.

Above left: Directly applied gelatine

(a) A splinter in a finger: A jelly piece wrapping around the finger; note that the piece is translucent, and colour was applied underneath so that the splinter can be seen through the material

(b) A quick effect for a disaster victim (following an explosion): Jelly is used as blood; concrete dust has been made from flour, powder paint, and chocolate sponge mix

Above: Lash wounds using latex and colouring

> **TIP**
> The non-stain 'blood' available from specialist shops is excellent, but expensive.

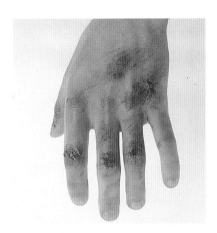

A wound

Equipment and materials
- congealed 'blood'
- modelling tool *or* dentist's scalpel
- blushing gel *or* red gelatine

When removing the make-up, do so with care. Never rub, and take plenty of time. Treat the other person's face as gently as you would your own.

An essential part of the learning process is that you should experience every make-up effect tried on *you*, as well as trying it on others: only then will you realise what it feels like. Students should practise on one another before attempting make-up on a model or an actor.

Manufacturers' instructions for the use of their products must *always* be followed. The **COSHH 1988 regulations** (see page 11) provide requirements and guidance for the safe practice and storage of potentially dangerous substances.

Cuts and wounds with colouring

1 Apply congealed 'blood' with a modelling tool or dentist's scalpel. Shape the cut or wound.
2 Put **blushing gel** (or red gelatine) over the cut or wound to give more depth.

Raspberry jam and warmed red gelatine will produce a good effect. Face powder, talc or flour can be used as a thickening agent.

Deep wounds

Apart from changing the shape of the face, wax can be used for building up an area which can then be cut into for a deep cut or wound.

Creating a wound with wax

(a) Wax has been smoothed onto the arm, and a wound cut into the wax with a palette knife

(b) Sealer has been painted on top of the wax

(c) Once the sealer is dry, a rose-coloured camouflage cream is stippled on top of the wax and then powdered. A flesh-coloured camouflage cream is then stippled on top, to match the natural skin tone of the arm

(d) The wax wound is coloured and filled with congealed 'blood'. Running 'blood' is added at the end when required, using a pipette

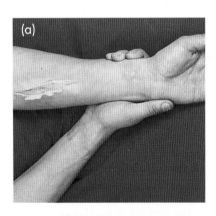

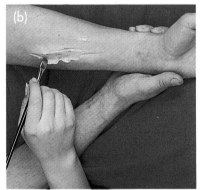

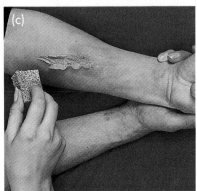

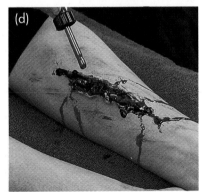

1 Spread the wax fairly thinly. Blend the edges as usual.
2 Cut into the wax with a palette knife or the end of a brush to make the required incision. Apply sealer.
3 When dry, colour the area to match the surrounding skin. Put red into the wound, and finally a trickle of 'blood'.

Slit throat

Before starting, think about what caused the wound. Was it a serrated or a smooth-edged knife? Think about the length, depth and shape of the cut.

1 Paint red and brown greasepaint onto the area of the wound.
2 Soften some morticians' wax in your hands, and apply it to the wound area with a modelling tool. Keep to the natural shape of the neck and blend the edges well.
3 Build up the wax in the centre of the wound to the required depth.
4 When the shape is right, apply two coats of sealer, allowing the first coat to dry before painting on the second.
5 Paint pink or red camouflage make-up over the sealer to blend it with the surrounding natural skin tones. Powder.
6 Add more camouflage make-up, stippling on the colour with a cosmetic sponge and paying particular attention to camouflaging the edges of the wax. Bruising and redness can be added around the area at this point. Powder again.
7 Now, using a palette knife, slit through the wax with a smooth sweeping movement.
8 Very gently, pull back areas of the wax, according to the desired effect.
9 Fill the wound with fresh scab material, wound filler, and raw-flesh colour.
10 Add some coffee granules.
11 Before the shoot, apply congealed and flowing 'blood'. Don't put on too much or the 'blood' will hide the wound make-up work you've done.

Bruises and black eyes

A bruise can usually be created using paint only. The colours used are red, grey, purple, greenish-yellow, and light cream or ivory and browns. The fresher the bruise, the redder it is; the older it is, the more yellow and brown it becomes. The stages of a bruise are as follows: red; reddish blue or dark purple; brown; paler brown; yellowish-green; yellow (in the last stages of healing).

Colours can be dabbed on and then blended well or brushed and stippled. Make sure that the edges are soft and the colours blended away. Rub the colour in well. (See page 128.)

For swellings, build up first with wax. Swellings look most convincing on bony areas such as the eyebrow bone.

Think about not just the particular bruise but the rest of the face. The victim might be bruised in other places, and appear pale from shock. What is the situation? What *caused* the bruise?

(See page 128.)

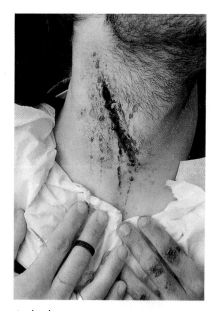

A slit throat

Equipment and materials
• wax
• palette knife *or* brush
• sealer
• colouring
• 'blood'

Equipment and materials
• greasepaint (red and brown)
• mortician's wax
• modelling tool
• sealer
• camouflage make-up (pink or red)
• powder puff
• cosmetic sponge
• palette knife
• scab material
• wound filler
• colouring
• coffee granules
• 'blood'

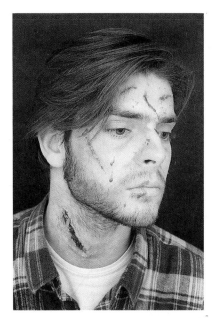

Scratches

Bruises should always look as though they have worked from the inside of the skin outwards, they must not look as if they were painted on. Think about the shape, the impact and the unaffected areas, as well as the 'age' of the bruise.

Never overdo the bruise (or any other casualty effect) for TV or film. If *your* critical eyes won't accept the effect as believable, the camera certainly won't either.

You may have continuity to consider. If so, you must be able to match the bruise exactly the following day, or even weeks later. Before gleefully creating hideous scars and burns, think carefully. Remember: more is less. In some circumstances you will need to apply dirt and scratches around the bruise or scar.

One way to build up a bruise is to work in the main colours and then smear a thin coat of wax over the top. Although bruise palettes are good, it is better to learn to mix your own colours from a normal basic colour palette.

1 Create the darkest part of the bruise first. Blend the edges. Don't make the bruise look too neat or too like eye shadows.
2 The bruise should look shiny, so add some Vaseline at the last moment.

Scratches

1 Use a coarse stipple sponge with a little grey-brown grease. Draw it quickly across the face. The sponge will leave small lines: these will act as realistic guidelines for your scratches.
2 With a fine brush, paint some 'blood' on different parts of the scratch marks. Add tiny dots of congealed 'blood', unevenly. (If the scratches look even they will not be convincing.)
3 Dot coffee granules here and there. Be subtle, or the 'scratches' will develop into severe cuts!

Equipment and materials
- stipple sponge (coarse)
- grease (grey-brown)
- fine brush
- coffee granules
- 'blood'

Stitched wounds

Although colourless adhesive strips are often used in casualty departments to bind wounds together, the old-fashioned stitches are still used in some circumstances. If a wound is irregular, the expertise of the stitching is of vital importance in helping the skin to knit together neatly.

1 Use black cotton (double thread). Calculate how many stitches you need. Tie double knots at about 25 mm intervals along the thread.
2 Cut between the knots, in the middle. Bend in the thread, halfway from the knot.
3 Use scar plastic in a very fine line to create a gather of skin. Quickly press the stitches into the plastic, before it dries. (If necessary, you can use spirit gum to stick them.) The knots should be stuck down at 12 mm intervals along the 'wound'.
4 Redden the area around the stitch line variably to look sore. With a fine black eyebrow pencil, draw in lines on either side of the cotton knots.

Equipment and materials
- black cotton
- scar plastic
- spirit gum
- colouring
- 'blood'
- scissors (sharp)
- Vaseline *or* oil

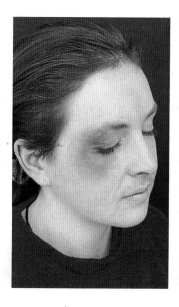
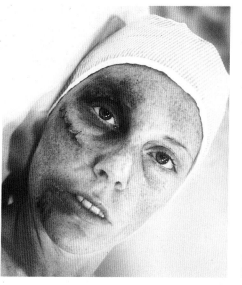
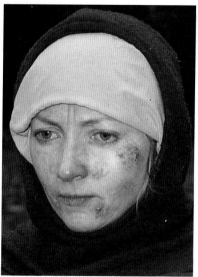

Above left: A bruised eye
Above centre: A stitched wound below a black eye
Above: A skin disorder, with acne

5 Put a small drop of congealed 'blood' at the base of several of the 'stitches'.

6 With sharp scissors (do not use hairdressing scissors or they will be blunted), cut the long ends of the cotton neatly all the way along.

7 Finally, add a little Vaseline or oil to give a shiny, stretched look to the area. (Sealer can be used instead.)

Burns

As always, *plan* the effect. How was the burn caused? How old should it be?

- A **first-degree burn** is slight, usually causing redness and sometimes a small blister.
- A **second-degree burn** causes severe blisters. Remember when creating a second-degree burn to *surround* it with a first-degree burn.
- A **third-degree burn** will cause much more severe lacerations: the flesh may even be charred and black. Around this you should place second-degree burns and, towards the edge, first-degree burns.

Alternative techniques for a third-degree burn

1 Place a single layer of cleaning tissue – tear the shape, do not cut it with scissors – across the latex while it is still wet. Cover the tissue with another layer of latex.

2 For a charred-flesh effect, add a small amount of cottonwool. Apply another layer of latex. When the latex is dry, spray the area with black hair colouring. When dry you can peel this all back to the skin in bits: this will resemble charred skin.

3 Put some gelatine in a bowl or plastic bag; place this in a container filled with hot water. When the gelatine has melted – but make sure it isn't *too* hot! – apply it to the burn to give

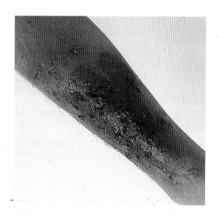

A third-degree burn

Equipment and materials
- greasepaint (red)
- stipple sponge
- latex
- cleaning tissue
- scissors
- cottonwool
- hair colouring (black)
- gelatine, in a bowl *or* plastic bag
- Vaseline

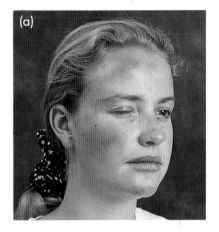
(a)

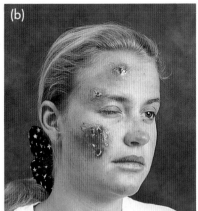
(b)

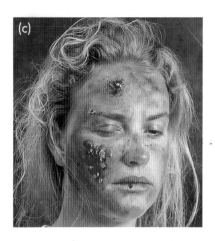
(c)

Creating a burn with latex, tissue, gelatine and colouring

(a) First-degree burn: Red greasepaint was applied to the face

(b) Second-degree burn: Latex* and tissue were applied to prominent areas with a modelling tool. For speed, the latex was dried with a hair dryer. When dry the latex was pulled to give a 'torn skin' effect. More redness was painted on, and gelatine added for the blistering effect

(c) Third-degree burn: Black colouring, another layer of gelatine and black smudges (using black powder) have been added

Equipment and materials
- hairpin
- scar plastic
- red colouring
- Vaseline

a shiny, blistered effect. Let the gelatine form small droplets around the burn, like blisters. (Alternatively, push Vaseline underneath areas of the latex.)

You can apply make-up over all of these products, but usually this is unnecessary.

Vaseline, KY Jelly or glycerine can also be used to give the shiny effect of blistered skin. Burn effects can make use of scar material, latex built up in layers, or gelatine. Scar material can be spread roughly and punctured when dry, with blood being pushed into the 'blisters'. Latex gives a shrivelled effect. Clear gelatine on top gives a watery, blistered look.

The most severe part of the burn should have the greatest depth: around this the effect should fade away, with blisters and redness.

Acne

1 Using a hairpin, place plastic scar material in tiny spots on the face to give the appearance of acne. Don't make the spots all the same size. Place them in clusters, particularly around the mouth and chin.
2 You can add redness, or Vaseline on each one to make them look 'weepy'.
3 Make the surrounding skin area look red and irritated.

Dirtying down

Dirtying down can be achieved using black and brown grease. The colour will be determined by the type of dirt needed, which in turn, depends on the location – desert, swamp, forest, street, mine, and so on. Apply the grease using a natural sponge with holes it it.

Head and face

1 Ask the artiste to frown and pull in the eyebrows. Apply brown grease over the wrinkles caused by frowning.
2 Put some grease around the nose and on the tip. Use a minimal amount and build it up.

Equipment and materials
- grease (brown and black)
- brush (thin)

3 Apply grease behind the ears, to the back of the neck, and under the chin; work into the neck creases and the ears.

4 If a darker effect is required, repeat lightly with black grease.

Hands

1 With a thin brush, put dark brown or black into the cuticles and rub around and under the nails.

2 Rub between the fingers and on the knuckles – in real life the creases always get dirty.

Dirtying down and blood

1 Dark brown grease or pancake applied using a damp natural sponge (bath-size) is excellent for achieving a fast natural look for dirt.

2 The large holes in the natural sponge prevent the make-up from going on too evenly. Repeat with black pancake, stippled all over and rubbed in well to add emphasis.

3 Pay attention to the neck area.

4 Remember to discolour and put brown or black under the fingernails and around the cuticles.

5 Fill two spray bottles, one with 'blood', the other with water. When the action is to be filmed, spray on first 'blood', then water, at the last minute.

> **Equipment and materials**
> - grease (brown)
> - pancake (black)
> - natural sponge
> - spray bottles (with 'blood' and with water)

Tooth blacking and dirtying

Teeth can be blacked out with **tooth enamel** to give the appearance, from a distance, that they are missing. Though this works well on stage the blacking out is obvious in film or television close-up. Enamel can also be used to 'break down' the teeth, making them appear dirty and irregular.

As with all make-up, use enamel sparingly. Often it is sufficient to paint small patches onto the teeth, close to the gums. The best approach is to paint the teeth first with a yellow nicotine colour, and then to dot black on once the yellow has dried.

Anything placed in the mouth is unpleasant for the actor, and such techniques should be used only with great caution. Few actors are comfortable about using tooth enamel, especially if they have expensively capped teeth. One American film actor demanded that the enamel first be analysed in a laboratory: although the result showed the enamel to be harmless, we didn't press him to use it. In any case, the added enamel quickly wears off with eating and drinking, so it is tricky to maintain during filming.

1 Dry the tooth with a tissue.

2 Using a small brush, paint nicotine-coloured tooth enamel onto an area of the tooth close to the gums.

3 Rub this gently with your fingertip so that it looks worn in. Leave it to dry.

4 To emphasise the dirtiness, add a tiny dot of black enamel.

> **Equipment and materials**
> - tissue
> - small brush
> - tooth enamel (nicotine yellow and black)

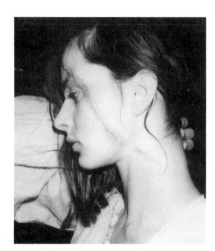

An old scar: Nastassja Kinski in the film *Revolution*

Removing the enamel

Put a small amount of surgical spirit on a cotton bud. Rub this over the tooth to remove the added enamel.

Scars

Scars may be new or old, inverted or protruding. As ever, you need to plan the effect according to the needs of the production.

Scars may be made using special plastic, available in several brands and packaged in tubes which make it easy to apply. The work is quick and the results realistic. Alternatively, latex can be used – any type will do.

You can even use the adhesive made for false eyelashes, as this too is made of latex. Once, on location in the middle of nowhere, I was asked by the director to provide a scratch and a scar. Caught without the special effects materials, I managed nevertheless using eyelash adhesive and a palette of grease colours.

Although it is desirable to have planned thoroughly and to be well organised, every professional make-up artist has had experiences of improvising effects at the last minute. The unexpected is part of the fun of the business, and some directors are a continual challenge to one's ingenuity.

1 Apply barrier cream and rub it in well.
2 Draw a line where the scar is going to be, using scarlet or crimson lake greasepaint or pencil.
3 Apply scar plastic or latex along the line, directly from the tube or with a modelling tool.
4 Before the material dries, shape it quickly using the tool.
5 For a *new* scar, paint crimson lake around the edges in an uneven way. Blend a little scarlet red as well, to look sore. Leave it shiny. For an *old* scar, paint brown around the edges and powder all over to give a faded effect.

Contracted scars

Paint **collodion** onto the skin and leave it to dry. Collodion causes the skin to pucker up, and looks like a very old scar. The result is very subtle in appearance. It gives a good effect for contracted scars around a plastic scar, and can also be used around burns.

Always test the skin for adverse reactions first, using a little where it won't show, and not on the most delicate skin. If using collodion on the face, be careful not to place it too near the eyes.

Broken noses

Broken noses are created by lighting and shading the nose to look crooked.

The skin must look inflamed and red. Wax can be used for any swelling, or sponge or cottonwool can be used, carefully, to plug the nostrils and so change the shape and create swelling.

Equipment and materials
- barrier cream
- modelling tool
- scar plastic *or* latex
- greasepaint (from palette or pencil – crimson lake, scarlet and brown)

TIP

A medical book is useful for reference. Cut out photos from the newspapers of accidents – these may be useful later as reference. Build up a varied collection to which you can refer when necessary.

A broken nose

(a) Before

(b) A broken-nose effect has been created using shading and highlighting

(c) A small piece of wax has been added and cut into with a palette knife; 'blood' has been added

ACTIVITY: THE 'BEATEN-UP' LOOK

This is a good exercise to practise on a male friend – usually it is male actors or stuntmen who have this type of make-up effect applied.

1 Place a piece of damp cottonwool in the mouth.
2 Model wax on either side of the nose, widening it at the top (to look swollen).
3 Place some cottonwool in the nostrils.
4 Using a rubber sponge, apply crimson lake greasepaint on top of a pale base across the forehead: rub hard. Apply crimson around the left eye, and on the chin and jaw also.
5 Paint blue-grey under the left eye and on the lid, and blend this into the red.
6 Use crimson lake pencil around the eyelids, close to the lashes. Blend it in.
7 On the same side as the red eye, highlight the bottom lip. Use cottonwool inside the mouth to make the lip protrude.
8 Shade under the bottom lip with dark grey greasepaint.
9 Ruffle up the eyebrow. (Use a toothbrush or small comb to brush the eyebrows the wrong way.)
10 Smear coffee, 'blood' and water over parts of the left eyebrow and under the left eye.
11 Paint scar latex on the lower lip, or apply wax.
12 Using the flat edge of an artist's modelling tool or palette knife, cut into the material to lift the edge.
13 Add coffee and 'blood' mixture over the latex edge, and a coffee granule on top.
14 Paint sealer over the waxed areas.
15 Clean the brush with isopropyl alcohol.
16 Paint grey greasepaint around the right eye.
17 Paint a burgundy bruise under it and on top of the eye, blending over the grey in parts.

Equipment and materials
- cottonwool
- wax
- rubber sponge
- greasepaints (crimson lake, blue-grey, dark grey, burgundy and ivory)
- foundation (pale)
- pencil (crimson lake)
- toothbrush
- comb (small)
- coffee granules
- 'blood'
- water
- scar latex
- modelling tool *or* palette knife
- sealer
- isopropyl alcohol
- stipple sponge

18 Blend burgundy over the mouth area (above the cottonwool inside). Add burgundy to the left eye.
19 Place congealed 'blood' into the wax on the nose.
20 Using a lake pencil or grease and a brush, make scratches on the forehead.
21 Put lake on a stipple sponge. Scrape this over the cheeks, and over the wax, to make stratches.
22 Add a running 'blood' and coffee mixture.
23 Blend ivory-coloured highlights onto the mouth swelling, and a little on the nose.

Illness

Equipment and materials
- foundation (pale and white)
- greasepaints (blue, mauve, brown, dark grey-brown, scarlet and blue)
- powder puff
- Vaseline
- glycerine and water in a spray bottle
- dropper

1 Apply a pale foundation, very finely. If using panstik, apply it sparingly. Work it in so that it is not sitting on the surface of the skin.
2 Add a tiny amount of white foundation to the forehead, cheeks and chin. Work it in well.
3 Put a little blue and mauve greasepaint under the eyes (lines going down) and around the nostrils. Add brown shading in the corners of the eyes (as in ageing). Hollow out the temples and under the cheekbones.
4 Use dark grey-brown, sparingly, in circles under the eyes. Blend the edges. Put scarlet red greasepaint – toned down on the back of your hand – onto the eyelids. Place it close to the lashes, and blend it upwards until it disappears. Do the same underneath the bottom lashes and add a little on the nostrils.
5 Use some high up on the cheekbones, unevenly, to look blotchy and feverish.
6 Place a little blue on the lips. Using a shading colour, emphasise the natural lines on the lips to make them look cracked. Frown lines can be added to denote stress.

Illness: before and after make-up

7 Powder the make-up to set it.

8 Smooth a little Vaseline on your fingertips and apply it lightly across the forehead and above the upper lip. Break the face up a little with shine, so that the light reflects on it.

9 To suggest perspiration, mix equal quantities of glycerine and water in a fine spray bottle. Spray it finely onto the forehead, where it will stick to the Vaseline. Dab the upper lip with water. (A dropper can be used for this – use a cleaned empty medicine bottle with a dropper.)

10 More red can be added to the eyelids and below the eyes, close to the eyelashes.

'Drug addict' effect

1 With your finger, dot purple greasepaint on either side of a vein on the inner wrist or arm. (Young girls tend to use the veins around the ankles.)

2 Fade the purple to look lighter away from the vein.

3 Put a darker purplish black *along* the vein.

4 Using a maroon colour, make patchy areas around the veins.

5 Mix in yellow, and blend this towards the outer edge. Don't do this uniformly: make it look raw and sore.

6 Using crimson lake, dot a few pinprick needle puncture marks.

7 Take a fine brush with black grease (or a felt-tip pen) and put a *tiny* black dot on top of the red needle marks. Make some stronger than others.

8 Lightly powder or spray the effect with a fixative spray.

> **Equipment and materials**
> - greasepaints (purple, purplish black, maroon, yellow, crimson lake and black)
> - fine brush
> - powder puff
> - fixative spray

'Drug addict' effect using collodion

1 Paint two coats of collodion on the vein, allowing each layer to dry.

2 Paint blue-grey grease irregularly on top of the collodion. Blend it in well.

3 For added bruising, paint maroon, dark red or burgundy on top.

4 Powder, to set the greasepaint.

Sealer or transparent nail varnish can be added on top to preserve the make-up for long shoots.

> **Equipment and materials**
> - collodion
> - greasepaints (blue-grey, maroon, dark red and burgundy)
> - powder puff
> - sealer
> - transparent nail varnish

Bullet wounds

1 Paint red lipstick, or red greasepaint from your palette, onto the skin.

2 With an orange stick, apply a wound filler (see page 124) to the red, sore-looking patch, leaving different areas of light and shade.

3 Use a thicker, darker wound filler (add more black treacle to the mixture) and create different levels.

4 Put blushing gel or melted red gelatine on top.

5 Add running 'blood' to the wound.

> **Equipment and materials**
> - lipstick *or* greasepaint (red)
> - orange stick
> - wound filler
> - black treacle
> - blushing gel *or* red gelatine
> - 'blood'

Tattoos

Draw the design on paper first. Take into account whether it is a modern-day tattoo, or an old tattoo for a period film.

Temporary tattoos

1 For a one-day video shoot you can draw the tattoo freehand with a dark blue-black ballpoint pen, filling in the colours with coloured pencils or felt-tip pens. Or you can transfer the design to the skin by drawing it first on tracing paper and then placing this on the skin, punching holes through the paper with the tip of your ballpoint pen to transfer the outline.
2 Fill in as usual with colour.
3 It is best to powder at the end when the design is dry: this gives a more natural-looking result.

Temporary tattoos can be bought in transfer form, but the designs are sometimes limited.

Longer-term tattoos

1 For a tattoo effect that needs repairing every day over a long period of time, such as for a feature film or TV series, it is best to have a rubber stamp of your design made up to the correct size.
2 Use a blue inkpad to ink the stamp. Apply the stamp to clean, grease-free skin.
3 Colour in the tattoo with felt-tip pens. (Felt-tip pens provide a translucent stain which looks suitably long-lasting.)
4 Finally, powder thoroughly when dry to take away the 'new' look.

HOW TO SUCCEED

Checklist

In preparing for assessments on special make-up effects, the following lists may be useful. Check that you have covered and fully understood these items.

Creating an effect using direct modelling
- The position and size of a directly modelled piece must exactly meet the original design specification, and the modelling technique must suit the individual's physical characteristics.
- The material must be safe for use on the skin, and appropriate to the artiste's skin type, the area of skin, the role, the effect to be achieved and the cost requirements.
- The artiste must be seated comfortably: the seating must be suitable to the length of time envisaged for modelling.
- Protection must be sufficient to prevent damage to the artiste's hair and clothing.
- Preparation of the artiste's skin must be thorough and suited to the materials to be used.

- Any adhesives used must be suitable for the skin area, the tenacity of adhesion required, and the intended removal technique.
- The effect must meet the requirements of the on-screen image.
- Application must observe all health and safety legislation and procedures.
- Where appropriate, edges must blend into the skin and match the characteristics of the surrounding skin area.

Creating texture to meet the required effect
- Application must observe all health and safety regulations and avoid any contact to the inside of the eye or cross-contamination.
- Any likely contraventions to health and safety regulations must be notified promptly to the production department, and steps taken to ensure that a qualified practitioner is present to take responsibility.
- The effect must be achieved on and/or off the set, within the allocated time appropriate to the type of production.
- The degree of the effect must be suitable given the watershed (TV) or certificate (film) and production requirements.
- The final effect must look realistic and natural on camera.
- The materials chosen must achieve the desired effect.
- Techniques must be suited to the materials and achieve the desired effect on screen.
- The artiste must be seated comfortably, the process carried out so as to minimise discomfort to the artiste, and a good relationship maintained at all times to ensure his or her continuing co-operation.

Questions
Oral and written questions are used to test your knowledge and understanding. Try the following.

1 When using wax to apply and model a false nose directly, how would you achieve a textured effect if needed?
2 When applying colour to a wax modelled nose, which colours would you use first?
3 Why is it necessary to avoid blending the wax onto the cheeks when modelling a wax nose?
4 When using wax to block out eyebrows on the face, which material should be applied to the brows before the wax?
5 Before applying wax for a deep wound effect, what questions should you ask?
6 What material would you apply at the last moment on a casualty effect?
7 There are six stages in coloration for bruising effects. Name them, in order of healing.
8 When using plastic scar material, which colour would you choose to paint it to give the appearance of (a) a new scar, (b) an old scar?

9 Which other materials besides plastic can be used to create a scar?

10 What type of sponge would you use to create scratch marks?

11 Describe what first-, second- and third-degree burns look like.

12 Describe what you would do to create: (a) a first-degree burn; (b) a second-degree burn; (c) a third-degree burn.

13 Which type of sponge would you use to apply natural-looking 'dirt' effects?

14 Which material would you use to black out teeth or make them look dirty?

15 How would you apply tooth enamel?

16 How would you remove tooth enamel?

17 Which material, used for creating contracted scars, should not be used near the eyes?

18 Which colour would you use on the lips to take away the natural redness when creating 'illness' effects?

19 What are the various uses by the make-up artist of a water spray?

CHAPTER 9

Bald caps

INTRODUCTION

The purpose of a **bald cap** is to cover some or all of the actor's hair so that the person looks bald-headed. In television and film work, this is often a key factor in making a character look older.

The cap needs to be strong enough to hold its shape, yet fine enough to be invisible – especially at the edges, which must be matched into the surrounding skin tones. Bald caps in the theatre are usually quite thick: they have to be put on and taken off many times, and in any case they are seen from a distance. Similarly, bald caps used in clown make-up are not intended to be realistic: traditionally these are of thick rubber, like a bathing cap, with brightly coloured synthetic hair sewn into or stuck onto them. In film and TV work, however, the material must be fine enough to look realistic even in close-up.

In ageing make-up the bald cap will often be worn with a toupee over the top, so as to show a bald patch or a receding hairline. In fantasy make-up the artist can instead use the bald cap as the basis of colourful designs.

Bald caps are easy to make, though time-consuming. Ready-made caps can be bought from professional make-up shops, ranging from the inexpensive thick ones to the more expensive types made of fine-quality plastic which can be stretched to fit any size of head.

A bald cap

MAKING A BALD CAP

Making a template

The method used in taking a pattern for a bald cap is similar to that used in taking a pattern for a wig.

Stage 1: Making the pattern

1 Tie back the hair. If the model has long hair, pull the ponytail band down lower, and add more clingfilm at the base. You need at the end to have a clingfilm head shape, reinforced all over with overlapping layers of adhesive tape.
2 Lay clingfilm across the head (see page 140).
3 Ask the artiste to pull the clingfilm down, making sure that the sideburns are covered.
4 Place one long strip of adhesive tape *around* the head. The

Equipment and materials
- clingfilm
- clear adhesive tape
- eyeline pencil or a crayon
- dressmaker's tape measure
- head block

actor can now let go of the clingfilm.

5 Slowly go round the whole head with adhesive tape, slightly overlapping it. When cutting lengths of tape, do so away from the actor – the noise can be irritating. Do not pull the adhesive tape too tightly on the head.

6 Go around the hairline with a crayon or eyebrow pencil. Draw in the ears as well. Cover the pencilled lines with adhesive tape, to protect them from being rubbed off.

Stage 2: Taking measurements

1 Using a dressmaker's tape measure, measure above the ears round to the bone at the fullest part of the back of the head. This is the *circumference* of the head.

2 Measure from the front hairline to the nape of the neck.

3 Measure from temple to temple.

4 Write these measurements and the person's name on the cap. Again, cover the writing with clear adhesive tape.

5 Draw a horizontal line across the front, to show the pattern's position when straight. When the cap is put on the block you will then be able to check that it is again straight.

6 Cut the pattern upwards to the top of the front of the ear, so that you can take it off the actor's head. Place your hands on top of the pattern to lift it off.

7 Cut around the hairline that you have drawn. Allow a 12mm margin in addition, as the plastic will shrink.

Stage 3: Transferring the pattern to the block

1 Turn the moulded head pattern inside out.

2 Place the pattern onto the **head block**. Check that it is straight and central.

3 Holding the pattern firmly with one hand, draw a line around the hairline, at least 12mm away from it. Go under the ear and down the back, marking the line on the head block.

4 You now have the pattern drawn on the head block and you can put the pattern aside.

Note: Sometimes the head block you are using will be either too small or too large for your pattern. Adjust by allowing more or less width.

Plastic caps

Bald cap plastic comes in liquid form, comprising **PVC** and **PVA** plus a **plasticiser**. A number of the formulations in use combine **acetone**, as a solvent, with a plasticiser to give elasticity to the product. Cap plastic can be tinted with any colour of your choice: you can add scrapings of pancake, powdered food colouring, raw pigments, or face powder.

The fumes of the solvents used are very strong: it is essential that the work be carried out in a well-ventilated room, with open windows and an electric fan to blow the fumes out of the windows.

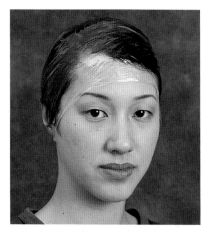

(a) Wrapping clingfilm around the head to make the head pattern

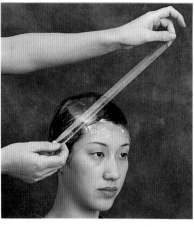

(b) Sticking adhesive tape over the top of the clingfilm to secure the head shape

(c) Drawing the hairline and the ears

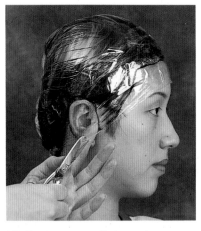

(d) Cutting a small slit in the middle of the drawn ear shape in order to remove the pattern

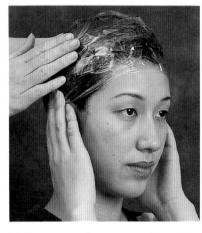

(e) Removing the pattern from the head

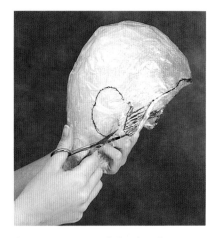

(f) Cutting around the hairline

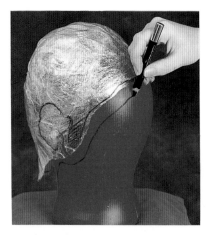

(g) The head shape is placed on the block and a line is drawn approximately 12 mm beyond the hairline

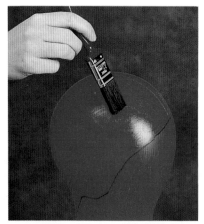

(h) Vaseline has been applied, and now cap plastic layers are being applied

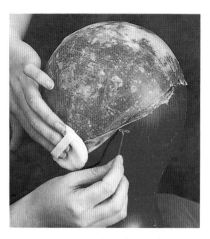

(i) Removing the bald cap from the block with a T-pin, and powdering

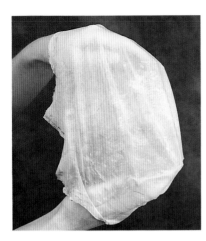

(j) The stretched bald cap

Equipment and materials

- head block
- mortician's wax
- Vaseline
- cap plastic
- brush (large)
- lidded jar containing acetone
- colouring materials
- talcum powder
- hairpin, T-pin *or* other fine, sharp object

Alternatively, if the weather permits, the work can be carried out in the open air.

The cap is made by painting layers of the plastic onto a solid head block. Unless you are using a metal block, you must first spread Vaseline on the block. Most people use plastic head blocks as these are lighter.

Each layer of plastic will take about ten minutes to dry. Do not apply the next coat until the previous one is dry.

Applying the cap plastic to the block

1 If there are any grooves in the centre join, file them down and smooth them out with mortician's wax.
2 Prepare the head block by smearing over it a very thin coat of Vaseline, which should then be wiped over with a tissue.
3 Apply the liquid plastic using a large brush – a small house-painting brush is suitable. Have to hand a jar of acetone, so that you can clean the brush after each layer. (You will need about three layers all over the cap and to the edges; and a further three, with colour, in the middle. Extra layers can be applied to the back to give more strength in attaching the cap to the head.) Apply the first layer of plastic thinly and quickly. Be methodical, and don't reapply plastic over the same area. Work from the top to the edges, keeping them as thin as possible.
4 Leave the layer to dry. You will be able to tell when it is dry because of the change in colour of the plastic. Clean your brush with acetone.
5 Apply two more layers, each time working slightly inside the outer edges so as to give the finest edge possible. Keep to your method, applying the plastic quickly using gentle strokes. Avoid air bubbles, and don't allow any hairs or clogged plastic to come off the brush. While waiting for layers to dry, keep your brush in acetone to prevent the hairs from sticking together.

Colouring the plastic

1 For the final three layers of plastic you will usually want to add some colour. Add a blob of your base colour – whatever is required, from natural to green – to the plastic and stir it well until it has been thoroughly mixed together. You can use prosthetic paints, ground-up pancake, or powder pigments.
2 Apply the final three layers to the top and back only. Each layer should finish slightly further from the edge than the previous layer, as with the earlier applications.
3 To reinforce the back, apply further layers or place very fine hair lace between the layers of plastic. Leave a small amount of lace free of the edge of the cap: this is what you will use to stick the cap to the skin.
4 When this third or final layer of plastic has been applied, leave the cap to dry thoroughly, preferably overnight.

Taking the bald cap off the block

1 Brush the edges of the plastic with talcum powder. Without tearing the plastic, carefully slip the T-pin between the cap and the block. Gently release the edge all the way around, powdering the inside as you go.
2 Ease the cap free a little further in, again with the pin and the powder.
3 Once you have enough to hold securely, pull the cap from back to front.
4 When the cap is free from the block, powder both sides. Put it back onto the block, inside out, until required for use.

Rubber bald caps

Though most bald caps nowadays are made of plastic, they can be made using latex rubber instead. The method then is to stipple the latex onto the block using a sponge.

To test a bald cap, stretch it out: on release it should return to its original shape quickly. Look also for unwanted air bubbles.

REFRONTING A PLASTIC CAP

Old caps can often be re-used, but you then need first to put a new edge around the hairline. This process is called **refronting**.

There are two sides to a cap made of plastic: the top side is shiny, the underneath is matt.

1 Put a tiny amount of Vaseline on the surface of the plastic head, and powder it with talcum or face powder.
2 Put the cap onto the plastic head, pulling the edges out.
3 Using acetone, gently wipe the edges underneath. This sticks the cap down and dissolves the edges. (Acetone is a solvent for bald cap plastic.)
4 Pour cap plastic into a jar.
5 Scrape some pancake of the appropriate colour onto a tissue, and sprinkle the scrapings onto the cap plastic.
6 Pour a little into a dish. Using a brush 50–75 mm wide, paint on the plastic a little at a time.

FITTING THE BALD CAP

1 Gel the hair back smoothly. If it is long, wrap it around the head, keeping as close as possible to the contour of the head.
2 If the skin is greasy, put a trace of acetone around the hairline.
3 Place the bald cap on the actor's head, stretching the cap down so that it is tight, with no air trapped inside – see page 144. (If you want to change the appearing shape of the head, you can add a foam piece underneath the cap.)
4 Slit up the plastic with scissors, cutting on the line that runs behind the ear. Trim around the ear, leaving a section in front of the ear.

> *Equipment and materials*
> * hair gel
> * scissors
> * acetone
> * Duo
> * cotton buds
> * tissues
> * spirit gum *or* surgical adhesive
> * powder puff
> * wooden modelling tool
> * stipple sponge
> * make-up

5 Stick the cap from the centre of the forehead to around the temples, using spirit gum or surgical adhesive. Use a powder puff to press the cap down. Let it settle for a minute, while the spirit gum dries.

6 Put a little spirit gum behind the ears and stick the cap down, pressing firmly with the powder puff. Make sure that the cap fits closely around the ears. Be careful that the edges do not buckle under. Use a wooden modelling tool to push them flat.

7 Once the cap seems securely stuck down, blend the edges into the skin. With a *plastic* cap, blend the edges with a little acetone (a tissue should always be held underneath the cotton bud to prevent acetone from dropping onto the actor's face) – do not allow the acetone to touch the actor's skin, just the edge of the cap. With a *latex* cap the edges may be blended using a latex-based surgical adhesive called Duo – apply this thinly on the edge and blend it into the skin.

Applying the make-up to the bald cap

1 Stipple on the colour: red, both dark and light. Use a rubber stipple sponge, or a natural one with plenty of holes in it.

2 *Keep* the specks of colour this method provides: do not smudge or blend them. Carry the make-up onto the forehead.

3 Powder; then apply make-up to the rest of the face, according to your design.

Colouring the cap

Bald caps are usually given a natural skin tone, to look realistic. For fantasy effects, however, you can use unrealistic colours – green, blue, gold, and so on.

For a realistic look, the bald cap should be stippled with pink and red before the foundation colour, in the same way as you would do with wax noses. Other effects can be achieved by adding hair, as for example clown make-up or a monk's tonsure. Or a wig can be applied to create a high forehead, as for a sixteenth-century look (like Elizabeth I).

For fantasy effects, watercolours can be used. For realistic effects, grease or cream is usually stippled on, using a sponge; when using greasepaint, powder must be applied to set it.

REMOVING THE BALD CAP

The procedure for removing a bald cap is the same as for removing all prosthetic pieces, wigs and facial hair. As the *adhesives* vary according to the materials, however, so do the adhesive *removers*.

Surgical spirit can be used, but use only a little on the tip of a brush. Work the brush gently under the edge of the bald cap to loosen it. Always hold a wad of tissues or cottonwool in the other hand, under the brush: if any of the adhesive remover drips down the forehead, wipe the skin dry immediately, before the remover

TIP

Be careful when applying powder. On bald caps the make-up tends to slide.

TIP

When removing a bald cap, take great care as you loosen the edges. Very often the fine hairs around the hairline can cause pain when they are pulled, especially if the adhesive has glued them to the bald cap.

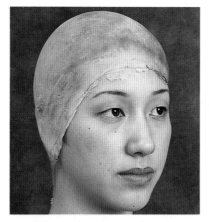

(a) The cap has been placed on the head

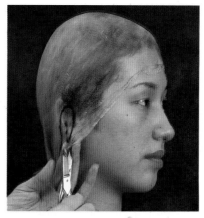

(b) Cutting a section from the drawn-on ear

(c) Sticking down the cap

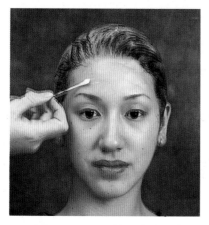

(d) The cap being blended with acetone

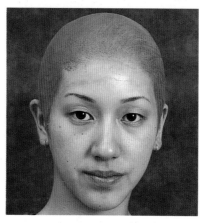

(e) Rose pink colour has been stippled onto the cap

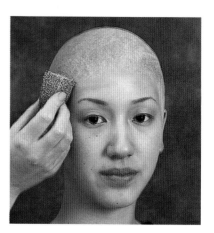

(f) Applying natural camouflage

reaches the eyes. This is the most dangerous part of removing the cap.

Once the edges have been loosened, the cap can be easily removed. When it is off the head you can remove the adhesive from the face gently and slowly. Then cleanse, tone and moisturise in the usual way.

Acetone should not be used on the face to remove spirit gum. (Use it to clean your brushes and tools.)

Adhesive removers

There are many adhesive removers made for use on the skin.

Spirit gum is sometimes called **mastix**, so some of the removers are called **mastix remover** or **mild mastix remover**. These are in liquid form, and are gentler than surgical spirit.

Isopropyl alcohol is used if the adhesive used was **Dow Corning 355**.

Various adhesive-removing creams are available which are especially kind to the skin; and there is an oil called **Klene-All** which removes most types of adhesive.

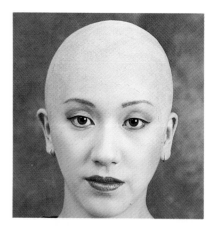

(g) The finished effect

INSERTING HAIR INTO BALD CAPS AND PROSTHESES

Hair can be laid *onto* bald caps and prosthetic pieces, but for tight camera close-ups the hair will look more natural if it is inserted *into* the latex or plastic.

For this method you need an adapted sewing needle. Remove the tip at the *eye* end, by rubbing the needle or by cutting it off with pliers; the eye of the needle should present a fork-like appearance. Insert the needle into a knotting hook holder.

The forked needle can now be used to punch individual hairs or tufts of hair into the bald cap or prosthetic appliance. Take the hair in the left hand, and hold the needle in the right hand. Catch hold of the hairs with the forked needle and push them through the latex or plastic *from the inside* of the piece. Pull the hair through until you have the desired outside length. The ends can be stuck down with adhesive inside the piece, where they will not show.

This technique works well when hair is needed for prosthetic animal faces, or in an ageing character make-up when you want a few strands of hair across a bald head.

HOW TO SUCCEED

Checklist

In preparing for assessments on bald caps, the following lists may be helpful. Check that you have covered and fully understood these items.

Making a bald cap
- Ensure that the block matches the artiste's head measurements.
- Materials and equipment must be available in sufficient quantities and ready to hand.
- Release agents must be suitable for the block surface and the material of cap.
- If required, colour and texturing techniques must be applied to achieve a realistic effect.
- Use of materials must strictly observe all health and safety legislation and procedures, and manufacturers' guidelines.
- Storage of materials must be safe and secure.
- The marking of the hairline and specialised designs on the block must exactly match the hairline of the artiste.

Removing a bald cap
- The edge must be loosened using the correct adhesive remover for the particular area of skin, the type of material used for the bald cap, and the adhesive.
- The adhesive remover used must be chosen to minimise irritation.
- The artiste must be protected and seated comfortably for what may be prolonged periods of time.
- Removal must be very gradual and gentle, and performed with the care appropriate to that area of the skin.

- In the case of skin irritation, medical advice must be sought promptly and the production office notified.
- Removal must observe all relevant health and safety legislation and procedures.
- A good relationship must be maintained with the artiste throughout to ensure her or his continuing co-operation.
- Storage of all removers, chemicals and materials must be safe and in accordance with health and safety regulations.
- All materials soiled with solvent must be placed in allocated containers and disposed of safely.

Questions

Oral and written questions are used to test your knowledge and understanding. Try the following.

Bald caps

1 When making a template or pattern for a bald cap, the procedure is similar to making a pattern for a wig foundation. Can you describe the process?
2 If the head measurements were larger than the block, what would you do?
3 How would you prepare the block before applying cap plastic?
4 Describe how you would remove the bald cap from the block when the plastic was dry.
5 When fitting a bald cap, how would you avoid the edges buckling?
6 When the bald cap is secured and stuck down, what method would you use for blending the edges into the face when the cap is made from (a) plastic; (b) latex?
7 When colouring the bald cap for a realistic look, as in ageing, which colour would you stipple on the cap before applying the foundation colour?
8 When removing a bald cap from the actor's head, which solvent should be applied to the edge of the bald cap to loosen the adhesive?
9 Why is it important to hold a wad of tissue under the brush when loosening the edges of bald caps?
10 Why is it so important to remove the adhesive from the face gently and slowly?

CHAPTER 10

Ageing

INTRODUCTION

Study the faces of older people around you and you will soon see the great variety of ways in which ageing affects people's appearances. Heredity, race, character, lifestyle and environment all play a part. A thin-faced woman who has worked for many years in a city office and suffered recurrent illness may appear pale, gaunt, and unhealthy-looking. A well-built, fit old man, on the other hand, who has spent his life out in the sun, rain and wind tending animals on the mountainside, will have a healthy, ruddy complexion, with weathered skin and many wrinkles. The lines on the face will reflect the person's character and temperament; there is a difference between the lines caused by frequent laughter and those caused by illness or bad temper. In *As You Like It* (Act II, scene viii) Shakespeare describes the 'seven ages' of man, from the 'mewling and puking' infant to the 'second childishness' of old age; it's a fine description of the ageing process, which you may like to read.

The creation of a convincing **ageing make-up** will draw on all the skills you have learnt so far. It must be as subtle as straight make-up, but in many respects you are trying to achieve the opposite. Go back to the beginning of your coursework and look again at the anatomy of the face. Recall the drawing of drapery folds, and the significance of light and shadow. As we get older our flesh becomes looser and the face starts to drop: in ageing make-up, therefore, you need to put in the shadows that normally you would be trying to conceal, adding bags under the eyes, lines from the nose to the mouth, and so on.

With thin faces it is quite easy to bring out the skull-like effect, by suggesting hollowing at the temples and drooping eyelids. Plumper faces stay looking youthful for longer, but you can add a double chin or sagging flesh, as well as highlights and shading. Hair becomes thicker and coarser in middle age, so you can give a man a dark beardline to take away the smooth look of youth. Broken veins on the face, age spots and greying hair at the temples all help to make the person look older. Don't overdo it: a woman of forty-five, for example, if she has taken care of her appearance, will not show extensive signs of ageing.

USING MAKE-UP

Start always from the real face of the person whom you are making up. Study the face; feel the prominences and notice the position and the colour of the natural shadows under the eyes and below the jawline – an overhead light will help you to see where these are. In adding the make-up, your aim is to intensify these shadows.

1 The shading colour must harmonise with the actor's own skin tone. Add a touch of grey to the chosen colour, mixing in a little brown and blue from the basic greasepaint palette. For pale, translucent skins, add a touch of blue or mauve.

2 Only use a foundation if it is necessary to change the skin tone. Apply the shading straight onto the face, emphasising the places where there are shadows already. Look for the age lines, checking that these move with the face. Strengthen the circles under the eyes, the nose-to-mouth lines, and the lines at the corners of the mouth. Keep the lines clean – don't let solid make-up smudge into the skin.

3 Add highlighting, blending the edges carefully with a clean brush. On more prominent areas, add more highlighting. Powder lightly between layers. Add the lightest highlights and the darkest shadows last.

4 Try adding a touch of grey and green in the hollows of the face.

5 Tone down the lips with a little blue (to disguise the red of youth). Don't apply much unless your intention is to make the person look ill.

6 If the face is plump and round, emphasise the skin folds: try to make them look as though they have sagged.

7 Whatever the shape of the face, be it plump or thin, you need to 'break up' the jawline and reduce the firmness of youth. On a thinner face, the shadows and highlights will tend to produce a skull-like effect. To produce a double chin on a fuller face, ask the actor to push his or her chin down, then put a shadow in the fold and highlight the bulge where the double chin forms.

8 Try to draw down the shape of the face. Using a stipple sponge, add a stipple of dark red and blue in the highlighted area. With a crimson lake pencil, lightly draw in the broken veins. Blend some of them, with fine brush.

9 Apply a little red to the upper eyelids, to make the eyes look sore; and sparingly outline the bottom eyelids to suggest watery eyes.

10 Paint in liver spots, with brown greasepaint.

11 For an ungroomed look, brush cream or white through the eyebrows, and then brush them down.

12 Age the neck by highlighting the bones and placing shading in the hollows and sockets. Blend the highlighting and shading softly at the edges: there must be no hard lines. Keep checking your work by looking in the mirror, turning the face sideways so that you can see the result.

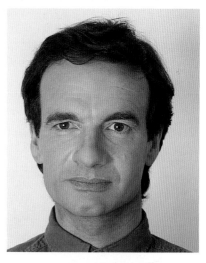

Equipment and materials
- greasepaints
- powder and brush
- crimson lake pencil
- fine brush

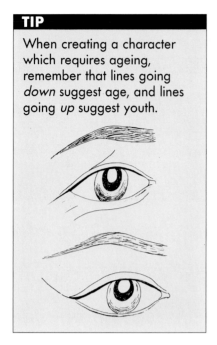

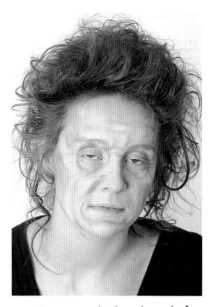

Ageing: before and (*right*) with ageing make-up applied and ready for blending

13 Age the hands also: apply highlight to the prominent knuckle bones and along the veins. Shade either side of the veins, and between the fingers.

Equipment and materials
- greasepaints
- powder and brush
- foundation (liquid)
- blusher
- eyeshadow
- eyeliner
- mascara
- lipstick

ACTIVITY: AGEING FROM YOUTH TO MIDDLE AGE

Work with a fellow student, ageing him or her from youth to middle age. The guidelines below are for a woman.

1 Apply shadows under the eyes — only in the darkest part of the circles.
2 Tuck your model's chin down, then look in the mirror to find the shadows. Paint shadow in the nose-to-mouth lines — not too much — and then blend the edges.
3 Put a shadow at the corners of the mouth.
4 Ask your model to frown. Put a tiny line where the frown lines appear.
5 Shade in the eye area, concentrating on the inner corners. Add highlight next to the shadows. Use very little make-up, or the effect will look too theatrical.
6 Shade softly in the temple depressions. On the forehead, don't paint in lines but highlight the prominences softly and shade the depression.
7 Lightly powder the areas you have made up. [Finish here if you do not wish to create a made-up look.]
8 On top, apply a light liquid foundation. Powder in the usual way.
9 Put on blusher and eyeshadow; strengthen the eyebrows; add eyeliner and mascara.
10 Finish off with carefully applied lipstick — red is a good colour.

Your model should look about 40 years of age.

Variations

To look middle-aged

1 Shade the eyes, from the top of the nose to the eyebrows.
2 Shade under the eyes, gently and lightly.
3 Hollow the cheeks a little more.
4 Add slight nose-to-mouth lines.
5 Break up the cheek muscle by adding a line around the bone.
6 Highlight for puffiness.
7 For a happy character, introduce warm colours into the shading; for a cold character, add cold colours.

To look sixty-ish

1 Accentuate the eyebags.
2 Break up the skin tone on the cheeks.
3 Deepen all ageing lines; highlight for puffiness.
4 Hollow the temples and the outside of the eyes.
5 Add a few frown lines and forehead lines.
6 Darken the inner eye sockets.
7 Break up the jawline.
8 Suggest puffiness with highlighting; lighten the cheeks so that they are not a rosy colour.
9 Add lines around the eyes. Whiten these a bit.
10 Add pale ends to the eyebrows, dragging them down.
11 At the centre of the forehead, shade and highlight the prominences.
12 Powder, to set.
13 Stipple in red veins, then stipple on pale colour to break up the skin tone.
14 Stipple on dark brown liver spots.
15 Powder again.
16 Ask the actor to screw up her or his eyes and nose. Tap on light colour with a sponge, to add a few wrinkles.
17 Darken the eyelids, top and bottom. Add more dark lines if necessary.
18 Rework the lines with a clean brush.
19 Broken veins can be emphasised with lake-coloured pencil or grease.
20 Add pale eyelids and eyelashes. Darken the sockets of the eyes to close them and bring them down. Use short strokes to create a crepe effect.
21 Make the lips paler.
22 Add a skin-tone coloured base and bleed lipstick into it.
23 Darken under the bottom lip to emphasise the cleft chin.

The highlighting colour 'ivory' is good for ageing.

People often shrink as they get older. One way of creating this effect is for the actor to wear a shirt a size too big.

The face becomes haggard and drawn sometimes, creating the illusion of a bigger nose and extended ear lobes.

USING LATEX

When painting is inadequate, **latex** is sometimes used to age the face. It does create wrinkles and it gives a very textured effect to the skin. One layer on the eye area can be sufficient to make a middle-aged actor look ten years older without having to age the rest of his face. Care should be taken, however, because latex can easily look mask-like.

Three people are needed when using latex: one to stretch the skin, one to apply the latex and dry the area with a hand-held hair dryer, and the third to powder the area before the skin is released.

Do not use brushes to put on the latex – they would be ruined.

> ### Equipment and materials
> - barrier cream
> - liquid latex
> - bowl for latex
> - powder, powder puff, powder brush
> - hair dryer
> - sponge cut into small pieces
>
> *Three students should work together as a team*

1 Place a protective wrap around the model's shoulders, and tuck a paper tissue around the collar line.
2 Apply barrier cream to the whole eye area. Allow this to sink in.
3 Powder to remove all trace of grease.
4 Pour a little latex into the bowl. If you need to add colour to the latex for use on a dark skin tone, do so now and thoroughly mix it with the latex. You can use dark powder or pigment for this purpose.
5 Working on one area of the face at a time, pull the skin tight with the fingers and, with your small piece of sponge, stipple some of the latex onto the stretched area. Do not overload your sponge piece or the latex will drip into the person's eyes. Discard the sponge pieces after use.
6 Take care to blend the edge of the latex into the skin very thinly. When putting it under the eye to create a pouchy effect, stipple the latex gently beneath the eyes, avoiding the bottom eyelashes; stop at the circle under the eye. Try not to take the latex out beyond the outer corners of the eyes – it would look strange if taken onto the cheekbones.
7 Use the hair dryer, at a good distance from the model's face – put your hand in front of it to test the heat. Take care not to irritate the skin with the dryer set too hot or too cold. Check with the model that he or she is comfortable. (The person stretching the skin should not relax her hold until after the area has been dried and powdered.) When the latex has become transparent and shiny, it is dry.
8 Powder on top of the dried latex with powder on a powder puff. Brush off the excess powder with a brush. The skin can now be released. It will form into wrinkles; these improve with time as they settle and become part of the model's face.
9 For a more exaggerated set of lines, repeat the procedure – however, one layer is usually enough for close-up work.
10 Clean the bowl by pulling off the dried latex. Remember always to put the tops back on bottles. This is particularly important with latex as the liquid becomes solid very quickly when exposed to the air.

If you apply latex to the whole face, work on small areas, overlapping each one. One layer applied above and one below the eyes is the most commonly used method. You can use the latex all over the face, to get an 'old crone' look.

Wrinkles are formed on the softest parts of the face, where you can stretch the skin easily. The direction in which you stretch the skin will determine the way the wrinkles form: if you pull the skin vertically, the wrinkles will be horizontal; if you stretch horizontally, the lines will be vertical. The *neck* can be stretched vertically simply by holding the model's head backwards.

If the whole face and neck has been done, the skin on the backs of the *hands* should be stretched and latex applied. Clench the model's hand into a fist to stretch the skin. (As you will find out, this is a time-consuming task.) To create a good set of wrinkles and so age someone, however, it is usually sufficient to apply latex around the eyes.

Make-up can be applied as usual on the rest of the face. Shading and lighting are not necessary on top of latex: the wrinkles are three-dimensional and create their own shadows.

Removing the latex

1 Use a pad of cottonwool, soaked in warm water and squeezed until damp.
2 Gently lift the edges of the latex with the damp cottonwool. Do not pull the latex off in one piece, especially around the eyes: instead, gently stretch the skin as you wipe with the cottonwool.
3 Oil can be used also to remove latex. Use baby oil or an oil face cleanser.

> **Equipment and materials**
> - cottonwool
> - baby oil *or* oil-based face cleanser

Take time and care in removing make-ups like this or you may damage the actor's skin. This type of latex work should be done in quiet, calm conditions. The actor should keep his or her eyes closed when you are working near the eye area.

FEATURE FILMS

In feature films your work will be very evident. On a cinema screen the close-ups are really big: every detail of the actor's face can be seen. The make-up artist's work is much more likely to be noticed and is therefore more open to criticism.

1 When ageing for film, study the person's face and let the person's natural markings, shadows and highlights be your guide. As before, the best lighting in which to see these shadows is an overhead light which casts straight natural shadows down the face.
2 First of all, put in your lighting and shading. As well as emphasising the nose-to-mouth lines, the temples and the bridge of the nose, begin to remould the face with patches and shapes of shadow rather than just lines. When you are satisfied, strengthen these so that you have two shades and two highlights.
3 The highlight need not run along the same lines as the shading

An eighteenth-century ageing make-up for grand opera
(note that the audience would be watching from a distance of 6–60 metres)

(a) Before

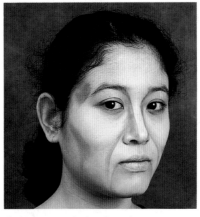

(b) Base and shading lines

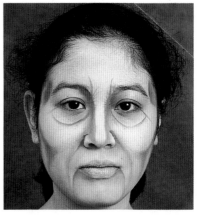

(c) Ageing lines have been added around the eyes

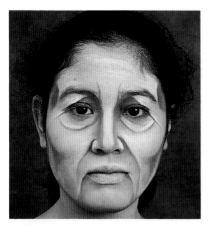

(d) Highlighting and blending

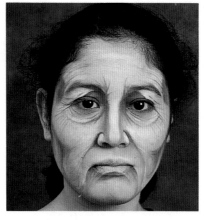

(e) Deepening shadows and strengthening the highlights

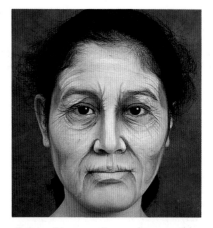

(f) Breaking up the make-up with points of colour, using lake red, blue and white

(g) The face is powdered with white talcum and the cheeks heavily rouged. A small mouth is painted in and two beauty spots added with a black pencil

– it can be thicker or more rounded. Create lines, folds and sunken skin around the side of the face, the jawline and mouth.

4 The eyes don't always need a shaded corner and highlighted brow bone. The emphasis can be on a smaller area, even just a blended line. Remember: a good result often follows from what you *don't* do – overworking can easily spoil the effect. Use the mirror constantly, and keep studying the natural lines and the shape of the face.

5 Once the light and shade is worked in and has graduated folds, the structure is finished. Powder and then texture.

6 Using a sponge, stipple on a red-pink; use your highlight colour to lighten this. Stipple again. You may also use an orange-red. Green can be stippled in around the temples and the beard or stubble line.

7 Age spots can be put on, from the receding hairline to the brow at angles. With red pencil, draw in broken and spider veins. Redden the ears.

8 To age the eyebrows, add grey, coarser hairs (rather than colouring the natural ones).

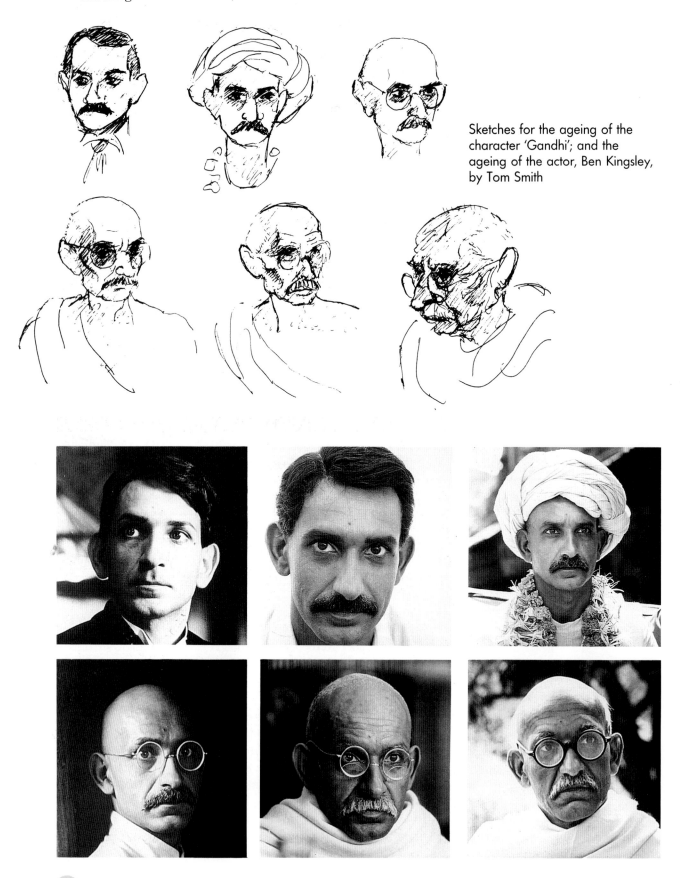

Sketches for the ageing of the character 'Gandhi'; and the ageing of the actor, Ben Kingsley, by Tom Smith

An ageing mouth

ACTIVITY:
Using sketches and photographs, compile a reference file. Cut out faces from newspapers and magazines. Place examples of fashion styles with make-up together in one section; in another, collate pictures of elderly faces. Shapes of noses, mouths, eyes, chins and so on are all useful also.

As you progress in make-up, add to this file. You will never finish collecting pictures as long as you work. Professional make-up artists refer to their reference files constantly. Start yours today!

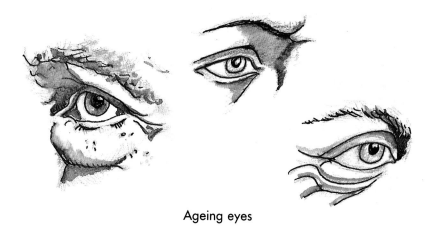
Ageing eyes

HOW TO SUCCEED

Checklist

In preparing for assessments on ageing make-up, the following lists may be useful. Check that you have covered and fully understood these items.

Ageing using make-up
- The degree of ageing required for the desired character effect, and for the intended medium (i.e. film, TV or theatre) must be determined.
- The areas of the face likely to sink or sag with age must be located.
- A design/chart must be produced with written notes to show the intended effect.
- The appropriate shading and highlighting colours must be mixed.
- Foundation may need to be applied to change the skin tone.
- Shading and highlighting must be applied effectively to produce a realistic-looking effect.
- The strength of colour and blending techniques must be suitable for the intended medium.
- Facial hair (eyebrows and eyelashes and the beard and moustache if worn) must be changed to assist the ageing effect.
- Health and safety rules must be observed throughout the procedure.

Ageing using latex

- The make-up location must be prepared, with a hand-held hair dryer, the latex, sponge, a bowl and powder ready in position.
- The colour process, if required, must be checked for completion.
- The skin must be stretched at right-angles to the direction of the lines required.
- Latex must be applied correctly to minimise the edges.
- A hand-held dryer must be used, on a cool setting, directing the air flow downwards to minimise discomfort to the actor.
- The latex must be powdered and then released.
- Additional layers may be applied if required.

Questions

Oral and written questions are used to test your knowledge and understanding. Try the following.

1 Which areas of the face would you age with make-up to give the appearance of: (a) middle age; (b) old age?
2 When creating the illusion of old age, which areas, besides the face, would you also 'age'?
3 When using latex to create wrinkles on the skin, in which direction would you pull the natural skin taut for (a) horizontal lines; (b) vertical lines?
4 What happens to latex if you do not replace the cap on the latex bottle immediately?
5 When planning ageing effects, which type of lighting is best for observing the effect of natural shadows on the face?

CHAPTER 11

Prosthetics

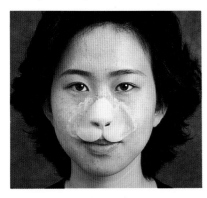

Ready-made prosthetics: a lion

(a) Before: The prosthetic piece is attached using spirit gum, and latex is placed around the edges of piece to blend away the hard edge

(b) After: The lion make-up was produced using water-based make-up by copying a drawing of a lion

INTRODUCTION

Prosthetics are appliances made out of rubber, plastic, gelatine or any other material which can be affixed to the actor's face or body in order to change the shape. These three-dimensional pieces can range from simple effects, such as warts, scars or wounds, which do not require a lifecast, to more complex additions, such as noses, chins, foreheads or eyebags which *do* require a lifecast – at least an impression of some part of the actor's face.

Ready-made prosthetics

Custom-made prosthetic pieces are available from professional make-up suppliers and are suitable for use in theatre and television for horror or fantasy effects.

Such pieces are attached to the skin according to the manufacturer's instructions. Usually they are made of latex or plastic, fixed in position with spirit gum; the edges are sealed and blended with latex (eyelash adhesive is suitable), and the pieces are painted with greasepaint or camouflage make-up to blend in with the rest of the design.

How prosthetics are made

First a *negative* **lifecast** or **life mask** is made to match the actor's face or body part. From this, a **duplicate positive** casting is made with a material such as plaster or stone: this is called a **facecast** or **bodycast**.

Based on this cast, a new shape is sculpted (positive); from this a *negative* is made of the newly sculpted feature. A positive copy of the sculpture can now be made in a flexible material such as plastic, rubber or gelatine: this, the **prosthesis** or **appliance**, is attached to the actor's face or body and coloured to blend in with the surrounding skin tone.

Materials used in casting and modelling

- **Plaster** This is the most basic ingredient, and the cheapest. There are different types of plaster. **Plaster of Paris** is soft; **dental stone**, such as **Crystacal D** or **R**, is hard. Plaster moulds are usually reinforced with fibres or fabrics such as **scrim**, **sacking**, **hessian** or **horsehair**.

- **Clay** A good-quality water-based clay is best. It must be kept wet, and sealed inside a plastic bag. An oil-based sculpting material called **plastilene** can be used; this has the advantage that it does not dry out, but the disadvantage that it does not give as smooth a finish as clay.

- **Alginate** This is used in taking accurate impressions of face or body parts. It takes about three minutes to set, and this can be accelerated by using warm water. (It is better to use cold water to mix it, however, as the setting time may be speeded up in hot weather: alginate is affected by temperature.) It is pleasant-smelling and harmless to the skin. It sets to a gelatine-like substance; because this is floppy it loses its shape, so it must be backed with plaster bandage to reinforce the shape.

- **Gypsona** or **plaster bandage** This is the material used in hospitals for setting broken bones. It is soaked briefly in water, wrung out, and then smoothed over the alginate.

- **Silicone rubber** This is an expensive room-temperature vulcanising rubber compound, used for making flexible moulds. It *must* be used on large gelatine moulds, and *can* be used on small moulds to give superior 'bite' to the mould halves. Silicone rubber work is usually done in specialist workshops as the material is expensive.

Ready-made prosthetics: a witch

The nose and chin have been attached using latex. The colouring was achieved with watercolour make-up

Materials used in making prosthetic pieces

- **Gelatine** A powder made from calves' hooves, used to make jelly. It is available as '300-grade technical gelatine'. It is mixed with glycerol and sorbitol and poured into hot moulds; when cool, it forms a rubbery compound. This is an easy and practical method you yourself can use.

- **Foam latex** This is a four- or five-part latex compound, which is whisked to a foam in a food mixer; the foam is poured into cold moulds and cooked in an oven to produce foam latex prosthetic pieces. These provide the best quality for large pieces and for close-up work for the screen. Foam latex work is usually done in specialist workshops as it is very time-consuming and expensive.

- **Liquid latex** This is a milky liquid which can be painted as layers inside moulds to produce a solid rubber piece. Each painted-in layer should be applied thinly and allowed to dry before applying the next layer. This is easy to do yourself.

- **Plastic** In liquid form, as it is used for making bald caps, plastic also can be painted into moulds to make small prosthetic pieces. This also is easy to do.

Of all these materials, only two can be re-used: gelatine, which can be heated, melted down and used again; and plastic, which can be cut into small pieces and melted down in acetone.

FLAT PLATE MOULDS

Flat plate moulds are among the most useful moulds; all moulding techniques can be considered as embellishments of this basic technique. It is ideal for making wounds, scars, stitched wounds, keloid scars, blisters, burns and so on. These can be made in advance and kept until you need them.

This type of mould-making can be done on any worktop or kitchen table, and does not require a lifecast of the actor's facial features.

Making the mould (negative)

Making the flat plate

> **Equipment and materials**
> - plastic box (about 50 mm deep)
> - dental stone plaster and scrim
> - small saw (for cutting the keys)
> - shellac (to seal the mould)
> - Vaseline
> - sculpting tools
> - clay
> - screwdriver (to separate the moulds)

1 Take a plastic box about 50 mm deep. Half-fill it (to about 25 mm) with dental stone plaster to create the flat plate. You will be sculpting on top of this plaster, so make it smooth on top. (Scrim can be added into the mix for reinforcement.)
2 When set, take the plaster slab out of the box and cut three **keys** in the sides (off-centre), using a small saw: these will allow you later to check that the mould halves are correctly fitted together.
3 Coat the flat plate with **shellac** and Vaseline, to seal the plaster. If you do not have time for this, use Vaseline only. (Clay put onto dry plaster will shrivel up.)
4 When dry, it is ready for sculpting on.

Sculpting

1 Sculpt your piece using wet clay – scars, wounds, bumps and flaps of skin are all suitable for flat plate moulds. Leave plenty of room around the piece. Blend away the edges, using a damp sponge or brush.

Casting

1 Make a low wall in wet clay around the piece, leaving 6–12 mm of clear plaster around the edge of the piece. *Do not cover the keys.*
2 Apply Vaseline all over the exposed plaster – the keys and the areas around the piece.
3 Place the whole plate inside the box; press the clay walls to seal against the edge of the box walls.
4 Mix another batch of plaster and fill the box to the brim, reinforcing with scrim. Take care that the plaster has filled the details of your sculpted piece.
5 Allow the plaster to set, which will take about 40 minutes. As it sets, the plaster will first get hot and then become cold.

Removing the mould

1 Take the completed mould out of the box. Separate the two halves carefully, using a screwdriver to lever if necessary.

Flat plate moulds

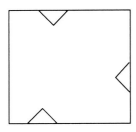

(a) Three keys are cut into the sides of the plaster slab

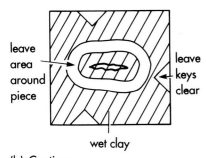

leave area around piece

leave keys clear

wet clay

(b) Casting

2 Clean all traces of wet clay from the mould.

3 Put both halves in the oven to dry (just over 100°C) for at least two hours.

4 When dry, shellac both halves of the mould (inside). The moulds are now ready for filling with gelatine.

The separator

A separating material, sometimes referred to as a **parting agent** or **releasing compound**, is used to help moulds detach easily when they are pulled apart. It is also used to seal the moulds, to prevent moisture from penetrating the surface. Vaseline (or petroleum jelly) is the most commonly used separator. Another separator is a saturated solution of soap and water; this is used when casting with foam latex.

Filling the moulds with gelatine

Using gelatine

Mould gelatine, as in the following recipe, *must never be used directly onto a person's skin*: it would cause burns. It must be used only for filling moulds.

1 Mix the liquid sorbitol and glycerine with the gelatine. Heat moderately, until the mixture has clarified. It will still contain many bubbles.

2 Mix together in a small bowl zinc oxide and pancake scrapings – 6W to 10W pancakes, depending on the required skin tone – with a little gelatine, until you are happy with the colour. Add this to the heated mixture.

> **Materials**
> - 100 g fine powdered gelatine
> - 200 g liquid sorbitol
> - 200 g glycerine (glycerol)
> - ½ tablespoon of zinc oxide powder
> - scraped pancake colour

Ideally, this mixture should be made up in advance, to allow time for the bubbles to rise and disperse. It can be kept indefinitely (cold) in a plastic bag or container, and reheated when needed.

Variations

- *Less* gelatine makes a softer, weaker appliance; *more* gelatine makes a harder, tougher one.
- To make a clear gelatine for blisters and the like, leave out the zinc oxide.

Colouring

- Any powdered **pigment** can be added to create a colour. It should be combined with glycerine in a separate bowl before being added to the mixture.
- Liquid **food colouring**, mixed with a little **isopropyl alcohol**, can also be used.
- **Chopped crepe hair** can be added to produce a vein texture.

Preparing the mould

The mould must be hot, but not *too* hot.

1 Place the mould in a moderately heated oven for 15 minutes.
2 Remove the mould from the oven and wipe the inside with Vaseline.

Filling the mould

1 Pour the hot gelatine mixture into the mould, making sure that the piece is well covered and that there are no air bubbles.
2 Close the mould halves, matching the keys to one another. Apply pressure evenly – do not press hard and then release, or air will be sucked back into the mould. Put a stage weight or similar on top of the mould and leave it for about two hours, until cold. (Do not try to open a warm mould: the gelatine inside will be a sticky mess.)

Opening the mould

1 Separate the mould gently, using powder to stop the edges rolling over, and a modelling tool to lift the piece. Care is needed here if you are to achieve the best possible piece.
2 When the piece is free, pull off the excess edges around the piece. It is tempting to leave them on, because they will be beautifully thin, but the *best* edges for application are close to the piece itself.

What went wrong?

If the edges are really thick, there are only four possible causes:

1 The mould did not close properly. Check it against the light for any trapped pieces of plaster or similar obstacles.
2 The gelatine was too cool. Try again, with warmer gelatine.
3 The mould was too cool when the gelatine was poured. Warm the mould.
4 Not enough pressure was applied during the cooling period. Add more weight.

LIFECASTING FROM THE ACTOR'S FACE

Caring for the actor

Many people – not just actors – are nervous of having their faces covered in plaster in order to provide a lifecast. This is quite understandable, and care should be taken in discussing the person's particular anxieties before the casting session. You should experience a lifecast yourself before undertaking one on another person – students should practise on one another to help them understand why lifecasting is sometimes frightening for actors. When lifecasting in a film studio, it is usual to have the unit nurse present during the procedure; in a classroom, a nurse or a teacher

Examples of lifecasts

with a knowledge of first aid procedures should be in attendance, in case of emergency and to provide a reassuring presence.

For actors, lifecasting sessions are similar to visiting a dentist; the procedure is out of their control, leaving them vulnerable and helpless. Take time to explain how they will breathe under the cast. Actors must be reassured that if they wish, at any time and for whatever reason the lifecast will immediately be removed if they simply raise an arm in a prearranged signal. The sympathetic, calm manner required of a make-up artist in all her work is of prime importance when lifecasting.

Taking the lifecast (negative)

All tools and materials must be laid out ready before the appointed time. The equipment must be neatly arranged and ready to hand.

Measure the required amount of alginate powder into the bowl. Make sure there are enough strips of plaster bandage in different sizes: you will need enough to cover the face with three or four layers.

Preparing the actor

1 Seat the actor comfortably and wrap the plastic cape around him. He should be wearing comfortable clothing – roll-necked sweaters are not suitable as the plaster may drip onto the neck. Use towels and tissues tucked into the neckline to protect clothing and to keep the actor warm.
2 Position the bald cap over his head to protect his hair, making sure that it covers the hairline.
3 Apply Vaseline, KY Jelly or any silicone grease to the eyebrows and eyelashes in a thin coating. Do the same with any other facial hair, such as a beard and a moustache. (Alternatively, these can be plastered down with wax, but *remember to apply grease on top of the wax* so that the alginate does not stick to it.)

It is important to talk to the actor while preparing him for the lifecasting. Make clear to him that if he signals you to remove the alginate from his face, you will remove it from the nose, the mouth and the eyes, in that order. This should help to relieve the claustrophobic feeling he may be undergoing. Explain to him that the alginate will feel very cold at first but will warm up later.

Applying the alginate impression material

Whilst the alginate is being applied the actor should remain as still as possible and in an upright position. The face must not be tilted in any direction – either up or down, or from side to side – otherwise the impression will not be accurate.

1 Having prepared the actor, start mixing the alginate by adding cold water to the powder. Stir from side to side to avoid trapping air in the mix.
2 When the mixture is a creamy paste, apply it to the face,

> ### Equipment and materials
> - 1 large plastic cape
> - 1 bald cap
> - alginate
> - plaster bandage (pre-cut in 150 mm and 300 mm strips)
> - scissors
> - petroleum jelly or silicone grease to cover facial hair (including eyebrows and eyelashes)
> - mixing bowls
> - spatulas
> - brushes
> - water
> - plaster
> - permanent marker
> - salt
> - tissues and cottonwool
> - towels

Taking a lifecast

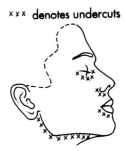

x x x denotes undercuts

The undercuts

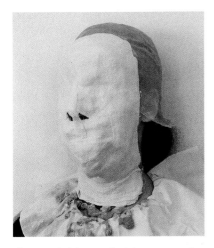

The model has a bald cap on, the alginate has been applied and plaster bandage put on top

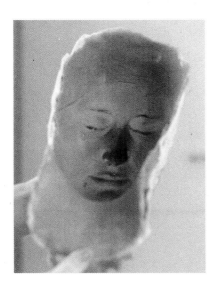

When dry, the plaster lifecast is removed

beginning on the forehead and working down over the face. Leave the nose and mouth until last. *Remember to leave breathing holes around the nostrils.* Use a brush to apply the alginate in particular areas: this will ensure that no air bubbles are trapped under the alginate. These areas, known as the **undercuts**, are under the chin and jawline, under the mouth, under the eyes and around the nostrils. (Instead of using a brush you can run your fingers gently along these points.) Keep the actor's nostrils clear: if there is a blockage, ask him to expel air sharply through his nose to shift it. An airway should be allowed through the mouth also.

Reinforcing the alginate with plaster bandage

3 When the alginate has been applied smoothly, dip the wads of pre-cut plaster bandages into warm, lightly salted water. Squeeze out excess water before applying the plaster bandage to the alginate. (For extra support, a layer of rough towelling can be placed over the wet alginate before applying the bandage – this should not be necessary if you use plenty of plaster bandage.)

4 The alginate will have set – setting takes approximately 3 minutes – and you can now begin placing strips of plaster bandage over the life cast. Keep inside the edge of the alginate: *plaster bandage should not directly touch the skin* as the alkali in the plaster can cause irritation.

5 Having covered the face, with four layers of the bandage all over the alginate, you may add an extra strip around the outside of the bandaged area to provide additional support when removing the cast. Keep an eye on the actor, talking reassuringly and watching for the agreed hand signal.

6 When you think the plaster bandages have set, run your fingers around the edge. About 10 minutes is usually sufficient for the plaster to harden.

Removing the lifecast

1 Ask the actor to wriggle his face gently under the lifecast in order to loosen the alginate. He should lean forward, holding the cast in his hands; as he moves his facial muscles the cast will loosen and fall into his hands. Alternatively, you can lift the edges of the lifecast – making sure that you are lifting the alginate and not just the plaster bandage – and work the lifecast loose.

Taking care of the actor and the lifecast

As soon as the lifecast has been removed, the actor's face must be restored to normal.

1 Remove any pieces of plaster and alginate from the face with damp cottonwool. The actor can now wash his face with warm water and soap.

2 After drying with a clean towel, an astringent may be used to close the pores of the skin; **rosewater** is excellent for this purpose. Finally, a mild moisturiser should be gently applied.

3 Insert plugs of wet clay or wax or plastilene into the nostrils of the cast, *so that the liquid plaster will not leak*. Position the cast gently on a bed of towels, ensuring that the nose does not get damaged. Alternatively, while you mix the plaster, ask a helper to cradle the cast in his or her lap, supporting the mould with cupped hands.

Making a positive plaster cast

Preparing the plaster cast

Mixing the plaster

1 Put 2 or 3 cups of water into a bowl, then slowly sift the plaster into the water until it barely rests on top of the water. Always mix plaster into cold water. Let the mixture stand until it begins to thicken. The plaster will draw up the water and become fully saturated: this process is called **slaking**.

2 Begin mixing with a side-to-side motion, then bang the worktop surface next to or underneath the bowl to bring any trapped air to the surface. Gently blow on any bubbles to disperse them. The consistency of the plaster should be like pouring cream.

Filling the mould

3 The shell, or mould, is ready to be filled with plaster. When the plaster has been mixed thoroughly, begin by painting some of it into the mould, using a soft brush. Brush the wash of plaster into all the cavities.

4 Pour the plaster into the mould, building it up slowly as the plaster thickens. *Pour from one end only*. When the plaster has thickened to a trowelling consistency, begin to apply it with increasing thickness to build up strength in the lifecast. There should be at least 25–50 mm thickness throughout the mould. Do not overfill or the cast will be too heavy to handle. Leave it for 1 hour.

5 When hardened, pick it up and turn it over. Remove the plaster bandage and alginate from the inner mould, taking care not to damage the face impression. Finish the cast by filing away any rough parts, and if necessary scratch the name of the artiste on the underside of the cast.

6 Leave the cast to harden and dry out overnight.

Finishing the plaster cast

1 Give the cast a coat of shellac to seal the plaster. The shape of the feature you wish to reproduce will be modelled in clay onto the facecast.

SCULPTING THE NEW FEATURE

Sculpting is the most important part of prosthetic work. The piece, however skilfully cast, and whichever material it is in – be it plastic, gelatine, liquid latex or foam latex – will only be as good as the shape you have created in clay. Whatever your concept, the skill of modelling and sculpting the piece requires much practice.

Modelling the feature

> ***Equipment and materials***
> - a sketch and/or Polaroid photographs of the required shape
> - various modelling tools, in wood or metal
> - bowl of water
> - spray bottle filled with water
> - clay *or* plastilene
> - rough towel, grapefruit peel *or* coarse stipple sponge

1 Place your facecast on a work surface, supported underneath by some lumps of modelling clay or plastilene to hold it in position. Place a small amount of wet clay onto the part of the face that you wish to change, often the nose.
2 When you have achieved the shape that you want, begin to put in the details. Keep the clay damp by spraying it with water; clay that is too dry does not produce good results. Remember to sculpt very thin edges, using your wet fingers to smooth away the base of the feature until it blends into the surrounding area of the facecast.
3 Take into account the final texture of the modelled feature. It should blend with the surrounding skin in the area to which it will be applied. Texture can be added by gently pressing a rough-textured towel or a piece of grapefruit peel onto the clay surface. Alternatively, a coarse-textured stipple sponge will have the same effect.

> **ACTIVITY: SCULPTING A FACE**
> Using wet modelling clay, sculpt a life-sized face using a photograph or a sketch for reference. Try to achieve a good likeness. Build up the shape of the face using small lumps of clay, a bit at a time. Remember to keep the clay damp by spraying it with water every few hours. When you are not working on the face, wrap it in plastic to prevent it from drying out.

Casting the mould

> ***Equipment and materials***
> - clay *or* plastilene
> - Vaseline
> - plaster
> - brush

1 To cast the newly modelled feature into a mould from which you can make your prosthetic piece, it is necessary to build a wall around the feature. Modelling clay or plastilene can be used for this. The wall should be even in height, and should be higher than the newly modelled nose (or other facial feature).
2 Using your fingertips, spread a thin layer of Vaseline on the nose and the surrounding area lying inside the clay wall.
3 Mix plaster as before, but less will be needed. Paint on a thin coat of the plaster using a brush, then pour plaster to cover the nose. Bang on the table with your fist, to disperse air bubbles in the plaster. Leave it to dry.
4 When the plaster is dry, remove the clay wall and separate the nose mould from the remodelled lifecast.

5 Remove the modelled nose from the interior of the mould and smooth away any imperfections with a file.

Cleaning the mould

1 Wash the mould in warm water, using a clean soft brush in all the cavities. Leave it to dry overnight, when it will be ready to fill with the chosen material.

Making the prosthetic piece

The prosthetic piece can be made out of plastic, latex or gelatine. There are three latex techniques: *painting in*, *slush*, and *foam*. The 'foam latex' method will be explained at the end of the chapter, as it is an advanced technique.

The painting method

The new nose shape can be made by painting the inside of the mould with successive layers of liquid latex. Prior to application, the latex can be coloured by mixing in scrapings of pancake or food colouring to give it a flesh tone or other effect, as desired. When the latex is dry it will be darker in colour.

1 Before applying the latex, brush the mould with liquid soap.
2 Pour a little latex into the mould, and use a brush to paint the inside of the mould until it is covered. Allow each layer to dry before painting the next.
3 Paint the next layer beyond the edge of the piece.
4 Apply about fifteen layers, so that the piece will hold its shape. Concentrate the most latex on the middle part of the piece, so that the edges are thin.
5 Leave the casting for 6 hours, during which it will become darker in colour.

> **Equipment and materials**
> * liquid soap
> * latex
> * brush

The slush method

The 'slush' method uses latex but without painting it in layers. As with the painting method, the area inside the mould should be brushed with liquid soap, which will act as a release agent.

1 Pour the latex into the mould and sluice it around, tilting it gently so that the latex runs into the required places.
2 Build up thickness in the middle, but leave the edges thin.
3 Leave the cast overnight to dry.

Colouring the latex

The liquid latex is milky white, and can be coloured by adding scrapings of pancake or food colouring to give it a flesh tone or other effect, as desired. Remember that when the latex is dry, the colour will be darker.

Using plastic

This method involves using liquid bald cap plastic and painting layers into the mould. Again, the positive mould is not used.

1 Spread a layer of Vaseline inside the mould (as a release agent).
2 Paint in layers of plastic, allowing each layer to dry before painting in the next. Scrapings of pancake colour and the like can be mixed into colour the transparent plastic.
3 As with the latex nose, more layers should be concentrated in the middle part of the nose mould and the edges left thin.

Removing the prosthetic piece from the mould

Caring for the prosthesis

1 Use talcum powder and a soft brush to lift and peel the edges carefully, powdering with the brush as you go. This prevents the material from sticking to itself as you remove it.
2 When you have removed the prosthesis from the mould, powder it inside and out with more powder: this is to remove any grease from the Vaseline, if the prosthesis is plastic, or soap, if it is latex. Keep the prosthetic nose in its mould to retain its shape until you are ready to use it.

Caring for the mould

The mould should be washed in soap and water and allowed to dry naturally. You can make as many pieces as you like from the mould, and it will probably be necessary to produce several before you get a good result.

Do not be disappointed if your prosthetic pieces do not turn out as well as you hoped. This happens all the time to experienced prosthetic specialists.

The facecast can be used for experiments in making all sorts of pieces: eyebags and jowls for ageing; a forehead for a monster make-up; a clown's nose; a witch's nose and chin – the possibilities are endless. Each piece must be modelled, and a mould made of each feature in the same way as you did for your first nose. To make a mask you can remodel the entire facecast with clay and cast it to produce a full face mask.

SECTIONAL LIFECASTING

When only a section of the face is needed – often the nose – instead of taking an impression of the whole face you can lifecast just the feature itself. This is less time-consuming and is also cheaper than casting the entire face.

Taking a cast of the nose

1 About half of the eye sockets and cheeks should be covered, as well as the nose itself, to allow sufficient room for good edges on the final positive.
2 The eyebrows, eyelashes, and any moustache should be coated with Vaseline to protect them and to allow ease of separation. The person's nostrils can be plugged with cottonwool covered with Vaseline, as he or she can breathe through the mouth.
3 The alginate and the plaster bandage are applied in the same way as for the previous facecast, using smaller quantities of plaster. Allow a few minutes for the plaster bandage to harden before removing the cast from the face. Ensure that the artiste's skin is restored to its normal state (see pages 163–4).
4 When the cast (*negative*) has been removed from the face it can be used as a mould. Pour in the freshly mixed plaster (dental stone – Crystacal D or R) and leave it to set.
5 When the plaster has hardened, remove the new plaster cast (*positive*) from the mould. Correct any minor defects, trim and smooth the surfaces.

Sectional casting

Making the plaster block for the nose

For sectional castings it is neater to **box** the features in a rectangle, making a block for the nose. The walls can be made of clay, metal, lead or damp-proof plastic.

Making the positive mould

1 Make a watertight wall around the feature, with a 12 mm gap all round.
2 Mix a batch of thick plaster (dental stone Crystacal D or R), and pour a base for the lifecast section.
3 Once the base is thick enough to support the lifecast feature without it sinking into the freshly mixed plaster, lay the lifecast on top of the base. Pour the plaster around the feature to set it in the block.
4 When the plaster is hard, remove the walls. Smooth out any lumps by sanding or scraping the plaster slab and feature.
5 Cut three keys in the sides, off-centre.
6 Apply Vaseline to the feature.

Sculpting the prosthesis

1 Sculpt the appliance, using wax, clay or plastilene on top of the stone feature. Blend the edges down and away from the feature so that the edges will be thin.
2 Sculpt an overspill or trench with clay around the sculpture, about 6–12 mm thick and 6 mm away from the edge of the

> **Equipment and materials**
> - Vaseline
> - cottonwool
> - alginate
> - plaster bandage
> - dental stone

Taking an impression of a nose

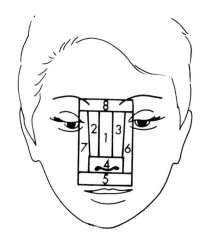

(a) Before

(b) Applying plaster bandages

168 PROSTHETICS

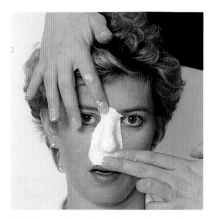

(c) Removing the plaster bandage when set

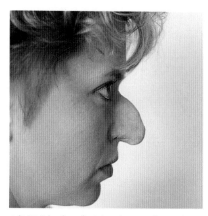

(d) With the finished prosthesis

Equipment and materials
- sponge *or* brush
- plaster (Crystacal)
- screwdriver or chisel

Equipment and materials
- Vaseline
- gelatine
- powder
- modelling tool
- plastic bag

sculpture. This creates an overflow, for use if you want later to use foam latex or gelatine to make the prosthetic piece. This overflow or trench is called the **flash**.

Making the plaster mould (negative)

This stage consists in building the other half of the mould.

1 Build a box wall in the same way as you did for the positive half. The wall should be high enough to reach 20 mm above the feature.
2 Using a sponge or brush, blend the outer edge of the flash to the walls to seal the edges and to make the box walls watertight.

To cast the mould, use Crystacal plaster, a little thinner than you did for the positive half of the mould.

3 Mix some plaster and water – always add the plaster to the water, and not the other way round – and pour it slowly *around* the modelled piece (not onto it). Blow on the plaster; and keep pouring until the piece is covered and the box mould filled. Tap the underside of the workbench to bring any air bubbles to the surface. Leave the plaster negative to set in its box.
4 When the plaster has set, remove the walls and trim the plaster.
5 Leave for 2 hours, then gently prise the mould apart. (You may need a large screwdriver or chisel to help.)

Cleaning the mould

1 Wash the mould in warm water, using a soft brush in all the cavities. Leave it to dry overnight, when it will be ready to fill with the chosen material.

GELATINE PROSTHETIC PIECES

Gelatine is good to work with because it is re-usable: if the piece is not as successful as you would have liked, you can melt it and try again.

Filling the mould

1 Seal the mould with Vaseline.
2 Heat the gelatine (using the same recipe and method as for the flat plate moulds) and heat the moulds in an oven until hot.
3 Sluice a little of the gelatine around the mould to pick up the surface detail, then pour in more gelatine to fill the mould.
4 Close the mould and leave for 2 hours or until cold.

Opening the mould

1 Separate the parts of the mould gently, and remove the gelatine piece from the positive mould: first powder it, and use a modelling tool to lift it; then powder it further, to stop the edges rolling over as you peel the prosthesis out of the negative mould.

Storing gelatine pieces

Keep all gelatine pieces in an airtight plastic bag.

APPLYING A PROSTHETIC PIECE

The adhesives

Various adhesives are available, which have different uses in applying prosthetics:

- **Spirit gum** will stick latex, gelatine and plastic.

- **Dow Corning 355 medical adhesive** will stick latex, plastic and gelatine – instantly. It can be thinned for easier application and for economy, using Tipp-Ex thinner or **trichlorotrifluoroethane**.

- **ProsAide** will stick latex pieces only, but when mixed with water it can be used as a sealer on foam pieces. When mixed with a thickener (**Cabosil**), it can also be used as a paste to conceal the edges of a piece; and when mixed with artists' acrylic paints, it can be used to artwork the piece. This should be done in advance, before application.

- **Duo** will stick latex and blend the edges of latex prosthetic pieces.

Sealing and preparation

1 Seal the prosthetic piece with sealer. Allow it to dry.
2 Prepare the piece for fixing, removing any unwanted edge material.

Affixing the piece

1 Position the prosthetic piece on the actor's face, and powder around it to show the outline.
2 Remove the piece, and put a thin layer of adhesive on the underside of the piece, in the middle. Do not apply adhesive yet to the *edges* of the piece.
3 Position the piece carefully, and press it with a cloth or powder puff.
4 Stick the edges last, using a modelling tool or small spatula to hold up the edges and to prevent them from curling or sticking together.

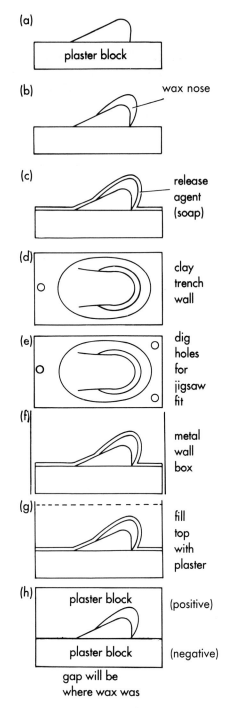

(a) plaster block

(b) wax nose

(c) release agent (soap)

(d) clay trench wall

(e) dig holes for jigsaw fit

(f) metal wall box

(g) fill top with plaster

(h) plaster block (positive) / plaster block (negative)

gap will be where wax was

Making the plaster block for a foam latex or gelatine nose

Equipment and materials
- sealer
- powder
- adhesive
- cloth *or* powder puff
- modelling tool *or* spatula

Blending the edges of the piece

Equipment and materials
- witch hazel *or* Duo *or* ProsAide with Cabosil *or* acetone
- cotton buds
- modelling tool
- palette knife

■ If the piece is *gelatine*, use witch hazel on a cotton bud to blend the edges. Use the dry end of the cotton bud to press firmly and roll on the edge.

■ If the piece is *latex*, use Duo on a modelling tool to seal the edge onto the skin. Smooth the Duo with a palette knife. Alternatively, you can use ProsAide mixed with Cabosil to a paste to blend the edges.

■ If the piece is *plastic*, use a cotton bud with a small dab of acetone to blend the edges of the piece. *Do not touch the skin*, only the edge of the piece.

Colouring the piece

Once the piece has been fixed and sealed you can paint it. Some make-up bases are made especially for prosthetic work. Camouflage make-up is excellent for coverage and for matching the skin tone of the surrounding skin area. Use rubber stippling sponges to achieve a dappled effect, and build up the textured effect using several colours. Powder between layers. Be careful not to overdo the colouring: you cannot wipe away unwanted make-up from a prosthetic piece. When painting prosthetic cuts and wounds, it is good to put colour into the cut early: the bright colour will draw the eye to it, and thereby distract attention from the edge.

When applying make-up to the piece, remember that the prosthesis will appear *lighter* than the skin – use a darker tone than on the rest of the skin, therefore. Warm pink tones should be stippled on the piece before the skin tone colour, exactly as when working with wax.

Take extra care when working near the eyes. *All adhesives are potentially dangerous*: avoid any prosthetic work involving the eye areas until you are experienced. Even then, undertake such work only with extreme caution.

REMOVING THE PROSTHETIC PIECE

Pieces attached with spirit gum

Equipment and materials
- brush
- mild mastix remover
- cottonwool

1 Use a small brush dipped in mild mastix remover to remove the prosthetic piece. Apply the remover to the edges around the piece; lift it with one hand, as with the other you work the brush to loosen it.
2 Clean the spirit gum from the actor's face with cottonwool dampened with the mastix remover.
3 Remove the make-up in the normal way.

Pieces attached with Dow Corning 355

1 Use a keratin-based oil called Klene-All. Isopropyl alcohol also will dissolve the adhesive.

Pieces attached with latex

1 Use warm water and cotton buds.

Equipment and materials
- Klene-All *or* isopropyl alcohol *or* warm water
- cotton buds

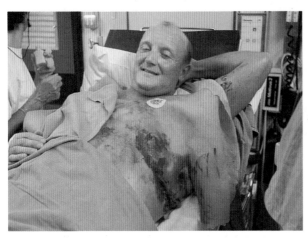

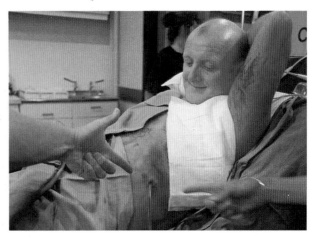

Prosthetics using gelatine (1): A whole chest piece done to show a chest drain

(a) The piece being applied

(b) The chest drain inserted — 'blood' is flowing through the drain (the gelatine has been melted in order to draw flesh up for a purse-string stitch)

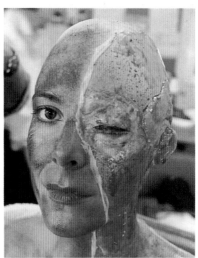

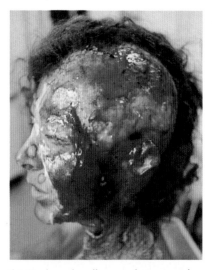

Prosthetics using gelatine (2): A head wound — the victim has been kicked on the head by a horse

A gelatine prosthetic piece (made from a cast taken from the actor's face) has been added from the middle of the forehead down to the temple. The 'blood' is directly applied gelatine

Prosthetics using gelatine (3): A burns victim

(a) A bald cap has been applied. The edges of the burn are made of bald cap plastic (made by painting layers of liquid plastic onto the glass); directly applied gelatine pieces have been applied to break up the flatness

(b) Red and yellow gelatine and black powder have been applied. For the finished effect, half a wig has been specially made. (The ear and eye patch were made from moulds using gelatine. Normal make-up colouring was used beyond the edge of the piece and kept matt for contrast against the shiny-looking burn)

The need for care

Great care should be taken when removing prosthetic pieces. Your understanding of the types of adhesives must include knowledge of the materials needed to remove them. As more products become available in the field of make-up there is greater choice – but with increased choice comes increased responsibility.

Some adhesives are not suitable for use around the eyes, but can safely be used on the chin or nose. This is not because of danger from the adhesive – which should always be safe for use on the skin – but because of danger from the product used to *remove* the adhesive.

Allowing time

In cases where there is substantial use of prosthetics, as with fantasy or 'cartoon' character make-up, you need to allow as long to remove them as to apply them.

On a film called *High Spirits* the make-up team took four hours to attach and colour the pieces, and at the end of the day it took us another four hours gently to remove the pieces and to clean off all the adhesive. We were doing this for hours after the rest of the crew had gone home! It was essential to work slowly and painstakingly at restoring the artistes' skin to normal. Any other way would run the risk of damaging the skin. That particular scene took several days to complete, and throughout it was very uncomfortable for the performers who had to ensure heavy prosthetics while working sixteen-hour days.

It is understandable if actors feel like tearing the pieces off, but it is crucial that you do not let this happen. Although patience and understanding are always essential parts of the make-up artist's job, they are absolutely vital when applying and removing prosthetics.

> ### ACTIVITY: PRODUCING A FACE MASK
> 1 Take an impression of a fellow student's face.
> 2 From this impression, make a positive cast.
> 3 Model new features onto the positive cast, for example to make a monster's or a witch's face.
> 4 Make a negative mould of the new face.
> 5 Use the 'slush' latex technique to produce the face mask.

USING LATEX: FOAM TECHNIQUE

Developments in technology

The advances in technology have affected the prosthetics laboratories and workshops more than any other area of make-up artistry. New methods, new materials – the technology advances all the time. To appreciate the time and effort involved, and to excel in this area, try to do some work experience or apprentice yourself to a professional prosthetics workshop and learn the art and the technology of this remarkable aspect of make-up. The specialist makers of prosthetics are part chemist, part artist and part engineer. Each tends to specialise in a particular area, such as sculpting, mould making, foaming latex, knotting hair into the pieces, colouring or artworking. A complicated ageing sequence or character change as it is eventually seen in a film may have used many prosthetic pieces and relied on the work of an entire crew of talented people.

Commissioning foam latex pieces

Prosthetic pieces that are large need to be made out of foam latex as this is the lightest material and the most similar to natural skin. Most make-up artists will commission a specialist to make the pieces for the production. In these circumstances, you will be required to take the actor to the prosthetic specialist's workshop for a lifecasting session. Several visits may be necessary to ensure the quality and the fit of the prosthetic piece or pieces required.

Here are some aspects to look out for:

1 Make sure that the piece fits exactly, when the actor's face is mobile.
2 Check that the edges of the piece are so fine and thin that they blend into the surrounding skin.
3 Check that there are no large air bubbles in the piece.

Don't be afraid to put forward your own ideas to the specialist – it is *you* who will be applying the prosthetics in the studio, and by that stage it will be too late to correct any faults. If you have a difference of opinion with the specialist, however, don't talk about this in front of the actor: sort out problems when he or she isn't there. If the actor thinks that anything is wrong, she or he will lose confidence.

When the foam latex pieces arrive from the specialist workshop, they should have been washed in soap and water (to remove the strong smell of the chemicals), and dried carefully. This is important, as the smell can be unpleasant and distracting for the person wearing the piece. The *number* of duplicate pieces will be whatever you have ordered – with foam latex you need a new piece on each day on the shoot.

Making foam latex pieces

Foam latex

The best, but the most expensive, method of casting is to fill the mould with foam latex and cure this in an oven. This approach requires much more preparation and time than any other type of prosthetic work. It is undoubtedly the finest method available for three-dimensional effects for the media. For large pieces in particular the foam latex surpasses all other methods; it is light and flexible and adheres well to the skin. If the film or TV budget

> **TIP**
>
> The ingredients for making foam latex can be purchased in small batches and mixed according to the maker's instructions. They are usually named 'Parts A, B and C' by the manufacturers.

can afford foam latex pieces at all it is advisable to contract the work out to an expert. Many make-up artists have neither the desire nor the skill to work in this area, but every make-up artist should have some knowledge of the techniques involved in making foam latex appliances.

Foam latex has the following ingredients:

- **Latex base** A high-quality chemically thickened latex, sterilised with ammonia.

- **Foam agent** An emulsion of soaps: when whisked with the latex base, these produce a foam.

- **Cure agent** A mixture of sulphur and other chemicals that **vulcanises** the foam latex when it is **cured** in the oven.

- **Gel agent** An acid that turns the latex from a liquid to a semi-solid: it coagulates the foam, preventing it from breaking down. **Warning**: *Before it has been cured, this is highly toxic.*

- **Soap release** The release agent which is painted onto the plaster moulds before filling them with foam latex. This ensures that the foam can be removed easily without sticking after the casting has come out of the oven.

> **TIP**
>
> Colour can be mixed into the gelling agent, using artists' tube colours thinned with water. For example, flesh colour can be obtained by mixing a teaspoon of burnt sienna with ¼ teaspoon of water.

The prosthetics room

The room should be equipped with an electric food mixer and bowl, weighing scales, a drill and a prosthetics oven for curing the moulds. **Warning** *An industrial mask should be worn as some of ingredients used in mixing foam latex are known to be toxic.* Inhaling plaster dust is bad for the health, so it is safest to assume that most of the work in the room is detrimental to one's health, and a surgical or dentist's mask should always be worn. For large effects, using full heads and bodies, catering mixers and ovens are used.

The temperature and humidity of the workroom affects the foaming process: higher temperatures cause faster setting, lower temperatures make it slower. It is not practical to attempt foaming operations at below 15°C (60°F). For professional results, you need air conditioning and heating. All other aspects of making prosthetic pieces can be carried out quite successfully in college, at home in the kitchen or in a garden shed – but it's not so simple for foam latex mixing and curing. Here chemistry and make-up overlap; successful results rely on dedication and experience.

Health and safety

The foam latex technician works with highly toxic and dangerous ingredients. **Warning**: *It is dangerous to inhale the products.*

To minimise the risks of accidents, follow these rules:

1 Keep all chemicals out of reach of children and inquisitive adults.
2 Do not decant chemicals into other bottles, especially bottles which have been used for drinks. To do so is an unnecessary

risk, and could prove fatal if someone mistook the chemical for a drink.

3 Always wear a respirator and goggles when opening bottles that are old or newly purchased: the vapours and fumes can build up to dangerous levels inside the containers.

4 Never sniff or breathe in any of the chemicals used in making foam latex.

5 Always put the lids back on the bottles, making sure that they are tightly sealed.

6 Wash any accidental splashes of chemicals from the skin with cold water immediately.

7 Keep eyewash solution and an eyebath near the sink in case of accident.

8 Never leave a mess in the workshop. Always wipe worktops with disinfectant and wipe machinery immediately after use. Wash used moulds. If the work area is clean, tidy and organised, it will also be safer.

9 The workshop should be spacious and well ventilated. Extractor fans should be used near open windows to get rid of the vapours from the ammonia present in the latex.

10 Wash your hands before and after working with foam latex.

11 Always read the labels on the bottles, especially the labels warning of risks. Always read the instruction sheets included with the products, and take heed of the health and safety warnings.

12 Wear goggles and gloves; if working in a poorly ventilated workshop, wear a respirator approved for ammonia vapour.

13 Never drink or eat in the foam lab or workshop. Food and drink can become contaminated with chemical vapours.

TIP

Small quantities of the ingredients for foam latex can be weighed in plastic cups which can be thrown away after use.

When measuring out the gelling agent, it is helpful to use a spoon that has been waxed: this prevents the gelling agent from sticking to the spoon.

Equipment

The actual process of making the foam latex is very simple; but, rather like making a soufflé, it can go wrong without one understanding why. As with cooking anything, variations in the mixture or the cooking times can upset the balance. When the foam fails to rise or has too many air bubbles, it is usually necessary to start all over again.

Filling the moulds and curing the latex

Preparation

1 Apply soap release to the plaster moulds and allow this to dry.
2 Weigh out the ingredients in plastic cups.

Mixing (foaming the latex)

3 Add the latex base, the foam agent and the cure agent to the mixing bowl.
4 Turn on the food mixer at *high* speed for 3–6 minutes, depending on the rise wanted; the greater rise (volume), the softer the foam.

Equipment and materials
- the moulds you wish to fill
- soap release
- soft brush (to apply the soap release)
- food mixer with a large bowl
- room thermometer
- plastic cups (for measuring the ingredients)
- accurate weighing scales
- spatula
- stopwatch (to time the process)
- electric oven (to bake the moulds)
- latex base (150 g)
- foam agent (30–45 g)
- cure agent (17 g)
- gel agent (4–10 g)

5 Turn down the mixer to *medium* speed, to refine the foam and break down the bubbles, for 4 minutes.

6 Turn the mixer down to a *slow* speed to refine the foam even more, for a minimum of 4 minutes.

7 Add the gel agent slowly, and mix it into the foam. Mix the two together for at least 1 minute.

8 Stop the mixer and fill the moulds carefully. Make sure that no air is trapped under the foam.

9 Close the moulds together.

10 Leave the foam until it gels. To test for gelling, with fingertips press the overspill of foam at the side of the mould.

Curing

11 Place the foam-filled moulds into a pre-heated oven at 100°C (212°F). Bake them for 3–4 hours until the foam inside the moulds has been cured.

12 Remove the moulds from the oven, and allow them to cool down before opening them. Test the texture of the foam by pushing a spatula into it: it should be springy and sponge-like. When fully cured, it will spring back to its shape.

13 Wash the pieces in soapy water, then dry and powder them.

Foam lab technicians usually keep a **log** of their foam runs. This helps them to compare temperatures and cooking times with the quality of the results. An accurate record provides continuity and encourages improvements in foam latex work.

What went wrong?

Just as when making cakes, there are many things that can go wrong:

- *Gelling occurs too quickly* This is caused by adding too much gelling agent, or by mixing it for too long.

- *Gelling occurs too slowly* This will cause collapse in the foam and the appearance of large holes; the result will be useless. Add more gel agent. If you are working at a temperature below 21°C (70°F), the reaction of the gel agent will be slowed down.

- *The foam does not gel at all* Again, it may be that the room temperature is too low (23°C, or 73°F, is ideal). Alternatively, it may be that more gel agent should be used, or that the mould was too cold – the mould should be at room temperature.

- *The mould details are poor* This could be caused by too much soap release. Always allow the mould release to dry before filling the mould with foam.

- *The foam is not springy enough* This is usually caused by undercuring. Extend the cooking time. It could also be that more curing agent should be used, or that the temperature of the oven was not high enough.

- *The foam is brittle and tears easily* This is caused by using too much cure agent, or by cooking at too high a temperature or for too long.

- *There are brown stains on the foam* These are caused by copper contamination. Always wash your hands before working with foam latex. If your hands are not the source, it may be that the entire stock of latex is contaminated.

- *There is a thick skin on the foam surface* This is caused by the mould being too warm (over 27°C, or 80°F). Allow the mould to reach room temperature before filling it with foam latex.

ACTIVITY: MAKING A PROSTHETIC NOSE

1 Take an impression of the subject's nose, using alginate compound and plaster bandage.
2 From the impression, make a positive cast.
3 Model the required nose shape onto the positive cast.
4 Make a negative mould from the modelled nose.
5 Separate the mould from the model.
6 Fill the mould with latex foam. Push the *positive* lifecast into the *negative* mould. Cook in a pre-heated oven at 100°C (212°F), or according to the manufacturer's instructions.

HOW TO SUCCEED

Checklist

In preparing for assessments on prosthetics, the following lists may be useful. Check that you have covered and fully understood these items.

Taking lifecasts and creating impressions
- Materials must be in sufficient quantities for the castings, and readily to hand.
- The artiste must be comfortable in the position required of the lifecast. A suitable working environment must be maintained throughout.
- The protection for the artiste's hair and clothing must be secure, and sufficient to prevent damage. Facial hair must also be sufficiently protected to avoid any damage or discomfort.
  A good relationship must be maintained with the artiste throughout, ensuring that she or he is safe, comfortable, and stress-free.
- Casting must strictly observe all health and safety legislation and procedures.
- Any particular concerns of the artiste must be elicited prior to taking casts. The procedure must be explained clearly to the artiste, and reassuring contact maintained throughout.
- The trimming of the cast must be accurate.

Sculpting and modelling

- Modelling must meet the design specifications.
- Modelling techniques must create the desired effect, as dictated by the design specification.
- Where appropriate, edges must be sculpted to blend into the skin and match the characteristics of the surrounding skin area.
- The modelling should be such as to allow the piece to hold its shape.

Creating prosthetics

- Walls and boxes must be firm and leak-free.
- Materials must be in sufficient quantity and be available to hand.
- Handling must strictly observe all health and safety legislation and procedures.
- Procedures for handling the material must be followed precisely.
- Where relevant, the quantity of material must provide central rigidity and the blending of edges.
- Edges must be neat.
- The time allowed for the drying of materials must take into account environmental conditions.
- The material must be completely set prior to removing the piece from the mould.
- Removal must be careful, avoiding damage and using a release agent appropriate to the material in use.

Positioning and affixing prosthetics

- The length of time to apply the prosthetic must be estimated accurately and conveyed beforehand to the appropriate personnel.
- The artiste must be seated comfortably and according to the length of time envisaged for modelling. A good relationship must be maintained with the artiste to ensure her or his continuing co-operation.
- Protection must be sufficient to prevent damage to the artiste's hair and/or clothing.
- The skin must be thoroughly prepared for the best adhesion and for maximum skin protection.
- The marking of the prosthetics position must be accurate.
- Anchor points and sectional hinge points should allow maximum anchorage and flexibility of positioning during adhesion.
- The adhesion of the appliance and its edges must be precise.
- The adhesion and the materials used must observe all health and safety legislation and procedures at all times.
- The adhesive must be chosen to suit the artiste's skin, and the adhesion technique must suit the size, weight, position and material of the prosthetic.

Applying make-up to prosthetics
- The art finish must create a realistic effect and a sound basis for matching the artiste's skin.
- The sealer, if used, must suit the prosthetic material, the area of skin, the make-up and the application techniques to be used.
- Edges must be carefully concealed.
- The make-up must be sufficiently durable for the effect required and allow retouching, maintenance on the set, and continuity of application.
- The make-up must suit the prosthetic material and the area of skin.
- The make-up must be well blended to achieve the required effect on screen.
- The colour and texture must be suited to the image on camera and must match the surrounding skin.

Removing prosthetics
- The edge must be loosened using the correct adhesive remover for the particular area of skin, the nature of the prosthetic and the adhesive used.
- The adhesive remover used should minimise irritation.
- The artiste must be protected and seated such that she or he will be comfortable for the necessary period of time.
- Removal should be very gradual and gentle, and performed with a level of care suited to the particular area of skin.
- In the case of skin irritation, medical advice must be sought promptly and the production office notified.
- Removal must observe all relevant health and safety legislation and procedures.
- Removal should be as quick and efficient as is practical.
- A good relationship must be maintained with the artiste throughout to ensure her or his continuing co-operation.
- The storage of all chemicals and other materials must be safe, in accordance with health and safety regulations.
- All materials soiled with solvents must be placed in allocated containers, and disposed of safely.

Cleansing and restoring the artiste's skin
- The cleanser and other materials used must be suitable for the artiste's skin type and the type of make-up to be removed.
- The artiste's preference for materials should be sought prior to cleansing.
- The artiste must be adequately protected.
- The artiste's skin must be restored to an acceptable condition.
- Cleansing must observe all relevant health and safety legislation and procedures.
- Cleansing should be as quick and efficient as is practical.
- A good relationship should be maintained with the artiste throughout to ensure her or his continuing co-operation.

Questions

Oral and written questions are used to test your knowledge and understanding. Try the following.

1 When taking an impression of the actor's face, what materials would you use?
2 Why is it necessary to use cold water, not hot, when mixing water with the alginate?
3 What is a 'parting agent' or 'release compound' used for? How and where should you apply it to moulds?
4 What material should you apply to the subject's facial hair, eyelashes and eyebrows before taking a facecast?
5 Name the *three* materials which can be used in the moulds to make the prosthetic pieces.
6 Describe the differences between the 'painting' method and the 'slush' method when making prosthetic pieces in latex.
7 What is the 'flash' on a prosthetic piece?
8 How does the use of foam latex differ from the 'painted' and 'slush' methods of making latex pieces?
9 What are the *three* adhesives that can be used for affixing prosthetic pieces to the face?
10 What are the *four* different uses of ProsAide?

CHAPTER 12

Character make-up

INTRODUCTION

A fine **character make-up**, like a fine painting or performance, is the result of thorough preparation, intelligent selection, and skilled execution. Through the script and rehearsals, the actor becomes acquainted with the physical appearance, background, environment, personality and age of the person he or she is portraying. As make-up artists, it is our job to translate this information into visual terms.

Often the actor and the director will have very firm ideas on how the particular character should look; the make-up artist must interpret their ideas. The script may specify the character's health, occupation and personal attributes: the make-up artist, through the make-up, should help the actor to interpret the role and add credibility to her or his performance. If a man is supposed to be returning from a long stint in the West Indies, for example, it would look wrong for him to be pale in colour; similarly, a suntan would look ridiculous on a woman of high birth in Victorian times, because such women never exposed their faces to the sun. Each character should be analysed thoroughly in this way, and the make-up tried out until everyone is satisfied with the result.

Physical appearance is determined by factors such as these:

- heredity;
- race;
- environment;
- temperament;
- health;
- age.

Though these factors are not of equal importance when analysing a character, they constitute a useful checklist when carrying out your preparation and research.

Planning the make-up

Every technique of media make-up is drawn on in creating a character make-up, yet the make-up should be limited to what is really necessary for the result to be convincing. Character make-up may therefore entail adding merely a moustache and a subtle ageing effect – or you may need the whole works: wig, facial hair, false nose, strong ageing effect and so on. Whatever the

> **TIP**
>
> Design the make-up on paper first. Spend time on planning and organising your selection of materials and resources.

production demands, it is up to the make-up artist to work out the best way to achieve it.

The type of production will impose practical constraints:

- whether it is for television, a feature film, a video, the theatre or a commercial shoot;
- how much the budget allows for materials and the costs of specialist suppliers;
- how long is allowed for the make-up artist to achieve the result.

In character work there are three categories:

- people in fashion;
- people no longer in fashion;
- people ahead of fashion.

Pay attention to the recorded evidence concerning when it was fashionable to have facial hair, for example, or when women wore heavy make-up. Remember, though, that always there are people who are not at all influenced by fashion: men who have beards and moustaches when others don't, and women who wear no make-up when others do. In period films, the make-up artist should try to recreate normal people, and not always what was in fashion.

When creating a character there are five important factors to consider:

1 age;
2 temperament;
3 social standing;
4 race;
5 period.

Bearing these factors in mind, here are some general guidelines in approaching character make-up:

- If you don't need it, don't use it.
- If you do use it, know *why* you're using it.
- Try to *draw out* the character through the use of make-up.
- Don't work *on* artistes – work *with* them.
- Don't stick rigidly to the rules – instead, draw on all the techniques you know to obtain the maximum effect.
- For character make-up, mix many different colours, and stipple them to give great depth and life to the face.

Contact lenses

It is not always necessary to use prosthetics and wigs to achieve a dramatic change in an actor. In feature films, **contact lenses** are sometimes used for dramatic specific effects – white contact lenses can make the eyes look blind, for instance; red ones can make them look horrific.

This type of effect is very expensive: the lenses must be made specially for the actor. An assistant make-up artist is needed, to look after the lenses, to clean them, and to stand by the actor at

ACTIVITY

Choose *one* of the following subjects, and create a character make-up for a colleague or a model:

1 *A witch* – using make-up, a false nose and chin (with prosthetic pieces): suitable for a stage performance.
2 *An elderly Victorian man* – using make-up, and including facial hair on lace or directly applied loose hair: suitable for a feature film.
3 *A geisha girl* – using make-up, and including oriental eyepieces made with plastic or latex: suitable for a photograph.
4 *Changing a woman into an Indian man* – using make-up, and including beard stubble: suitable for TV.

Three different character make-ups:
John Carter, Art Malik and a crowd artiste in *Covington Cross*

all times to check that he or she wears them only for the time allowed, and in case of problems such as dust particles. The optician will advise on how long the actor should wear the lenses each day, and the make-up artist should observe these instructions for the actor's safety. This kind of effect is out of the question unless the production can afford the necessary time and money.

LOOK-ALIKES

In recreating a well-known person the make-up artist aims to achieve as accurate a likeness as possible. Where possible the actor will be cast with the likeness in mind, but even so there are often adjustments to be made.

Begin by comparing the face of the character and the artiste. Analyse the differences and similarities. Examine the skin tones, the shape of the face, the colour of the eyes and hair, and the shape of the eyebrows and nose.

When the character is relatively modern – such as Marilyn Monroe or Marlene Dietrich, for example – there will be numerous photographs available for use as reference, and details of the person will be widely known. For instance, it is common knowledge that Marilyn Monroe never sunbathed, even though it was fashionable to do so: as well as having the famous blonde hair and the arched eyebrows, the lookalike would need to have a pale skin. Similarly, if the subject were Abraham Lincoln it might be necessary to model a nose for the actor in order to achieve a likeness. Points of similarity should be emphasised and differences minimised.

In the case of famous people from history who predate photography, such as Elizabeth I, we have to rely on portraits or caricatures. Very often the painting or engraving will have simplified the personal features. Go back further still into history

Look-alikes

A Rembrandt painting

A model made up to look like the painting

Sid Little as 'Nigel Kennedy'

and we have only the information handed down to us through historical records. The tombs of Tutankhamen, for example, provide evidence of the fashions in make-up and hair in the days of the ancient history of Egypt. Many people think of Cleopatra in terms of how Elizabeth Taylor looked in her film role opposite Richard Burton as Anthony, but in fact these portrayals had sixties overtones reflecting the period in which they were filmed.

When a portrait or engraving is the only evidence of how the person looked, bear in mind that the artist has used brushmarks or cross-hatchings to represent shading or lighting. As the make-up artist, however, you must create a realistic effect with subtler shading and lighting, and you may also be required to adapt the look somewhat for present-day audiences. Thus, a very long beard for a mediaeval period production might be disallowed by the director on the grounds that it would seem too bizarre, even though an existing portrait of Edward II of England shows that he actually had such a beard. A film accurately based on eighteenth-century life would look unbelievable to us; we may know from records that the ladies at court wore thick layers of white lead on their faces, but it would *look* extraordinary to our eyes. The make-up artist would therefore use pale skin tones, but would avoid the overpainted look that was in fact accepted in those days.

Some historical figures who are household names, such as Winston Churchill, J. F. Kennedy or Charlie Chaplin, are within living memory and are so well known that they *must* look right when played by actors. There is an abundance of photographs and archive material to help the make-up artist achieve the likeness, but it is then particularly important that the actors should be physically similar to the characters they are to portray, so that they can easily be transformed by the make-up artist. Make-up and hair must be carefully researched and planned in such cases. With the help of photographs from books and old newspaper

Character make-up

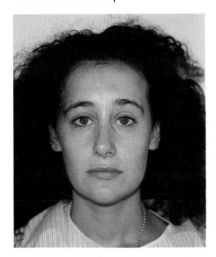

Without make-up

Fashion make-up

Ageing make-up

cuttings, make notes and sketches. Photographs of the actor will be useful so that you can compare the two faces and plan what you will need to do for the make-up and hair.

You will need to experiment on the actor's face, and maybe change your design accordingly. Adapting the make-up to the face requires that you study it from every angle; whereas a photograph or painting is frozen for all time at one angle, the actor must move and be seen in three dimensions, and may need to be filmed in bright sunshine and in dimly-lit interiors.

Character make-up is as important in characterisation as are the clothes and the lines. If the likeness has been recreated skilfully, the actor will be able to perform the role with much greater effectiveness.

ETHNIC APPEARANCES

Caucasian to oriental

It is possible to give a subject an oriental appearance simply with make-up, using highlights and shadows (see page 188).

Chinese eyes using make-up

1 Highlight the entire eyelid, and add shading at the inner corners and underneath the outer corners.
2 The effect can be improved by plaiting the hair on either side of the temples and by pulling to lift the skin.

> **Equipment and materials**
> - greasepaints
> - powder
> - brushes

Chinese eyes using eyepieces

A more realistic look can be obtained by using plastic **eyepieces**. The eyepieces are made by painting PVC and PVA into a *negative* mould taken from modelled oriental eyes.

To place them in position:

1 The actor must be sitting upright and looking straight ahead, with both eyes open.
2 Dab the eyepiece with spirit gum.
3 Place the eyepiece above the actor's eye on the inner (nose) side. Draw it across the eyelid so that the lower edge is covering the lid, allowing the lid to open and close freely.
4 Stick the false eyepiece at the outer corner of the eye.
5 Apply make-up to match the rest of the facial make-up.

> **Equipment and materials**
> - eyepieces
> - spirit gum
> - make-up

Caucasian to Indian

For a female

1 To change the nose shape, apply wax; press with a towel, to give texture to the wax. When modelling around the nostrils, put a cotton bud in the nostril and model around this. Seal the wax.
2 Use a brown eyeliner on the inner eyelid to give an almond shape.

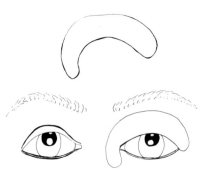

Oriental eyes: the eyepiece, and the eyepiece in place

3 Apply a dark brown grease as a base.

4 Go back to the nose, adding another coat of sealer; powder when dry.

5 Add Chinese yellow and dark brown to colour the nose.

6 Apply eyeliner on the upper lid, and smudge this.

7 Add more dark base on top of the nose, coming down the nose in patches (use a rubber stipple sponge).

8 Place yellow highlights over this – on the forehead and on top of the mouth, to break up the skin texture; also above the cheekbones, and in the inner corners of the eyes, blending into the dark colour. Do the same *under* the eyes.

9 Put some dark brown on the lips, lightly and unevenly.

10 Put dark brown down the side of the nose. Blot with a tissue, and powder.

11 Put brown shadow over the eyelids, and a tiny amount of matt navy blue shadow under the eyes.

12 Draw the upper eyelines with dark brown and black pancake.

13 Fill in the eyebrows, with dark brown drawn underneath; extend this to the ends of the brows.

14 Darken the skin a little more if necessary, with dark brown and green.

The main points to remember are these:

- the dusky stain around the eyes and the lips;
- taking the redness out of the skin;
- the colour – yellow, to counteract the red;
- the curve of the nose characteristic of Indian people.

For a male

When making up a Caucasian man as an Indian, use pencils and grease (dark brown) to draw in lines, as in ageing make-up, and apply hair to make and dress a moustache. The method of make-up is this:

1 Apply the base in patches, not all over.

2 Put dark brown on the forehead (two sections above the eyebrows).

3 Stipple burgundy on the cheeks, the beardline and the chin. Blot with a tissue.

4 Stipple green greasepaint onto the beardline to put it back. Use a little red also.

5 Use Dermablend to cover any spots or shadows under the eyes.

6 Add grey or brown grease on the upper lids.

7 Paint grey eyeliner underneath, to break up the texture and remove the 'made-up' look.

8 Pencil grey on the eyebrows if needed – just one or two strokes.

9 Stipple dark brown onto the forehead.

Oriental make-up: before and after

SUNTANS

Applying a suntan

Ask the actor what colour he *normally* turns in the sun. Remember that some areas, such as the forehead and the cheeks, may go browner than others.

1 Stipple crimson lake panstik on those areas.
2 Go over the top with a yellow-brown colour to avoid the colour looking too pink.

Applying sunburn

1 Stipple red on the areas mentioned above.
2 Ask the actor to crinkle up his eyes: pat over the resulting wrinkles at the outer corners of the eyes.

Do not powder the make-up: leave it to shine.

HOW TO SUCCEED

Checklist

In preparing for assessment on character make-up, refer to the checklists at the ends of the previous chapters, depending on whether you are using wigs, facial hair, prosthetics, directly applied modelling effects, or simply make-up. You are now using all the techniques you know to create a character.

Questions

Oral and written questions are used to test your knowledge and understanding. Try the following.

1 When analysing a character make-up after having read the script, which *two* people from the production would you consult first with your ideas?
2 Which *six* characteristics determine the physical appearance of a character?

3 In what ways does the type of production determine the materials used for a character make-up?

4 With fashion in mind, what are the *three* categories to remember when planning a character make-up?

5 When using special contact lenses on an actor, what arrangements must be made and carried out to ensure the actor's safety?

6 Why would using special contact lenses for an effect be impractical on a low-budget production?

7 When planning the make-up for a 'look-alike' character, how would you research the effect you were trying to achieve?

8 Why is it necessary in some circumstances to 'tone down' an authentic representation of the period?

9 When changing a Caucasian to an Indian by means of facial make-up, what are the *four* points to remember to achieve a realistic effect?

10 When applying a suntan or sunburn effect, what question would you put to the actor before applying the make-up?

11 Which make-up techniques may be used to create a character make-up?

CHAPTER 13

Designing the make-up and hair

INTRODUCTION

The make-up artist should be involved as early as possible in the production. Sometimes, as in the case of ageing and character work, it is important that the make-up artist be involved in casting actors.

DEVELOPING THE DESIGNS

Having first read the script, the make-up artist should attend a preliminary meeting with the producer, the director and the costume designer to discuss the interpretation of the script and the style of the production.

The make-up artist then researches the *style* of the production, using books, old photographs, magazines, videos, old films and the like. If there are special requirements, such as make-up for illnesses, burns or wounds, the make-up artist may need to consult medical experts or police records.

Having completed the research, the make-up artist begins to make plans. She:

1 **breaks down** the script, marking items needing her attention (e.g. when a character needs a 'wound with running blood');
2 lists the number of characters and **walk-ons** (extras, or crowd artists) involved;
3 compiles a cost breakdown for the producer;
4 discusses this with the producer and agrees the budget;
5 contacts the artistes, through their agents or the production office, to discuss the 'look' required, determine whether wigs, facial hair or prosthetics are needed.

A more detailed breakdown of the script must be made to choreograph any make-up changes during filming. This is done in consultation with the director and the costume designer so that everyone is working to a common end; it is vital if continuity is to be maintained when scenes are shot out of sequence. The actors will want to discuss their ideas too, and when everything has been taken into consideration, the make-up artist will be ready to design the make-up and hair.

Providing sketches

Drawing the idea on paper is the best form of communication; one sketch can save hours of talking. The drawings can be passed on to the various specialists, to show precisely how the wigs, facial hair or prosthetics should look. Once the design is on paper it must be approved by everyone involved: these include the director, the actors and the producer, and – in the case of wigs, facial hair and prosthetics – the specialist makers.

The initial design is a starting point, which can be discussed and modified where appropriate. The *final* design, once agreed, can be photocopied and distributed to the wigmaker, the facial-hair maker or the prosthetics expert, as necessary. The design element in make-up is present throughout the make-up artist's work; despite this ideal procedure, in practice many make-ups are designed directly onto the actor's face, if time does not allow pre-production sketching.

If there *is* enough time for planning the schedule and breaking down the script, however, time is well spent in thinking through the entire project. After the research, perhaps relating to an idea already at the back of your mind, the intended result should be captured on paper where it can be improved until it seems to work well.

Sketches should be well presented, with additional notes and instructions as necessary to help those involved to achieve your concept. Copies can then be sent to the specialists where postiche or prosthetic pieces need to be made.

Make–up design for an 'accident victim'

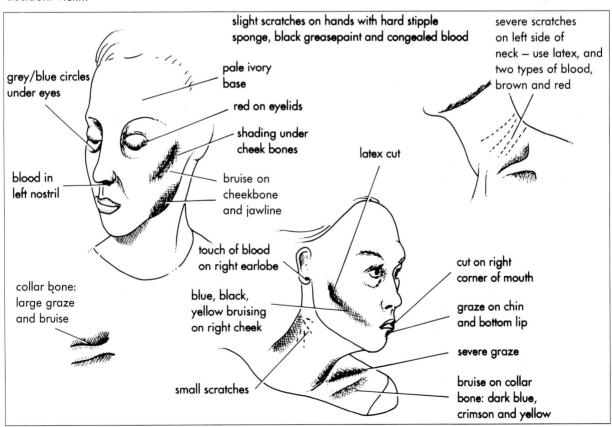

slight scratches on hands with hard stipple sponge, black greasepaint and congealed blood

severe scratches on left side of neck – use latex, and two types of blood, brown and red

grey/blue circles under eyes

pale ivory base

red on eyelids

shading under cheek bones

latex cut

blood in left nostril

bruise on cheekbone and jawline

touch of blood on right earlobe

collar bone: large graze and bruise

blue, black, yellow bruising on right cheek

cut on right corner of mouth

graze on chin and bottom lip

severe graze

bruise on collar bone: dark blue, crimson and yellow

small scratches

It is a good idea to cover the drawing with a layer of tracing paper; this will protect the artwork and prevent it from getting dirty. Notes and comments can be written on the top layer of greaseproof paper.

Make-up and hair designs can range from a simple chart with written explanatory notes, to a detailed drawing filled in with colour.

One method of working out the design is to use a photograph of the actor, drawing the face on paper and then superimposing the design on top. This is a good way of working out the shape of a nose, or how the face might be successfully aged with make-up.

MAKE-UP CHART

TITLE OF PRODUCTION: ....

ACTOR'S NAME: ....

CHARACTER NAME: ....

Foundation: ....

Concealer: ....

Shading: ....

Highlight: ....

Eyes: ....

Cheeks: ....

Eye make-up

Lips: ....

Eyebrows: ....

Body make-up: ....

Hair notes: ....

A make-up record chart

(a) A Polaroid of the actor

(b) A sketch of the make-up

(c) The final effect

Make-up designed for Anthony Hopkins as 'King Lear'

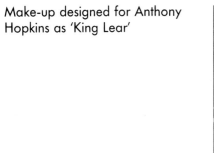

Make-up designed for a 'fantasy' character

(a) A Polaroid of the actor

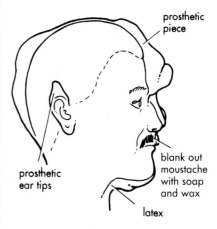

prosthetic piece

prosthetic ear tips

blank out moustache with soap and wax

latex

(b) A sketch of the proposed make-up and prosthetics

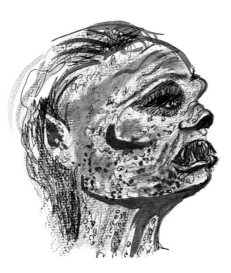

(c) A sketch of the final effect

(d) The final effect

Checklist

In preparing for assessments on designing the make-up and hair, the following lists may be useful. Check that you have covered and fully understood these items.

Commissioning, hiring or buying specialist supplies for wigs, facial hair and prosthetics

- The supplier must be furnished with full design specifications and research material to enable an accurate reproduction of the design idea.
- If possible, the make-up designer (who may also be the hairdresser) should be present at all fittings.
- Fittings must be arranged between artistes and suppliers at relevant intervals to enable the progress of the design.
- Every effort must be made to ensure that the materials used are suitable to the design and are within the allocated budget.
- Time spent on the design must be justifiable within the agreed overall limits.
- Any problems with the design must be identified as early as possible to allow modifications or to find alternative solutions.
- Any alterations needed must be made as soon as possible to meet deadlines; solutions must be as cost-effective as possible.
- Contact must be maintained on a regular basis to monitor the progress of the design.
- Any changes to schedules, scripts and deadlines must be highlighted promptly; the ability to meet them realistically must be assessed with the supplier and the production team.
- Items must be collected or sent on time, to and from the correct locations.
- Supply lines must be arranged to ensure reliable deliveries throughout the production.

Producing make-up and/or hair designs

- Designs must be presented in the manner best suited to convey the ideas and to gain agreement: where necessary, alternatives must be presented.
- Any changes or suggestions must be discussed and agreed, and modifications made where appropriate.
- Charts and notes must be as detailed as necessary for the work needed.
- Charts and notes must be clear and legible.

Researching

- Maximum use must be made of all available sources of information.
- Information must be clearly set out to provide the necessary reference material.
- Sources must be relevant to the particular brief.

Meeting the requirements of the script and production
- Designs must meet the production and script requirements.
- Designs must provide a level of detail suited to the type of production and the production team's needs.
- Designs must be realistic in terms of materials and budget.
- Designs must meet the technical requirements of the shoot.
- Where necessary, designs must allow for continuity.
- Designs must be as simple as possible to facilitate repetition; they must be easy to translate; and they must be workable for the make-up team.
- The colours used must harmonise with the overall design concept and theme.

Questions

Oral and written questions are used to test your knowledge and understanding. Try the following.

1 When designing the make-up and hair for a period drama, how would you set about researching material to inform your preliminary sketches?
2 Name the available sources of information used by a make-up artist.
3 If when reading a script, you saw the words 'The army advances', what questions would you need to raise at the production planning meeting?
4 Which specialist suppliers would you need to provide with sketches, photographs, verbal and/or written information?

Make-up artist Tom Smith first worked with Richard Attenborough when Attenborough was acting in the film *Dock Brief* in 1962. Tom gave him a nose which was so successful that no one could see that it was false. Attenborough strolled around the studios and was amazed to find that his changed nose made him unrecognisable.

Tom himself insists that it was a lucky accident – he had taken a cast of Attenborough's own nose at a board meeting, and cast it that night using cap plastic, powdered pancake and water, leaving it to set in a warm oven overnight. It was so successful that Tom couldn't find the edges to peel it off, and had to cut it down the middle with scissors.

Perhaps it was this early experience that made Sir Richard Attenborough, as he by now was, determined to have Tom do the make-up on *Gandhi* in 1980–81, more than twenty years later. At the time, Tom was working on *Raiders of the Lost Ark* for Steven Spielberg, and he found himself deluged with photos of Gandhi, Nehru and other characters of the period.

He accepted the job and went to India, not knowing who the actor would be but expecting to have to make prosthetic changes to the actor's face. He took a laboratory oven, a mixing machine and scales, and all the other laboratory equipment. But he couldn't take the actual chemicals because Indian customs would not allow them through; they told him he could obtain all his chemicals in Delhi. When he got there, the chemicals were delivered in old bottles without labels. He experimented with the chemicals in the garage of the hotel in Delhi, and modelled some prosthetic pieces.

At this point, Ben Kingsley was cast to play Gandhi. Tom had already read the script, of course, and had made some preliminary sketches of five different ages of Mahatma Gandhi's evolution from young man to emaciated old age. (He was 79 when he was assassinated.) The importance of the sketches served to remind Tom not to go too far – to hold back, so that there was always something left in reserve.

When Ben Kingsley arrived Tom tried out the pieces, but they decided that the prosthetics interfered with the characterisation: psychologically, it was like putting a mask on him – the make-up was getting in the way of the performance. They agreed to do it without prosthetics.

The sense of Gandhi ageing throughout the film was achieved by Tom with greasepaint. His intention was to make it imperceptible, so that through the film Ben Kingsley, as Gandhi, grows older

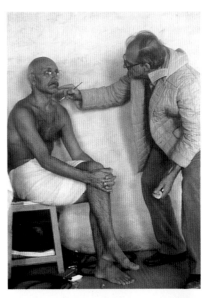

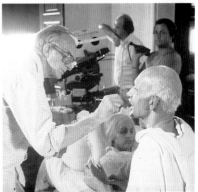

Tom Smith working on 'Gandhi'

without you noticing. In real life, when you live with someone you are unaware of the ageing process because it is so gradual.

If you get a chance, view *Gandhi* on video. I think you'll agree that Tom achieved his goal superbly.

The make-up artist's attitude

In 1992, Tom Smith was given a Lifetime Achievement Award by BAFTA.

When Tom was doing the make-up on *Macbeth* in 1968, director Roman Polanski asked him, 'How many awards have you got, Tom?'

'None,' replied Tom.

'Baftas, Oscars – you must have won some?' said Polanski.

'No,' said Tom. 'Nominations, yes; but winning, no. You see, if you can notice the make-up, you've failed. You've destroyed the illusion.'

'I see,' said Polanski: 'you're in the kitchen.'

'Yes,' said Tom. 'I'm in the kitchen.'

When an actor has thought through, developed and rehearsed his or her part, when the director has given assistance and constructive criticism concerning how the role fits within the film or play; when they are in accord, the lighting is arranged, and the costumes are ready, then the only remaining contribution to a good, or even a great, performance is the visual appearance of the performer.

This is in the hands of the make-up artist. If the make-up is true, in combination with the feelings of the actor it will afford the audience a true appreciation of the production.

Allsworth, Joyce 1985. *Skin Camouflage*. Stanley Thornes.

Baker, Patsy 1993. *Wigs and Make-up for Theatre, Television and Film*. Butterworth Heinemann.

Baygan, Lee 1984. *Make-up for Theatre and Television*. A & C Black.

Baygan, Lee 1988. *Techniques of Three-Dimensional Make-up*. Watson-Guptill.

Buchman, Herman 1973. *Film and Television Make-up*. Watson-Guptill.

Buchman, Herman 1989. *Stage Make-up*. Watson-Guptill.

Corson, Richard 1972. *Fashion in Make-up*. Peter Owen.

Corson, Richard 1986. *Stage Make-up*. Peter Owen.

Corson, Richard 1991. *Fashion in Hair*. Peter Owen.

Green, Martin *et al.* 1994. *Professional Hairdressing*. Macmillan.

Hogarth, Burne 1989. *Drawing the Human Head*. Watson-Guptill.

Innes, Jocasta 1981. *Paint Magic*. Frances Lincoln Publishers.

Kehoe, Vincent 1985. *The Technique of the Professional Make-up Artist for Film, Television and Stage*. Focal Press.

Kehoe, Vincent 1991. *Special Make-up Effects*. Butterworth Heinemann.

Nunn, Joan 1990. *Fashion in Costume 1200–1980*. Herbert Press.

Palladino, Leo 1989. *The Principles and Practice of Hairdressing*. Macmillan.

Palladino, Leo 1991. *Hairdressing – The Foundations*. Macmillan.

Palladino, Leo & June Hunt 1992. *The Nail File*. Macmillan.

Wickham, Glynne 1985. *A History of the Theatre*. Phaidon.

PRODUCTS

Foundations

During the 1920s a Polish immigrant wigmaker named Max Factor started mixing up different colours in grease to beautify his Hollywood clients for the silver screen. With his son, he created a range of hundreds of colours. The numbers he used for his pancakes and panstiks are still quoted as standard colours by other brands.

Other Hollywood make-up artists, such as Bob Kelly, Ben Nye, Joe Blasco, William Tuttle (Custom Color Cosmetics) and Vincent Kehoe (RCMA), also invented brands. In general their greasepaints are finer than European equivalents, but they are relatively expensive in the UK. For straight make-ups, fashion cosmetic brands such as Clinique, Elizabeth Arden or Estée Lauder can also be used. Christian Dior's 'Visiora' – now sadly discontinued – was the finest beauty range for professional use.

Kryolan is probably the most widely used professional brand. Leichner grease sticks are used by actors who do their own make-up (Mehron is the equivalent of Leichner in the USA); Grimas and Fardel are the 'face-painting for fun' ranges. Add a drop of moisturiser to your sponge if you find grease foundations in these brands are too thick. Indio panstiks are probably the finest European cream bases, although they are not widely stocked.

All of these brands offer water-based pancakes as well.

Pressed-powder eyeshadows and blushers

The fashion cosmetic brands tend to make their eyeshadows very glittery. This is largely because the glitter acts as a net, holding the powder loosely – the customer uses it more quickly because it is softly pressed, and such shadows are cheaper to produce than matt shadows.

Ranges of professional matt shadows tend to be sold locally rather than widely distributed. If you are fortunate enough to travel, look out for eyeshadows from:
* Le Maquillage in New York, USA;
* La Femme in Los Angeles, USA;
* Make-up Studio in Milan, Italy.
* Make–up Centre, London, UK.

In the UK, Cosmetics à la Carte has a good range of inexpensive matt colours. The Make-up Centre's Delamar brand matt shadows are larger and very popular.

BRUSHES

Ox, goat and pony are quite floppy. In small sizes they are perfectly adequate for eyelines or face-painting; in medium sizes they are used for applying blusher; in large sizes they are used to brush off excess powder. The softest powder brushes are made from squirrel hair.

Sable-hair brushes are firmer and should be used for all other make-up purposes. This is important; if you find it impossible to blend your eyeshadow powders properly, or if the lip colour won't follow the shape of the mouth, it may be that your brushes are to blame.

OTHER ITEMS

For straight beauty and fashion

- Baby wipes
- Barrier cream
- Blisteze
- Blushers – powder and cream
- Bowls – for brush cleaning, sterilising, etc.
- Brushes (in brush bag)
- Cleansing milk or oil
- Cologne
- Concealer creams
- Cotton buds
- Cream bases
- Cuticle clippers
- Cuticle remover stick and oil
- Emery boards
- Eyebrow pencils
- Eyebrow sealer
- Eyelash adhesive
- Eyelash curlers
- Eyelash dye
- Eyelashes
- Eyeliners
- Eye pencils
- Eyeshadows
- False nails (tips)
- Gowns
- Hairbands
- Hairbrush
- Mascaras – for sensitive eyes and waterproof
- Moisturiser
- Nailbrush
- Nail buffer

- Nail clippers
- Nail-polish remover
- Nail scissors
- Nail varnish – clear and coloured
- Orange sticks
- Palette knife
- Palettes
- Pancake (or liquid water-based) foundations
- Pencil sharpener
- Plastic spray bottles
- Polaroid camera
- Powder, translucent
- Powder puffs
- Razor
- Reference books
- Section clips
- Shading colours
- Shaver (battery)
- Shaving brush
- Shaving foam or soap
- Thimble, needle and cotton
- Tweezers

For facial hair

- Adhesive tape (clear)
- Beard blocks and holders
- Beards and moustaches on lace
- Brushes
- Clingfilm
- Combs
- Hackle drawing mats and clamps
- Hackles
- Hair – yak belly and wool crepe
- Hair streakers
- Indelible marker (fine)
- Knotting ('ventilating') needles and holder
- Moustache wax
- Plastic spray
- Postiche pins
- Scissors
- Spirit gum
- Spirit gum remover
- Tong heater
- Tongs – various sizes
- Ventilating nets – soft film and hard theatrical
- Wahl clippers and attachments; lubricating oil
- Wahl trimmer and recharger

For hair

- Acetone
- Adhesives
- Adhesive tape (clear)
- Boxes – for pins and rubber bands
- Bowls – for wig cleaning
- Brushes – for applying adhesive or colour
- Chamois leather
- Cleaning solvent
- Clingfilm
- Clipper disinfectant
- Clips
- Combs
- Conditioner
- Conditioning oil
- Cottonwool
- Crimpers
- Curling irons
- Diffuser
- Drawing mats
- Drying hood (portable)
- Drying hood stand
- Dry shampoo
- Electric benders
- Electric clippers – large Wahl and spare guards
- Electric tongs
- Electric trimmer – small Wahl with charger
- Face shields – for hair spraying
- Fixer spray
- Fuller's earth
- Gel sprays
- Gloves – useful when cleaning postiche
- Glycerine
- Hackles and holders
- Hair – wool crepe and real
- Hairbrushes
- Hairgrips
- Hairnets
- Hairpins
- Hair oil
- Hair removing cream
- Hairsprays
- Hair treatments
- Heated roller clips
- Heated rollers
- Klene-All
- Knotting needles and holders
- Kool-Aid
- MME mild mastix remover
- Mortician's wax
- Mousse

- No-shine hairspray
- Pincurl pins
- Pins – assorted
- Pipecleaners
- Polystyrene heads
- Postiche pins
- Razors – wet and disposable
- Rubber bands
- Scissors
- Section clips
- Set bag or box
- Setting clips and pins
- Setting rollers
- Shampoo
- Shaver (electric)
- Shaver sterilising cleaner
- Shaving foam
- Skullcaps
- Spirit gum
- Spirit gum remover
- Sponge
- Styptic pencil
- Teabags – for staining wig lace
- Tissues
- Tong heater
- Toupee tape
- T-pins
- Tweezers
- Ventilating nets – soft film and hard theatrical
- Wig blocking pins and tape
- Wig blocks (malleable), holders and stands
- Wig boxes
- Wig measurement charts
- Wig repair kit

For special effects

- Acetone
- Bald cap plastic
- 'Blood', non-staining
- Brushes (inexpensive)
- Burn and exposure colour creams
- Cereals
- Cleaning solvent
- Collodion
- Dental (or modelling) tools
- Hair dryer and diffuser
- Head block – for making bald caps
- Isopropyl alcohol
- Klene-All
- Kool-Aid

- Latex
- Modelling tools
- Mortician's wax
- Nose putty
- Old-age stipple
- Prosthetic colours (grease)
- Prosthetic pieces – ear tips, noses, cheeks
- Scar plastic
- Sealer
- Spatula
- Spirit gum
- Spirit gum remover
- Sponges – stipple and natural
- Surgical spirit
- Tear stick
- Vaseline

acetone A liquid solvent which melts plastic. It can be used for cleaning hair lace, but should never be used directly on the skin. Commonly it is used for removing nail varnish. It is available from chemists.

adhesive A means of sticking different surfaces together. Various types are available, for use with wig hair laces, eyelashes, prosthetics and so on. Adhesives are available from theatrical suppliers and chemists.

ageing stipple A latex product used for wrinkled ageing effects. It can be obtained in different flesh colours from theatrical make-up suppliers.

alginate A dental impression material used in lifecasting. It is available from dental suppliers.

analysing a character The technique of determining the make-up requirements of an actor, according to the script.

appliances Prosthetic pieces which are applied to the actor's face or body.

aquacolour A cake make-up which is grease-free and is applied with a damp sponge or brush. It is used for body make-up and fantasy painting.

blending The technique of graduating the intensity of the colour from its strongest tone to its lightest until it disappears into the natural skin tone.

block A head-shaped template for use in wig work, or a beard-shaped one for facial hair work. It can be malleable, wooden or plastic, and is available from hairdressing suppliers.

breaking down The technique of applying make-up to achieve a natural weathered or discoloured effect according to the action and location, such as for a coal mine, a desert, a fight scene, or the aftermath of an earthquake.

breaking down a script The technique of going through a script systematically in order to organise crowd scenes, locations, continuity needs, and changes of make-up and hairstyles.

camouflage make-up Ointment-based creams used for covering scars and for other remedial work. It is available from chemists and theatrical make-up suppliers.

castor oil An oil used with make-up for colouring prosthetic pieces.

chamois leather A piece of leather used in attaching hair-lace wigs, beards and all facial hair. It is available from paint or hardware stores.

Chinese brushes Long, pointed brushes for watercolour painting to produce various effects, including marbling.

compressed powders Powders in a variety of colours, shiny or matt, used as colouring for the eyelids (eyeshadows) or for the cheeks (blushers or rouge); they are also used for colouring eyebrows. They are available from make-up suppliers.

contact lenses Lenses used for special effects in films or television productions, to change the eye colour. They must be supplied and fitted by a qualified optician.

continuity The technique of achieving a seamless sequence in productions (which are usually filmed out of order) by making sure that the make-up and hair 'match' the preceding and following shots.

double knotting The technique of using two knots together when knotting hair onto a foundation net.

drawing mats Mats used in postiche work for drawing hair.

dressing out a wig The technique of styling the hair with tools such as rollers, tongs, a hair dryer and brushes to produce the finished effect.

duplicating material A material used for taking impressions, as in lifecasting. Dentists' alginate is used; this is available from dental suppliers.

eyelashes, artificial Lashes used for extra emphasis on the eyes, available in different lengths and thicknesses. They are trimmed, then applied with a latex adhesive.

face powder Powder used over the foundation to set it and to reduce shine. An all-purpose translucent loose powder is enough to suit all occasions, though many colours are available. Face powder in compact form (compressed face powder) can be applied directly to the skin without a base, or used on top of the foundation base to give a matt finish.

fantasy make-up A make-up that does not look natural – it might be bizarre or stylised, such as for a witch or a statue.

flash The edge of a prosthetic piece made of gelatine or foam latex. The flash is sculpted prior to casting to provide an overflow for the foam or gelatine.

foundation (face) The make-up base used to achieve a complexion in the desired colour.

foundation (wigs) The base, made out of net, into which hair is knotted to make a wig.

gelatine A material used for directly-applied casualty effects and for making prosthetic pieces.

glycerine A material mixed with water and used to simulate perspiration and tears. A spoonful of glycerine mixed with a bottle of rosewater is a good refresher or toner for dry skins. Glycerine is available from chemists.

hackle A tool used in combing and mixing loose hair.

Constructed of metal spikes set in a wooden block, it is rather like a miniature bed of nails.

hair, human Hair used for making fine wigs, toupees and other hairpieces.

hair, synthetic Hair generally used for stylised wigs, and normally made into weft for wigs, beards and moustaches.

hair, yak Hair from the yak: it is coarse and is used for laying on directly-applied hair for beards and moustaches.

hair lace A net-like material, also called ventilating net, into which hair is knotted for many types of postiche.

highlighting The technique of using a light colour to make a feature more obvious.

Karo syrup A type of syrup, used in the manufacture of artificial blood. It is available from specialist grocers.

knotting hooks Hooks attached to needles, used for inserting hair into gauze when making postiche.

latex A natural rubber in milky-white foam, available in varying densities. It is used in creating wrinkles in ageing make-up; in casualty effects, for peeling skin and the like; and in making bald caps and filling moulds in prosthetic work.

laying a beard The technique of making a beard by applying loose hair directly onto the face.

laying on hair The technique of sticking loose hair directly onto the face and then dressing it with tongs.

lifecasting The technique of taking an impression of the actor's face or body, and casting it in stone.

lifecasting, sectional The technique of taking an impression of a section or piece of the actor's face or body, and casting it in stone.

look-alike The character make-up required to make the actor look like someone else.

luminous make-up Fluorescent make-up for fantasy make-up effects, for use under ultra-violet lights. It is available from theatrical make-up suppliers as a cream, a liquid or a gel.

modelling clay Clay used for sculpting features in prosthetic work. It is available from pottery and artists' suppliers.

modelling tools Tools used for building and modelling in clay, plastic and wax. Sculpting tools and dentists' tools are useful to the make-up artist.

modelling with wax The technique of building up a natural feature and changing its shape using wax directly applied to the face or body.

mortician's wax Wax used for modelling directly onto the face, when blocking out eyebrows, changing the shape of the nose, and so on.

moustache wax A coloured wax used to curl the ends of moustaches.

pancake A cake make-up which is grease-free. It was first made by Max Factor.

panstik A cream stick make-up base, also available in paintbox-style containers, obtained from the theatrical make-up shops.

pencils Wooden pencils with soft grease lead, used for colouring eyebrows and outlining eyes and lips.

plaster A material used for making positive and negative moulds in prosthetic work. It is available from dental or artists' suppliers.

plaster bandage Bandage used to reinforce the impression when lifecasting.

plastic A material used in liquid form to paint layers when making bald caps and prosthetic pieces. Glatzan is a well-known make available from theatrical make-up shops. Plastic should never be used directly on the face.

plastic head blocks Blocks used in making bald caps.

plastic scar material A material in tube form used for modelling scars and the like directly onto the skin. Although especially formulated for use on the skin, this material should always be tested on the back of the actor's hand first, in case of irritation.

plastic spray An artificial latex spray used for setting facial hair when making hair on a block. It is not for facial use.

plastilene A material used for modelling in prosthetic work: though not as good as clay, unlike clay it does not need wetting. It is available from artists' suppliers.

powder brush A soft brush used for removing excess powder from the face.

rubber-mask greasepaint A castor-oil-based product, available in various colours, used for painting on top of latex.

sealer A material used on top of wax, nose putty and prosthetic pieces before applying make-up.

shading The technique of using a darker colour to make a feature less obvious.

spirit gum The adhesive most commonly used in attaching wigs, beards, moustaches, bald caps and the like. It is available from theatrical make-up shops.

standing by Staying near the actors on the set, ready to retouch the make-up when necessary.

stippling The technique of using an open-pored sponge and applying make-up with a dabbing movement in order to provide a textured effect.

straight make-up The technique of defining and correcting a face with make-up.

stubble paste Wax in stick form, used on the face before applying chopped-up hair to create a beard stubble.

T-pins Pins used to attach wigs to blocks. They are available from hairdressing suppliers.

test shots (cinematography) The filming and viewing on a screen of the lighting, hair, make-up and costume, to try them out.

test shots (photography) Photographs taken by the

photographer, the model and the make-up artist working together unpaid to produce picures for their portfolios.

tong heater An electronic heater for heating iron tongs used in dressing postiche.

tongs Iron tools heated up to dress hair.

toning down a colour The technique of making the colour less bright by adding a complementary one, such as toning down red by adding green.

toning down a period look The technique of making a look more modern.

tooth enamel A material used for painting the teeth. It is available in white, cream, nicotine, yellow, black, gold and silver, from theatrical make-up shops.

watercolour brushes Brushes used for applying sealer, collodion or spirit gum: they should be cleaned in acetone immediately after use. They are available from artists' suppliers.

waterproofing the make-up The technique of protecting the make-up for filming in water.

waxing out The technique of using a layer of wax to cover a feature such as the eyebrows before applying make-up.

wig stand A stand used to hold a wig or moustache block while dressing postiche. Stands are available either free-standing or as a shorter version that clamps to a workbench or table.

witch hazel A material used for blending the edges of gelatine pieces. A spoonful mixed in a bottle of rosewater makes a good refresher or toner for greasy skin. Witch hazel is available from chemists.